A
Maryknoll Book
of
Inspiration

A
Maryknoll Book
of
Inspiration

READINGS FOR
EVERY DAY OF THE YEAR

Michael Leach and Doris Goodnough,
editors

ORBIS BOOKS

Maryknoll, New York 10545

Third Printing, May 2011

Founded in 1970, Orbis Books endeavors to publish works that enlighten the mind, nourish the spirit, and challenge the conscience. The publishing arm of the Maryknoll Fathers and Brothers, Orbis seeks to explore the global dimensions of the Christian faith and mission, to invite dialogue with diverse cultures and religious traditions, and to serve the cause of reconciliation and peace. The books published reflect the views of their authors and do not represent the official position of the Maryknoll Society. To learn more about Maryknoll and Orbis Books, please visit our website at www.maryknollsociety.org.

Manufactured in the United States of America.

Library of Congress Cataloging-in-Publication Data

A Maryknoll book of inspiration : spiritual readings for every day of the year / Michael Leach and Doris Goodnough, editors.
     p.   cm.
   Includes index.
   ISBN 978-1-57075-901-7 (pbk.)
   1. Devotional calendars.   I. Leach, Michael, 1940–   II. Goodnough, Doris.
   III. Title: Book of inspiration.
   BV4810.M37 2010
   242'.2 – dc22   2010018834

In gratitude
to
Miguel d'Escoto
and
Philip Scharper
for
a dream come true

Contents

CONTENTS

CONTENTS

CONTENTS

APRIL

MAY

CONTENTS

CONTENTS

CONTENTS

CONTENTS

AUGUST

SEPTEMBER

CONTENTS

DECEMBER

CONTENTS

Preface

Do not let a day go by without some spiritual reading.
— St. John Bosco

Lectio divina is not only an ancient tradition but a daily habit that can lift our spirit and deepen our understanding of God. Literally it is reading the Bible and contemplating its wisdom. Pope Benedict XVI observes:

> The diligent reading of Sacred Scripture accompanied by prayer brings about that intimate dialogue in which the person reading hears God who is speaking, and in praying, responds to him with trusting openness of heart. If it is effectively promoted, this practice will bring to the Church — I am convinced of it — a new spiritual springtime.

The purpose is to listen to the word of God with what St. Benedict called "the ear of our hearts," and to hear "the still, small voice of God" (1 Kings 19:12) that whispers to us when we are silent. No sound could be more beautiful.

An offshoot of *lectio divina* is the practice of spiritual reading. Books, poetry, essays are often wellsprings of inspiration that nourish our souls. St. Bernard of Clairvaux said that spiritual reading accompanied by prayer "are the arms by which hell is conquered and paradise won." Spiritual reading triggers connections between the world we stumble in and the loving God "in whom we (really) live and move and have our being" (Acts 17:28). A passage or excerpt from a good spiritual book makes us pause, reflect, and sometimes see what we never saw before. The poet Cyrano said, "There comes a moment to everyone when beauty stands staring into the soul with sad, sweet eyes, and God help those who pass that moment by." That moment has come to many of us as we have read a spiritual book.

This book, *A Maryknoll Book of Inspiration,* features 366 selections from Orbis Books from its birth in 1970 to the present. It's a celebration of Orbis' 40th anniversary and its parents' 100th anniversary, The Catholic Foreign Mission Society of America, also known as the Maryknoll Fathers and Brothers.

In 1911, Father Thomas Frederick Price of Raleigh, North Carolina, and Father James Anthony Walsh from Boston, Massachusetts, with the blessings of the bishops of the United States and the permission of the Holy See, founded the first American missionary order. Accompanying them in this great adventure was Mary Josephine Rogers, who in turn founded the Maryknoll Sisters of St. Dominic in 1912. The third "branch" of the Maryknoll family, now officially the Maryknoll Mission Association of the Faithful, began in 1937. Like the first Fathers, Brothers and Sisters, the first Maryknoll lay missioner, Dr. Harry Blaber from Brooklyn, New York, served in China.

Maryknoll, the shorthand for all three branches, serves the poor and fosters self-worth and dignity among marginalized peoples on four continents. Maryknollers are known throughout the world as the heart and hands of the U.S. church overseas.

The Maryknoll Fathers and Brothers founded Orbis Books in 1970 to be a bridge between the people it serves and readers in the "global North" beginning with theology and mission studies from Latin America, Africa, and Asia. Since then, Orbis has published hundreds of books that enlighten the mind, nourish the spirit, and challenge the conscience. Like Maryknoll itself, Orbis books explore the global dimensions of Christian faith, invite dialogue with diverse cultures and religious traditions, and serve the cause of reconciliation and peace. Each book is a missioner, reaching out to both believers and seekers in the United States and overseas.

Maryknoll and Orbis Books remind American Catholics that we belong to a world church, that we are truly our global brothers' and sisters' keepers, and that we are not truly disciples of Christ unless we share his mission to bring the Good News to the world. Unexpectedly, by being true to this vision, Orbis Books has also become a brand name known around the globe. Orbis books have been translated into thirty-five languages, including Afrikaans, Arabic, Chinese, Croatian, Indonesian, Korean, Polish, Slovak, Swahili, Tamil, and Vietnamese.

Like Maryknoll Orbis has come to represent integrity, idealism, and service to the church. This is reflected in the 150 awards it has received from the Catholic Press Association in the past ten years, more than any other Catholic publisher, and in its 12 Pax Christi awards, including one in 2005 for Orbis itself in recognition of its unique contributions to the cause of peace and justice. It has become impossible to think of Maryknoll without thinking of Orbis, or to think of Orbis without thinking of Maryknoll.

Orbis publishes books on mission, Catholic social teaching, current affairs, church history, theology, biography, ethics, inter-religious dialogue, world religions, Latino/a studies, spirituality and inspiration. *A Maryknoll Book of Inspiration* features excerpts primarily from books that inspire but also from other categories because they too have the power to move our hearts and minds and encourage us to become "the salt of the earth" (Matt. 5:13). Some of the selections draw on religious traditions other than Christianity because Maryknollers not only bring the Gospel to all nations but often find their own faith enriched by the cultures in which they serve. As the *Catechism of the Catholic Church* teaches, "All religions bear witness to the essential search for God."

So please sit back then and read the selection for today's date, or any date, or many dates, and be still. That last is the best part!

— *Michael Leach and Doris Goodnough*

Acknowledgments

The editors are deeply grateful to the following individuals who joined them in selecting and preparing the 366 inspirations in this book: David Aquije, Janet Carroll, M.M., Mary T. Connell, M.M., Catherine Costello, Wayman Deasy, M.M., Marie Dennis, Robert Ellsberg, Marge Gaughan, Joseph Healey, M.M., Steve Judd, M.M., Ivy Kelly, James Kroeger, M.M., Claudette LaVerdiere, M.M., Marie Ann Lipetzky, M.M., Lynn Monahan, Dennis Moorman, M.M., Sue Perry, Helen Phillips, M.M., Bernadette Price, Leo Shea, M.M., John Sivalon, M.M., and Joseph Veneroso, M.M. Without their generosity and good judgment this book would not have been possible.

JANUARY

. . . .

Time to Pray

I don't mind telling you that during my twelve years in prison I was not unhappy a single day. I dreamed — well, first I woke up one morning and found myself in prison. I had been taken there the night before — handcuffed, surrounded by six guards. When I woke up the next morning, I thought: "This is what I've dreamed of — time to say all the prayers I couldn't say while I was working."

I had time to pray for my family, for my friends, for people all over the world, everybody under the sun. And I knew you were praying for me during those years. God put us here on earth to help each other. The best way to help people is to pray for them. That's why you're here. Keep it up. I felt that I was being helped during those years by your prayers, by the prayers of my friends, and, I hope, my own. Prayer is so powerful. I am a living example of what prayer can do.

— Bishop James E. Walsh, M.M., from *Zeal for Your House*

Knowing How to Pray

I met a woman from our parish at a gathering of the wives and children of Filipino overseas workers. Her husband was working on a ship that exploded and sank in Norway in early 2004. His body had not been recovered. She said, "Sometimes I tell God that I know my husband is safe somewhere, when a part of me tells God to forgive my husband and grant him eternal rest." As she talked, I could see how her heart was torn between denial and acceptance. She continued, "I go to the Blessed Sacrament but no words come out of my lips. Many times I do not know what to say. I do not know what to pray for. I just catch myself crying before the Lord. My tears — that is the best that I could give God. I trust God will take good care of my children and keep me strong for their sake." With a forced smile to keep her tears from falling, she asked me, "Do you think I am praying?" "Yes" I told her, "you just taught me how to pray."

— Bishop Chito Tagle, from *Easter People: Living Community*

Give Us This Day Our Daily Bread

Another day. Another long, hot, hard, exhausting, exasperating day in Ethiopia. Well, better one day in Your tent, O God, O suffering, saving, compassionate God, than a thousand in the security of my own home in Connecticut. It is time to celebrate the "liturgy" for which I was ordained. I pull on my jeans and my thick-soled shoes. God, I believe, help my unbelief. God, let all that I do praise you.

It is just after dawn and already the long, brown, deathly silent line snakes all around the perimeter of our camp and loses itself in the distance. Our intense feeding center for emaciated children is a temporary refuge. Daily, every two hours, what serves as bread is figuratively blessed, broken, and distributed under a variety of disguises: soybean porridge or hotcake; high protein biscuits; thick, sweet powdered milk laced with oil and sugar; and once in a while, God be praised, a very, very small banana.

Seven times a day I take, break, bless, distribute, and all around give thanks as the Author of life restores to life those physically diminished. Seven times a day, a miracle, when fully present to the Presence, I can see the shape of grace. It is 10:00 a.m., time once again for me to fulfill my primary daily function, presiding over a liturgy of the eucharist, presiding over the distribution of desperately needed "daily bread." When you see a hungry person and feed that person, you are feeding me, said Jesus. I look out over the beautiful brown faces of my sisters and brothers, broken bodies with unbroken spirits. This is my body, said Jesus. Amen, I say. Amen.

—Miriam Therese Winter, from *The Singer and the Song*

The Transformation of the World

Therefore, if anyone is in Christ, he is a new creation; the old has gone, the new has come!
— 2 Corinthians 5:17

Thomas Merton used to travel from the monastery to the city of Louisville when he was a young monk. At first everything of the world seemed repulsive. But in prayer he learned to see. Later, when he went to town, he was astounded at how beautiful everything was. He stood on a corner one day, and it was as though the entire city glimmered with the grace of God. "How do you tell people," he asked himself, "that they are walking around shining like the sun!"

In the movie *Field of Dreams* a tourist asks the hero Ray Kinsella, "Is this heaven?"

"No," he says. "It's Iowa."

Now neither Louisville nor Iowa are literally heaven, but when we have eyes to see, all things become new and we behold a new heaven and a new earth right in front of our eyes.

We are now "in the world but no longer of the world." The world has become our cloister.

— John Michael Talbot, from *The World Is My Cloister*

The Everywhere God

It makes a big difference how we pray if we view God as a person in heaven or, as the Baltimore Catechism put it, if we view God "everywhere." For many of us prayer has been an effort to contact an "elsewhere God." What happens when we shift our attention to an "everywhere God" — a sustaining Presence in all, through all, never absent, never distant, not in one place more than in any other place, a Presence "in whom we live and move and have our being"?

There is a new story emerging in consciousness, one that evokes awe, wonder, and reverence as it expands our notion of God. We are beginning to understand that God is not limited to a place and only vaguely present in the universe. We are beginning to appreciate a God alive in every particle in the billions of galaxies beyond us and in the grass or pavement beneath our feet. God is here, everywhere, and always with us.

> *May we open our minds and hearts*
> *to the presence of God in us.*
> *May God-in-us,*
> *the "everywhere God,"*
> *find generous and courageous expression*
> *in our words and actions*
> *as we undertake*
> *to make the reign of God*
> *evident in our world.*
> *Amen.*

— Michael Morwood, from *Praying a New Story*

Charity Is Love in Action

Sam was an older man, a Vietnam veteran who lived on the streets, had teeth missing, and a body odor from not bathing. He would stop me and ask me for a dollar. "I'm not going to lie to you, Father. I want a dollar for a beer. I'm so ugly nobody wants to talk to me. A cold beer helps me feel good."

Instead of giving him a dollar I invited him to go with me to a bar nearby so we could have a beer together. He started to cry. "Father, nobody wants me around. How come you want to hang around with me?" I simply told him, "because you are my friend and I don't want you to drink alone."

One time, in a beautiful handwriting, Sam wrote me one of the most beautiful and poignant poems I have ever read about pain of total aloneness and the hunger for mere acceptance. I'm not sure how much I helped Sam but he helped me by giving me valuable insights into the sufferings of street people. Sam was not ugly. He was simply a human being in need of being acknowledged. One of the greatest acts of charity, I keep learning, is befriending the lonely, the lowly, the excluded, and the rejected of society.

— Virgil Elizondo, from *Charity*

The Glory of God

At the end of the day, it is not our achievements, our doing, that will count the most. Rather, true brilliance is the glory of God transforming each and all of us into sons and daughters of the Father through Christ in the Spirit, bonding all together in a communion in the one Love. Transformed by the very light and life of God, this is what we become: a blessed communion of persons both human and divine.

Those who have very little in the way of worldly goods, or in the ways of the wisdom of this earth, invite us to this way of perceiving and being. So, too, do all those who open up the human heart to the superabundance of Love's loving in our own time and place, inviting us into communion with the three in one Love, embracing diminishment and anguish, relishing the gift yet to be given even in dying and death. For even and especially in our brokenness and failure, when there is nothing left but loss, and yet more loss, the glory of God shines: alight in the face and piercing eyes of the one who faced diminishment, darkness and death — the Son of the Father, perfect icon of Love, Given and Gift/ing.

— Michael Downey, from *Altogether Gift: A Trinitarian Spirituality*

Joy in Struggle

There is a sense of profound joy and delight in giving oneself to a cause or mission that is greater than oneself, that aims in small yet real ways to make a difference in how social and ecclesial life is understood and lived. This is joy, not in the sense of an ephemeral happiness or fleeting pleasure, but rather of deep satisfaction that what one is doing is fundamentally worthwhile. Such joy can be pervasive even while feeling tired and spent after a day of intense labor, teaching, lecturing, and writing. Amid the tiredness there is the inner satisfaction of having spent one's energies on a cause that is meaningful, purposeful, and attuned with the promptings of the Spirit.

— Bryan N. Massingale, from *Racial Justice and the Catholic Church*

Come to the Party

While visiting the Open Door Community in Atlanta, Georgia, I heard the following story. A dedicated young American woman was doing some sort of human rights work in El Salvador. She was invited to a party but declined because she had too much work to do. Later the people who had invited her told her, "You're not going to last here, you're going to go back North." She was hurt and indignant: "What do you mean?" "The ones who don't come to parties always leave." They knew that unless we make a place for play and for beauty in our work we will begin to do harm to ourselves and others. Any change movement without joy or beauty is not sustainable.

— Laurel A. Dykstra, from *Set Them Free: The Other Side of Exodus*

Claiming Your Corner

I knew a man once. No one seemed to remember his name. He had always just been there. He sold balloons on a street corner in Washington, D.C., mostly at night. In the snow and rain and on windy days he stood there under his splotches of color, holding onto them, keeping them close to the earth. He didn't talk much and never asked you if you wanted one. He just stood there like he was reminding you of something even he couldn't remember well enough to put into words. Tall and black, white-haired and alone, the man belonged on that corner. During the day when he was often absent, the corner looked bleak and empty — crying out for his presence and his colors. The corner lived only at night. You weren't aware of it until there was nothing there to look at or to look for when you passed by.

And now, the man comes no more to the corner. Someone said he died over the holidays. But when I come to the corner, he's still there. I remember. I see and know he still waits for someone to buy his balloons. And I wonder if there's any place that my presence fills up and makes whole, or whether I move so fast that there is no space that is touched so intimately and thoroughly by me that it is truly mine. And you — where's your space?

— Megan McKenna, from *Keepers of the Story*

Rosary and Relationships

Whether prayed in a spirit of supplication, praise, petition, or simple exhaustion, the rosary never strays far from the events of the day. We know deep within us the mysteries these prayers evoke. As we move our fingers along the beads, the mysteries of our own lives find redemptive expression in the mysteries of the rosary. The rosary is about the relationship between God and humanity; it is about mother and child, divine mysteries flowing through our veins in a transformative journey that takes us to Bethlehem, Cana, Calvary, Pentecost, and the promise of eternal life. Each of the mysteries reveals something specific about a relationship with God that is as certain and as palpable as the love between Jesus and the woman who gave him birth.

— Teresa McGee, from *Mysteries of the Rosary*

Salvation Events

Hope is the most feared reality of any oppressive system. More powerful than any other weapon, hope is the great enemy of those who would control history. What salvation events bring to the world, most of all, is hope.

Real social change is not just about great leaders, it's about releasing the aspirations of millions of ordinary people. The truly great leaders know that they are servants of ordinary people and of the god of history. Nelson Mandela's first speech in Cape Town began with these words: "I stand before you not as a prophet, but as a humble servant of you, the people."

When salvation events occur, we are all surprised. We don't expect they could or will ever happen. . . . Through salvation events, we can also be set free from the illusions that so often govern us. The most appropriate response to salvation events is thanksgiving. The jubilant crowds on the Berlin Wall and the dancing South African masses welcoming Nelson Mandela are both fitting signs of it. Both show us the way to respond to the salvation events of hope. In the words of C. S. Lewis, we are "surprised by joy. . . . "

From the perspective of the Bible, hope is not simply a feeling or a mood or a rhetorical flourish. Hope is the very dynamic of history. Hope is the engine of change. Hope is the energy of transformation. Hope is the door from one reality to another. . . . Hope is believing in spite of the evidence and watching the evidence change.

— Jim Wallis, from *The Soul of Politics*

Ingrown Toenails and the Body of Christ

A few years ago I hiked the White Mountains of New Hampshire with my family. What I hadn't shared with anyone was that for weeks I had been suffering from an ingrown toenail in my big toe. After a couple of hours my toe was throbbing. I could hardly walk and was slowing down the group. The children were getting frustrated. Finally, my brother stopped and said, "Sit on that rock and give me your boot." In shock I watched him cut off the entire top part of my boot with his hunting knife. "Here," he said, "the toe won't bother you anymore. It has all the space it needs now to move freely without hurting."

That experience stayed with me as a pastoral minister. How many "ingrown toenails" are in the Body of Christ? How many members of the Body seem to bring only pain, infection, and frustration to the rest of us? But what do we do with those who cause us pain? Do we try to heal them and make them comfortable? Do we give them some space so they don't hurt so much? Or do we ignore, reject, and get rid of them?

1 Corinthians teaches: "If one part suffers, all the parts suffer with it; if one part is honored, all the parts share in its joy." My ingrown toenail taught me to respect and have compassion for every member in the Body of Christ.

— Adele Gonzalez, from *The Spirituality of Community*

The Vicar and the Mother Superior

One day John XXIII visited the Hospital of the Holy Spirit in Rome, which is administered by a religious sisterhood. The mother superior, deeply stirred by the papal visitation, went up to him in order to introduce herself.

"Most Holy Father, I am the Superior of the Holy Spirit!" she said.

"Well, I must say you're lucky," replied the pope. "I'm only the vicar of Jesus Christ!"

— Pope John XXIII, from *Pope John XXIII: Essential Writings,* edited by Jean Maalouf

We Are What We Pray

Prayer is the sum of our relationship with God.

We are what we pray.

The degree of our faith is the degree of our prayer. The strength of our hope is the strength of our prayer. The warmth of our charity is the warmth of our prayer. No more nor less.

Our prayer has had a beginning because we have had a beginning. But it will have no end. It will accompany us into eternity and will be completed in our contemplation of God, when we join in the harmony of heaven and are "filled with the flood of God's delights."

The story of our earthly-heavenly life will be the story of our prayer. Thus, above all it is a personal story.

Prayer is a word of infinite variety, were it repeated into infinity with the same syllables and in the same tone of voice.

What varies is the Spirit of the Lord which gives it life, and this is always news.

Understanding prayer well means understanding that one is speaking with God.

God's inspiration searches out our will. The spirit of Jesus settles where the will desires it, because it is love. And two are needed to make love.

When I bow before his love he is not slow to come; rather he has already come, for he loves me much more than I, poor creature, can ever love him.

And love shows itself in action, as for the Prodigal Son.

The soul must say with sincerity, "Now I will arise and go to my Father."

— Carlo Carretto, from *Letters from the Desert*

What Is Prayer?

When Brother Bruno was at prayer one night, he was disturbed by the croaking of a bullfrog. All his attempts to disregard the sound were unsuccessful, so he shouted from his window, "Quiet! I'm at my prayers."

Now Brother Bruno was a saint, so his command was instantly obeyed. Every living creature held its voice so as to create a silence that would be favorable to prayer.

But now another sound intruded on Bruno's worship — an inner voice that said, "Maybe God is as pleased with the croaking of that frog as with the chanting of your psalms."

"What can please the ears of God in the croak of a frog?" was Bruno's scornful rejoinder.

But the voice refused to give up. "Why would you think God invented the sound?"

Bruno decided to find out why. He leaned out of his window and gave the order, "Sing!" The bullfrog's measured croaking filled the air to the ludicrous accompaniment of all the frogs in the vicinity. And as Bruno attended to the sound, their voices ceased to jar, for he discovered that, if he stopped resisting them, they actually enriched the silence of the night.

With that discovery Bruno's heart became harmonious with the universe, and, for the first time in his life, he understood what it means to pray.

> — Anthony de Mello, from *Anthony de Mello:*
> *Selected Writings,* edited by William Dych, S.J.

Love Everything

Love people even in their sin, for that is the semblance of Divine Love, and is the highest love on earth. Love all of God's creation, the whole and every grain of sand of it. Love every leaf, every ray of God's light. Love the animals, love the plants, love everything. If you love everything you will perceive the divine mystery in things. Once you perceive it, you will begin to comprehend it better every day. And you will come at last to love the whole world with an all-embracing love.

— Fyodor Dostoyevsky (*The Brothers Karamazov*),
from *Lenten Prayers for Busy People,* edited by William J. O'Malley

We Have Work to Do

Some years ago I visited a middle school in Denver. The occasion for the visit was a Martin Luther King Day assembly. When the assembly was finished I was surrounded by a dozen or so students. One of them, an African American young man who looked about 13 or 14, sidled up closer to me and said, "Dr. Harding, I've got a question to ask you." With an interesting combination of boldness and wonder, he asked, "If Dr. King knew that he could be killed at any time, why didn't he just back off? Why didn't he just chill out for a while?"

As I stood there, considering how I might share with my young friend the reality of Martin's commitment, courage, and compassion, a young woman who looked about the same age as the questioner moved in to my aid. "What do you mean, 'chill out'? Dr. King *couldn't* chill out. He had work to do."

There it was. The word. For them, for me, for all of us, especially in times like these, when it seems so much easier to chill out, to back off and away from the hard, sometimes dangerous work of challenging the racism, the extreme materialism, and the militarism that threaten to undermine our best possibilities for creating a humane, compassionate, and nonviolent democracy, King's kind of place. So the word continues: We have work to do, not just to celebrate, admire, and praise him. But, like him, we have work to do, to be.

— Vincent Harding, from *Martin Luther King:*
The Inconvenient Hero

A Chance Encounter

One day on a long flight the place next to me was empty. A young fellow came from his empty row to the seat next to mine. He asked me whether he could join me. We talked. He told me about himself. We compared notes and noted sympathies for points of view. We spoke about Jesus' place in human life, and what we thought history would lead to. We talked about what lies beyond this world, and what we expected it all would lead to. An unexpected conversation. Things I had never thought of fell in place. He spoke about his expectations, and I about mine. A new horizon opened up before me. The flight was over before I realized it. The voice of the plane's captain surprised me when he announced that we were descending to our destination, asking us to fasten our seat belts. I left the plane another person. A chance encounter.

The memory of such meetings doesn't wane. The experience is at times so enlightening that the enthusiasm created does not fade. Human history is full of stories about such meetings. No wonder that the Bible sometimes compares these strangers with angels! A chance encounter — and life changes forever.

This is how it was for those who encountered Jesus. People met him in the street, along the lake shore, at a well, during the night, on a boat, on the road from Jerusalem to Emmaus, in the Temple, at their work. They met, and they started to talk. We are inclined to forget that the good news began in such a common way.

— Joseph G. Donders, from *Charged with the Spirit*

Beautiful the Feet

The jet broke suddenly through the clouds as it continued climbing. There, on the right side of the plane, but at an angle from which I had never seen it, was the very sight which greeted me on my first day in the missions, the peak of Kilimanjaro, 20,000 feet high. Seventeen years had passed since seeing it that first time, and now I counted it a blessing to be able to see it for the last time. In all my years of wanderings and safaris on this continent, I had never really got out of range of this gigantic mountain of snow on the equator. . . . And looking down on it now made everything I had been involved in down there seem small and insignificant. Seeing the mountain for the last time reminded me of the only description of missionaries I could ever find in the bible, a description repeated three times with just slightly differing emphasis from one author to another: "Behold upon the mountains the feet of him that brings good tidings and that preaches peace" (Nahum 1:15).

. . . But maybe, most of all, as I looked down for the last time, I remembered people like Ole Sikii making the painful climb, foot by foot, up the volcanic side of Oldonyo L'Engai, on his lonely quest to see the face of God. And Abraham Ndangoya. And Keti, with her baby strapped to her back, walking happily over the green hills of Africa to bring the gospel to Masai kraals that had never heard it. And the old man who had taught me of the relentless, untiring, pursuing feet which seemed forever to be stalking all of us.

St. Paul confirms the description: "How beautiful are the feet of those who preach the gospel of peace, of those who bring glad tidings of good things" (Rom. 10:18).

— Vincent J. Donovan, from *Christianity Rediscovered*

Walk with the Spirit of God

Our relationship with god is the most basic relationship we have. To the degree that we draw near to him, we also draw near to our brothers and sisters, and in drawing near to our sisters and brothers, we draw near to God. Let us pray without ceasing.

Andar con el Espíritu de Dios

Nuestra relación con Dios es la más fundamental relación que tenemos. En la medida que nos acercamos a él, nos acercamos a nuestros hermanos y hermanas, y en cuanto nos acercamos a nuestros semejantes, así nos acercamos a Dios. Oremos sin cesar.

— Linda Unger and David Aquije, from *Un solo mundo, una sola familia / One World, One Family*

Happiness

Happiness is accepting and choosing life, not just submitting grudgingly to it. It comes when we choose to be who we are, to be ourselves, at this present moment of our lives; we choose life as it is, with all its joys, pain, and conflicts. Happiness is living and seeking the truth, together with others in community, and assuming responsibility for our lives and the lives of others. It is accepting the fact that we are not infinite, but can enter into a personal relationship with the Infinite, discovering the universal truth and justice that transcends all cultures: each person is unique and sacred. We are not just seeking to be what others want us to be or to conform to the expectations of family, friends, or local ways of being. We have chosen to be who we are, with all that is beautiful and broken in us. We do not slip away from life and live in a world of illusions, dreams or nightmares. We become present to reality and to life so that we are free to live according to our personal conscience, our sacred sanctuary, where love resides within us and we see others as they are in the depth of their being. We are not letting the light of life within us be crushed, and we are not crushing it in others. On the contrary, all we want is for the light of others to shine.

— Jean Vanier, from *Jean Vanier: Essential Writings,*
edited by Carolyn Whitney-Brown

Hope: Gift and Choice

For those of us who believe in the crucified and risen One — the cosmic Christ — this is a hopeful *and* a demanding vision. It doesn't appear that injustice will be defeated anytime soon, or that the world of violence is about to end. Perhaps this is precisely the challenge of discipleship in our time — to trust that our prayer and action on behalf of justice will make a difference despite all indications to the contrary. It is possible that, in the first decades of the twenty-first century, believing has less to do with doctrinal details and more to do with embodying the gospel vision, even when it is not politically correct or religiously approved. Perhaps, like the carpenter from Nazareth, we must choose to live and act without the assurance of significant outcomes or measurable results.

Like most of my sisters and brothers in the human community, I do not have a clear view of the future — no magic lantern, no crystal ball, no personal revelation, no apocalyptic secret. But, whatever the future will be, this is what I trust. The nonviolent coming of God is unfolding as surely as scattered seeds will find good soil; as certainly as there is hidden treasure in the field of human history. And as confidently as grains of wheat fall into the ground in search of a harvest that is still to come.

Hope has feet. And we are still walking.

— John Heagle, from *Justice Rising: The Emerging Biblical Vision*

Prayerful Moments

I remember well my first visit to the Beuron Abbey. It was evening. We went from the train station directly to the abbey and were welcomed into the cloister itself, since the guest wing was not yet built. Residing in the cloister made our stay warm and life-giving. The rooms were simple, with much brown wood and an indescribable something that made a person feel good in one's depths. Then we received something to eat, and after that we went to evening prayer. The church was already dark, with only a light in the choir. The monks stood in their places and prayed the beautiful psalms of the evening prayer. A sense of mystery, holy and momentous, dominated the entire church. Later I saw that the liturgy has many powerful and glorious aspects. But evening prayer was the door through which I initially entered into the sacred world of worship. At the start, it was a better entrance for me than the great liturgical ceremonies.

— Romano Guardini, from *Romano Guardini: Spiritual Writings,* edited by Robert A. Krieg

Nurturing the Inward Life

Bring the whole of your life under the ordering of the spirit of Christ. Are you open to the healing power of God's love? Cherish that of God within you, so that this love may grow in you and guide you. Let your worship and your daily life enrich each other. Treasure your experience of God, however it comes to you. Remember that Christianity is not a notion but a way....

Do you try to set aside times of quiet for openness to the Holy Spirit? All of us need to find a way into silence which allows us to deepen our awareness of the divine and to find the inward source of our strength. Seek to know an inward stillness, even amid the activities of daily life. Do you encourage in yourself and in others a habit of dependence on God's guidance for each day? Hold yourself and others in the Light, knowing that all are cherished by God.

— Michael L. Birkel, from *Silence and Witness: The Quaker Tradition*

Jesus Our Model

Christians are not only to imitate Jesus, but to be closely united to him. He invited his disciples and friends to join him in his unique offering on behalf of the whole of humanity. The bread and wine for which he gave thanks symbolized the entire creation. They became his body "given" and his blood "poured out for the forgiveness of sins."

Through the ministry of the Church, the one Eucharist is offered by Jesus in every age and place, since the time of his passion, death and resurrection in Jerusalem. It is here that Christians unite themselves to Christ in his offering which "brings salvation to the whole world" (Eucharistic Prayer IV).

Such a prayer is pleasing to God who "desires all men to be saved and to come to the knowledge of the truth" (1 Tim. 2:4). Thus, they offer thanks for "everything that is true, everything that is honorable, everything that is upright and pure, everything that we love and admire, whatever is good and praiseworthy" (Phil. 4:8). Here they draw the grace of discernment, to be able to read the signs of the Spirit's presence and to recognize the favorable time and right manner of proclaiming Christ.

— William R. Burrows, from *Redemption and Dialogue*

In Touch with God

There is no single method of prayer. Prayer is a word we have for all that we do in our efforts to be in touch with God, or our ways of exploring God coming to know through actual experience who God is. This is mystical life. To see it from another angle, our spiritual life is a process of doing all we can to rid ourselves of those things in our lives — ideas, ideologies, vices, obsessions — which get in the way of awareness of God and block us from God.

"If the only prayer you ever say in your whole life is 'thank you,'" wrote Meister Eckhart, "that would suffice." To the extent we know God, we are drawn to expressions of praise and gratitude. At our most blessed moments, what moves us to pray is not a sense of duty but is similar to what happens to people in love. They can hardly stop thinking about how wonderful the other person is. We pray out of our joy in who God is.

— Jim Forest, from *Praying with Icons*

Authority

Jesus was a person of great authority, but he came "to serve and not to be served," and he taught his disciples that their authority should contrast radically with the "princes of this world" who "know how to make their authority felt...."

The secret of the authority of Jesus was his ability to respond to the real aspirations, hopes, desires, and needs of others. He allowed them to use his power to work their wills — their deepest, most authentic good wills for healing, for empowering, for liberating. For him authority was service and it was empowerment. He asked us to be in the midst of the world as "one who serves."

It takes a great deal of discernment to know how to serve in this way.... We all have great power to author life — or to stifle it. Discernment is first of all our effort to distinguish what will really be life-giving in the exercise of the personal authority we all have. Obedience is a listening process that empowers us to use our authority in a way that seems to be in tune with the will of God here and now.

— David A. Fleming, S.J., from *Pilgrim's Notebook:*
An Experience of Religious Life

Using Our Gifts

It seems to me that the greatest misuse we make of God's gifts to us is the misuse of our talents. There is a false sort of humility that makes us say, "I cannot do that; I am not fitted for that work." We sometimes hold back, and do not expend all our abilities on the task at hand.

On analysis, we discover that the work we hold back on is a task assigned to us by others, and not some pet project of our own. If we propose a plan of work and it is given to us to carry out, we go into it with heart and soul. Then someone else suggests a modification of our plan, and our ardor slackens. We discover reasons why we cannot cope with the task any longer. This is not humility, but the pettiness of wounded pride.... "To those who love God, all things work together unto good" (Rom. 8:28). Come, Thou Giver of all gifts and create in us by the fire of love a new heart, so that Thy invitations may be visible to us alike in the ordinariness of our earthly pilgrimage and in the glory of the firmament studded with stars.

— Bishop Francis X. Ford, M.M., from *Come, Holy Spirit*

A Vision

"I will shed my spirit on all humankind." A spirit of partnership. The rich woman will sit down at the same table with a poor woman and learn how good corn bread and collard greens are, and the poor woman will find out what a T-bone steak tastes like. Neither will shiver in a drafty house, nor have to move her furniture when it rains. Both will rejoice in the robust health of their children, who are not listless from having too little nor bored from having too much. They will discover the blessedness of sharing, the warmth of compassion, the quiet strength of humility, and the glow of gentleness, the clearness of honesty, the peace of justice, and the ecstasy of love. . . .

God's spirit will call the people from the East to join hands with the people from the West, and the people from the North to join hands with the people from the South, and all will seek the other's good. . . .

God's spirit will join an old woman's wisdom and a young woman's strength and they will be partners for the Lord. They will respect one another, and will be slow to take offense and quick to forgive. They will be as mother and daughter. The old woman will be filled with compassion and understanding, and the young woman with gentleness and loving concern. They will find joy in bearing one another's burdens.

God's spirit will give eyes to humankind with which to see the glory of the Lord. God's spirit will give ears to humankind to hear the sound of God's trumpet as well as God's still small voice. God will dwell with us and be our God, and we shall be God's people. God will wipe away our tears, dispel our doubt, remove our fears, and lead us out. God will heal the broken-hearted, open

31

the eyes of the blind, release the captives, preach the good news to the poor, and usher in the acceptable year of the Lord. God will bulldoze the mountains and fill in the valleys. God will make the rough places smooth and the crooked ways straight. God'll stand all people on their feet so that all humankind may see God's glory together.

— Clarence Jordan, from *Clarence Jordan: Essential Writings,* edited by Joyce Hollyday

Liberation

Ours is not a watchmaker God who creates the world, winds it up, and then withdraws into some separate spiritual abode, leaving us to fend for ourselves. God does not liberate us by leaving us alone. (This is precisely what the modern understanding of freedom has become: a demand to be left alone.) On the contrary, the God of Jesus Christ liberates us precisely by refusing to leave us alone, by refusing to withdraw from any aspect of our lives, even the most insignificant or banal. The wounds, blood, and tears that cover his face and body are what make him present and, hence, real, for those are the source of our hope for ourselves, our community, our church, and our world. By accompanying us in our own crucifixion, Jesus witnesses to the truth of his resurrection as the source of life, for suffering shared is already suffering in retreat.

— Roberto S. Goizueta, from *Christ Our Companion*

FEBRUARY

Burning Questions

For any visitor, the Anne Frank House raises burning questions. What would I do if I lived in a country under military occupation? How successful would I be in not having my thoughts and actions shaped by intimidation, fear, and propaganda? How would I respond to harassment, arrest, and deportation? What would I say if a friend or neighbor in danger plead for my help? Might fear play so decisive a role in my life that I would say, "I'm sorry, but there is nothing I can do"? Far from helping the hunted, might I even be one of those who decide that helping the hunters is a prudent and even profitable thing to do? But the most urgent questions raised by a visit to the Anne Frank House are not about what I might have done had I lived in Holland when it was an occupied country. Rather, they are these: What am I doing about endangered people in the world right now?

— Jim Forest, from *The Road to Emmaus*

On Being a Leader

Sometimes people in Christian groups lament that their leaders have taken over too much control and authority. However, this matter cannot be solved solely by criticism and complaints. It requires people to step in and assume the responsibilities of a follower of Jesus and not leave these tasks to others. In the ideals presented by Luke at the Last Supper, the real church leader is "one who serves at table" — one who is unique because he or she does not strive for dominative power but rather delights in the humble role of developing the talents and gifts of others so that they can be effective witnesses of the kingdom preached by Jesus. In this way real leaders make themselves "useless" by selflessly helping each person to be "useful."

— Joseph Grassi, from *Broken Bread and Broken Bodies*

A Calling

God calls all the souls he has created to love him with their whole being, here and thereafter, which means that he calls all of them to holiness, to perfection, to a close following of him and obedience to his will. But he does not ask all souls to show their love by the same works, to climb to heaven by the same ladder, to achieve goodness in the same way. What sort of work, then, must *I* do? Which is *my* road to heaven? In what kind of life am *I* to sanctify myself? Apart from the universal calling of all of us to perfect love, to holiness, to the following of Jesus, and obedience to his will in everything, however small, a calling at the last to heaven, what is the particular and social vocation that he puts before me and each one of us?

This question: "What kind of life am I going to undertake?" is the question of *vocation*. And it has got to be answered rightly. For if it is answered rightly and we take the way to which God calls us we shall be living obediently to him, we shall be strengthened by his help, and so we shall come to heaven. . . .

There can never be any question of *choosing* a vocation: the word "choice" is excluded by the word "vocation," which means "calling," a call from God. Therefore we do not "choose a vocation" but seek to find *our* vocation, to do all we can to hear the divine Voice calling us, to make sure what he is saying — and then to obey him. Where vocation is concerned God speaks, calls, commands: we have not to choose but to listen and obey.

— Charles de Foucauld, from *Charles de Foucauld: Essential Writings,* edited by Robert Ellsberg

The Global Jesus

Like us "in everything but sin," as the tradition insists, Jesus can be understood only in global terms. He is the cosmos become conscious; he provides it with soul-space. But in him the cosmos finally finds adequate soul-space, a cavern of interiority big enough to contain the fullness of divine love and compassion. (Unlike us, he isn't a shallow container; he doesn't babble nonsense or go haywire under the strain of too much possibility.) We don't take his words as some freak, unprecedented event in the history of the world. Jesus was a Jew. He recapitulates a lineage, a crowd of witnesses, without which we, their descendents, would hardly be able to imagine that the dizzying process whereby dark matter, the galaxies, and black holes occur is "parented," fathered-forth by a boundless Love. Without these witnesses, without their boldness in pulling back the curtain of obscurity, we would not have the courage to call the creator of this vast cosmos "Father." Much less utter the more familiar term that Jesus himself uses for the "illegible Force" — namely *Abba*.

— David Toolan, from *At Home in the Cosmos*

Incarnation

Christ plays in ten thousand places,
Lovely in limbs, lovely in eyes, not his,
For the Father, through features of our faces.
— Gerard Manley Hopkins

Every time I board a plane or fear death I pray these words: "Dear Lord, if I am to die, please let people remember of me only that which was you. Let my life serve merely as a witness to your love."

It's an abbreviation of St. Francis' classic prayer, "Make me an instrument of your peace..." and resembles this one by Mother Teresa: "Dear Jesus, help us to spread your fragrance everywhere we go. Flood our souls with your Spirit and life. Penetrate and possess our whole being so utterly that our lives may only be a radiance of yours."

Whomever I got it from, the prayer works for me because, like a compass for my soul, it directs me to my Creator and to my purpose on earth. It's the Incarnation in my own words: God's becoming human in each and every one of us.

Whatever you do, in word or deed,
do everything in the name of the Lord Jesus,
giving thanks to God the Father through him.
— Colossians 3:17

— Therese Borchard, from *Winging It:*
Meditations of a Young Adult

The Value of Joy

Laughter has long departed from the church and theology. Once stepping into the church, we Christians leave our laughter behind. We forget to laugh. We think it not proper during worship. Even when singing: "Hosanna, in the highest!" we are straight-faced and solemn. We are too conscious of the straight-line God staring at us from a pedestal high above. He seems ready to catch any sign of mischievousness in us. But a religion that has done away with laughter can be a dangerous thing. . . .

A laughing and dancing God — this is the god of most Asians and Africans outside the Christian church. This God laughs with them as well as weeps with them. This God dances with them as well as mourns with them. Worshiping this God, Africans "beat their drums, play musical instruments, dance and rejoice. Religious singing is often accompanied by clapping and dancing, which express people's feelings of joy, sorrow or thanksgiving." How different this is from Christian worship in a solemn assembly!

Worship is celebration of God who gives life and takes it away. Celebration must be a noisy thing. Clapping, singing, and dancing — such noisy assembly is a communion of God and people in deep ecstasy. Worship in ancient Israel must have been very much like this. Listen to Psalm 47, for instance: "Clap your hands, all you nations; acclaim our God with shouts of joy" (47:1).

— C. S. Song, from *The Compassionate God*

Solidarity

There is a beautiful story of a young man with a disability who wanted to win the Special Olympics; he got to the hundred meter race and he was running like crazy to get that gold medal. One of the others running with him slipped and fell; he turned round and picked him up and they ran across the finishing line together last. Are we prepared to sacrifice the prize for solidarity? It's a big question. Do we want to win or do we want to be in solidarity with others? Why is the gap between the rich and the poor growing? Or the gap between the powerful and the powerless. Between those who are the oppressors and the oppressed? We have to look at the poorest and the weakest. They have a message to give us. Living with these people — different, fragile, vulnerable, anguished people — has revealed what is the most beautiful in me, but also what is the most terrible. I have discovered that the anguish of some people with disabilities has awoken my anguish.

We need transformation because there is so much tension and egoism in us. We see the world only through our own eyes; we are not liberated to see people as God sees them. We see people through our wounds, through our difficulties, through our prejudices. We need to be liberated to see people of other cultures as God sees them. . . . It is important to find a way of transformation so that fear and hate can be transformed into positive energies. It's a long road. The water has to be changed into wine. The whole of the vision of Jesus, which is the vision of peace, is about coming out from behind barriers and discovering people as they are.

— Jean Vanier, from *Jean Vanier: Essential Writings,*
edited by Carolyn Whitney-Brown

The Sunflower of the Soul

Christ concealed his divinity and nobility.
He clothed his power in power.
We clothe our poverty in power.

We are shackled by fear, loneliness,
hatred, and egotism.
Christ came to liberate us . . .
so we in turn can liberate others.

The garden of solitude produces
many beautiful flowers,
the most beautiful of which is
compassion.

Compassion is the sunflower of the soul,
turning its face toward
the Son of God.

— Gerard Thomas Straub,
from *Thoughts of a Blind Beggar:
Reflections from a Journey to God*

Jesus and the Power of Touch

Jesus' life helps us to appreciate the power of touch. He is frequently in contact with other people. At dinner one evening, a woman anoints Jesus' head with expensive, fragrant oil. This sensual act startles and offends his companions. Jesus tells them, "Leave her alone." He welcomes being touched in this way.

Throughout Mark's gospel we read about the sick who seek Jesus out. Jesus responds to them in a way that changes their lives. And he seems to need to touch, to make contact with them. When he heals a blind man, Jesus mixes dirt with his own spit and presses the mud into the man's eyes; gradually the man regains his sight. A sick woman approaches him with the conviction that if she can even touch his clothes, she will be healed. Jesus comes to a halt, aware that he has been touched in some special way and that power has gone out of him. There is a lesson here: Touch has the power to heal if we honor its sensual/spiritual force.

— James Whitehead and Evelyn Eaton Whitehead,
from *Holy Eros: Pathways to a Passionate God*

God's Disguise

If sometimes our poor people have had to die of starvation it is not because God didn't care for them, but because you and I didn't give, were not instruments of love in the hands of God, to give them that bread, to give them that clothing; because we did not recognize him, when once more Christ came in distressing disguise — in the hungry man, in the lonely man, in the homeless child, and seeking for shelter.

God has identified himself with the hungry, the sick, the naked, the homeless; hunger, not only for bread, but for love, for care, to be somebody to someone; nakedness, not of clothing only, but nakedness of that compassion that very few people give to the unknown; homelessness, not only just for a shelter made of stone, but that homelessness that comes from having no one to call your own.

— Mother Teresa, from *Mother Teresa: Essential Writings,* edited by Jean Maalouf

Charity and Justice

We must go beyond "aid" or "charity" and demand justice that will bring peace. Many people falter at this point. He who asks the powerful to give aid to the poor, or helps the poor himself by being imprudent enough, or bold enough, to mention these or those rights or demands this or that justice, is regarded as a splendid man, a saint. But he who chooses to demand justice generally, seeking to change structures that reduce millions of God's children to slavery, must expect his words to be distorted, to be libeled and slandered, viewed with disfavor by governments, perhaps imprisoned, tortured, killed. . . . But this is the eighth Beatitude:

Blessed are you when men revile you and persecute you and utter all kinds of evil against you falsely on my account. Rejoice and be glad for your reward is great in heaven, for so men persecuted the prophets who were before you. . . . "

An enormous effort will be needed to create awareness in the marginalized masses to prepare them to fight their way out of their subhuman situation. . . . An enormous effort is also needed to create awareness in those who are privileged. . . .

But if the effort is not made the scandal will continue and the rich will go on getting richer and the poor poorer. The spiral of violence will get worse. . . . When will governments and the privileged understand that there can be no true peace until justice has been established?

— Dom Helder Camara, from *Dom Helder Camara: Essential Writings,* edited by Francis McDonagh

Saints

What significance does yesterday's saint have for today's Christian? What meaning has the sanctity of the past for the holiness of the present? On broad lines, three solutions may be suggested. One extreme insists that usually the lives of the saints are normative for us; the other extreme affirms that the lives of the saints have little or nothing to say to contemporary man or woman; their experiences were too different. The position I have learned to take is a *via media,* an effort to harmonize and unify what is valid. The lives of the saints, or aspects of their lives, or individual episodes in their lives, even legends surrounding saints who did or did not exist illustrate in striking fashion certain principles or facets of Christian spirituality that are permanently valid, that have a relevance transcending persons and places, eras and situations. And even where saintly actions seem embarrassingly eccentric or bizarre, they often lend credence to G. K. Chesterton's contention: "A saint is one who exaggerates what the world and the church have forgotten."

. . . Centuries old but as fresh as today. That's the meaning past sanctity has for present holiness.

— Walter J. Burghardt, S.J., from *Short Sermons*
for Preachers on the Run

Enlightenment

Enlightenment is the ability to see beyond all the things we make God to find God. We make religion God and so fail to see godliness where religion is not, though goodness is clear and constant in the simplest of people, the remotest of places. We make national honor God and fail to see the presence of God in other nations, particularly non-Christian nations. We make personal security God and fail to see God in the bleak and barren dimensions of life. We separate spirit and matter as if they were two different things, though we know now from quantum physics that matter is simply fields of force made dense by the spirit of Energy. We are one with the universe, in other words. We are not separate from it or different from it. We are not above it. We are in it, all of us and everything, swimming in an energy that is God. To be enlightened is to see behind the forms to the God who holds them in being.

— Joan Chittister, from *Illuminated Life*

A Mass on the World

Since once again, Lord...I have neither bread, nor wine, nor altar, I will raise myself beyond these symbols, up to the pure majesty of the real itself; I, your priest, will make the whole earth my altar and on it will offer you all the labors and sufferings of the world.

Over there, on the horizon, the sun has just touched with light the outermost fringe of the eastern sky. Once again, beneath this moving sheet of fire, the living surface of the earth wakes and trembles, and once again begins its fearful travail. I will place on my paten, O God, the harvest to be won by this renewal of labor, into my chalice I shall pour all the sap which is to be pressed out this day from the earth's fruits....

Receive, O Lord, this all-embracing host which your whole creation, moved by our magnetism, offers you at this dawn of a new day.

This bread, our toil, is of itself, I know, but an immense fragmentation; this wine, our pain, is no more, I know, than a drought that dissolves. Yet in the very depths of this formless mass you have implanted — and this I am sure of, for I sense it — a desire, irresistible, hallowing, which makes us cry out, believer and unbeliever alike: "Lord, make us *one*."

— Pierre Teilhard de Chardin, from *Pierre Teilhard de Chardin:
Essential Writings,* edited by Ursula King

The Nature of Faith

There are some who assume that it is wrong to doubt, that one is somehow less Christian if one doubts. But doubt is an element of faith; faith is not certainty that can be scientifically proved, or else it would not be faith. Recall that the author of the letter to the Hebrews writes, "Now faith is the substance of things hoped for, the evidence of things not seen" (11:1, KJV). The Easter story is a matter of faith. No one saw the resurrection, but something happened of such magnitude that it transformed frightened men and women into bold, courageous witnesses willing to die to proclaim the Risen Christ. And the power of this witness has been so great that it is brought down to us over the centuries as if the event happened yesterday. It is a mystery that we cannot understand with our sense; we can only comprehend it through faith. . . .

On the evening of his resurrection, Jesus, the Risen Christ, spoke not only to Thomas, but also the multitudes of us who have followed over the centuries. "Because you have seen me you have found faith. Happy are they who never saw me and yet have found faith."

— Pauli Murray, from *Pauli Murray: Selected Sermons and Writings,* edited by Anthony B. Pinn

That Little Cup of Oil

A monk was seeking salvation in the wilderness. He continually read his prayers and even got up twice a night to do so. A peasant used to bring him food. The monk started to wonder whether his way of life was holy enough, so he went to the saintly elder monk for guidance. He told the elder monk about his life, his way of praying, the words of his prayers, his getting up at night to pray, and his being fed by charitable offerings. He asked whether he was living right.

"All is fine," said the elder monk, "but go and see how the peasant who feeds you lives. Maybe you can learn something from him."

The monk visited the peasant and spent a day and night with him. The peasant got up early and said only, "Lord." He went to work and plowed the fields the whole day. At night he came home and again said, "Lord." Then he lay down to sleep. The monk thought, "There is nothing I can learn here," and wondered why the elder monk had sent him to the peasant.

He returned to the elder monk and told him, "The peasant hardly thinks about God — he mentions Him only twice a day."

So the elder monk told him, "Take this cup full of oil and walk around the village and come back here without spilling a drop." The monk did as he was told. When he returned, the elder monk asked him, "How many times did you think about God while you were carrying the cup?" The monk admitted that he did not think about God even once. He said, "I only thought about not spilling the oil."

The elder monk said, "That little cup of oil kept you so preoccupied that you did not remember God even once. But the peasant fed himself, his family, and you with his labor and care and still remembered God twice a day."

— Leo Tolstoy (*Path of Life*), from *Leo Tolstoy: Spiritual Writings,* edited by Charles Moore

A Talisman

I will give you a talisman. Whenever you are in doubt, or when the self becomes too much with you, apply the following test.

Recall the face of the poorest and the weakest person whom you have seen, and ask yourself if the next step you contemplate is going to be of any use to that person. Will that person gain anything by it? Will it restore that person to a control over his or her own life and destiny? In other words, will it lead to freedom for the hungry and spiritually starving millions?

Then you will find your doubts and your self melting away.

— Mohandas Gandhi, from *Mohandas Gandhi:*
Essential Writings, edited by John Dear

Looking for God
in All the Wrong Places

I searched for God in my heart, not quite convinced
I'd find anything of worth or holy there.
And I was right — or so I thought.

I looked for God in my home with greater doubt
the Lord of Hosts would dwell amid such messy madness,
no matter how great the joy or strong the bonds of love.
And sure enough the Lord eluded me again — or so I believed.

So I took my quest to fields afar,
confident the farther I went,
    the more desolate the desert,
    the starker my surroundings,
the greater my chances of finding the One
who alone could make me whole.

I climbed each sacred mountain,
I fasted and prayed and
    offered sacrifice
    before various altars at sundry shrines.
I chanted, sang or kept silent,
doing works of charity along the way
— all to no avail.

Tired, sad and discouraged
    I gave up my quest
and mourned the passing of a dream.
Then, a child, curious, poor,
watched me — and smiled.
A woman, too, older than the hills,
nodded approval.

So I gave the child my dream
  and handed the crone
  my empty, broken heart...
And in that instant
  angels filled the sanctuary and
  rocked the Temple
  with their eternal
  "Holy, holy, holy!"

— Joseph R. Veneroso, M.M.,
from *God in Unexpected Places*

Go Out into the World

I remember the closing words of the Latin Mass: *"Ite, missa est* — Go, get out!" which we try to soften in the English translation as "Go in peace." But the Mass is a dismissal: *missa, dismissa.* We are sent away; we are shown out. We are driven by the Spirit of affirmation we have enjoyed in the Mass to go out into the desert of the world around us to be emissaries of Christ, occasions of blessing. We are to draw the springs up from the desert in which we walk, so that, wherever our steps take us, the secret running rivers of divine friendship and grace will flow.

— Mark Gruber, O.S.B., from *Journey Back to Eden*

A New Communion

The pictures on my wall reveal my thirst for communion, but as I gaze on them with great love, I feel immense pain rising up within me: "Why can't I speak with him? will she never write? Why did they die before we were ever reconciled? Why can't we feel safe with each other?" And as I light a candle in front of my icon of Jesus and look into the eternity of his eyes, I say, "When, when Lord, will you come and fulfill the deepest longing of my heart?" the thirst for communion is evoked every time I look at Veronica's veil with the face of Christ on it and the faces of all whom I love . . . and pain deepens as I grow older.

I know that I have to lose my life to find it — to let go of my pictures and to meet the real person — to die to my sentimental memories and trust a new communion will emerge which is beyond my imagining. But how can I trust to a new life when I see the blood and sweat-stained life of Jesus and all those who suffer in prisons, refugee camps, and torture chambers? Jesus looks at me and seals my heart with the imprint of his face. I will always keep searching, always waiting, always hoping. His suffering face does not allow me to despair. My sorrow is a hunger, my loneliness a thirst. As we meet, we know that the love that causes us pain is the seed of a life where pain cannot abide.

— Henri Nouwen, from *Walk with Jesus*

To a College Student

I think that this experience you are having of losing your faith, or as you think, of having lost it, is an experience that in the long-run belongs to faith; or at least it can belong to faith if faith is still valuable to you, and it must be or you would not have written me about it.

I don't know how the kind of faith required of a Christian living in the twentieth century can be at all if it is not grounded on this experience that you are having right now of unbelief This may be the case always and not just in the twentieth century. Peter said, "Lord, I believe. Help my unbelief." It is the most natural and most human and most agonizing prayer in the gospels, and I think it is the foundation prayer of faith....

If you want your faith, you have to work for it. It is a gift, but for very few is it a gift given without any demand for equal time devoted to its cultivation.... To find out about faith, you have to go to the people who have it and you have to go to the most intelligent ones if you are going to stand up intellectually to agnostics and the general run of pagans that you are going to find in the majority of people around you....

Even in the life of a Christian, faith rises and falls like the tides of an invisible sea. It's there, even when he can't see it or feel it, if he wants it to be there. You realize, I think, that it is more valuable, more mysterious, altogether more immense than anything you can learn or decide upon in college. Learn what you can, but cultivate Christian skepticism. It will keep you free — not free to do anything you please, but free to be formed by something larger than your own intellect or the intellects of those around you.

— Flannery O'Connor, from *Flannery O'Connor: Spiritual Writings,* edited by Robert Ellsberg

What Is Happiness?

In the early 1960s Pearl, a frail little old lady in her 70s, was demonstrating outside the White House against racism. She was arrested and imprisoned. While in prison she had a heart attack, but refused to go to the nearest hospital because it did not admit black people. And having survived the prison and the heart attack, back she went to demonstrate against racism in front of the White House.

Twenty years later I met Pearl at a meeting protesting the nuclear threat. To me she seemed a most experienced, wise and holy person. So I thought I would put an important question, perhaps the most important question, to her. "Pearl," I asked, "what is happiness?"

Without hesitation, out of her long experience and great wisdom, she replied, "Happiness is *belonging*."

How right she was. Happiness is belonging to a family where I am loved and accepted as I am. Happiness is belonging to a community where I am loved and accepted as I am. Even the happiness of heaven consists in being absorbed into the community of the Trinity. Hence the relevance of the small Christian communities, or basic Christian communities, that have appeared in the Church over recent decades.

— James O'Halloran, from *Signs of Hope*

Suffering

Show me someone who hasn't suffered and I'll show you an insufferable bore. Difficult as it is to accept, suffering and loss are necessary to humanity. Who could value warm, sunny days who hasn't known dreary, rainy ones? Who could appreciate good health who has never been ill? Who could value the people we love if we felt no acceptance of death? Who could offer grateful worship who takes everything for granted?

In order to experience humanity fully, even the Son of God suffered. This is a God who willingly stripped himself of all defenses to show us how humanity is "done."

With dignity. And faith. And love.

— William J. O'Malley, from *Help My Unbelief*

The Light Comes from God

When I was a child in the 1960s I remember visiting old relatives in rural Ireland. When the electric light was switched on, the man said, "God, give us the light of heaven!" I took electricity for granted, yet it had only arrived in that house in the previous decade and customs from the time of lamps and candles still survived. The moment impressed itself on my memory for everyone in the house, including my parents, could chime back "Amen" in unison — but I had not heard this happen before. It is a liturgy of just two lines, but it linked that day, and that physical light, with a future "day" and the notion of the incomprehensible light of God.

When we speak of a sacramental understanding of the universe, it is that simple kitchen liturgy that we should keep in mind. Those people would have had little need to explain with words "the symbolism" of candles in the liturgy; every time they lit lamps, they knew that somehow they pointed toward heaven, and that to speak of heaven using lamps and candles made perfect sense. The action *now* in this reality was a petition for a *future* in another reality. It was many years before I recognized the richness of that simple act in a kitchen lit by one light bulb, but this was a spontaneous trace of an attitude to life that makes those Christians of long ago so interesting to us.

— Thomas O'Loughlin, from *Journeys on the Edges*

The Mystic

A great development has taken place in the twentieth century as Christians everywhere become aware of the social dimensions of their religion. Christians see that to follow Christ they must resonate with the suffering of the world — with the poor and afflicted and distressed.

And if men and women are moving toward a sense of solidarity, those called to the mystical life cannot claim exemption. The authentic mystic can never flee from the world.

Active mystics who live in the hurly-burly enter into the same inner silence as those who live in the desert. They experience the inner fire and the inner love. Now the inner fire drives them — no longer to the wilderness but to the crowded marketplace and to the inner city. The living flame of love drives them to walk in peace marches, to denounce oppressive structures, to go to prison and to die. Like the mystics in the desert they pass through agonizing dark nights and come to profound enlightenment. The mystic in the silent desert and the mystic in the noisy city are alike in following one who emptied himself taking the form of a slave and was given a name that is above all names.

— William Johnston, from *Mystical Theology*

Our Life Is Our Prayer

To wish to learn from the Celtic Christian is to wish to sense the passionate presence of God in all of life. It is to find God in the ordinary events of life, love, eating, working, playing. It is to learn that everything is grace and blessing and we are to aim at bringing into consciousness the holiness of every moment.

Prayer needs to be not just part of us but all of us. We need to pray with the whole of ourselves, my full person in harmony with all creation, not just with words but going beyond words, using heart, images, and body. This tradition is a call to return to our roots in the clay of the earth from which we come and to the Spirit of God in whom we dwell. If we can do this, we will find our prayer is our life and our life is our prayer.

— Timothy Joyce, from *Celtic Christianity*

The Laity

The laity I knew, patronizingly described as *vulgus indoctus,* were still immature and inert, a flock of sheep, with a cleric on whose shoulders fell the full weight of the apostolate.

Then came a new age.

Beginning with the pontificate of Pius XI and increasingly through the reigns of Pius XII, John XXIII and Paul VI, a process of development took place on a vast scale within the Church.

The laity became aware of forming the Church and grasped the fact that their faith didn't merely urge them to acts of piety but required them to live out the gospel message in the world.

Everything became the material of religion: home, politics, social relations, job, life, love.

The Second Vatican Council — the most extraordinary event to have taken place in all the centuries of Christianity — effected the Church's transit from childhood to maturity, obliging everyone to see the Church as *the people of God* and no longer as a clerical pyramid.

This achievement was of enormous significance and in fact formed the theological basis for the new concept of Church-and-world. Even though we haven't yet achieved in entirety what the new perspectives, afforded by the Council, may reveal, we have made a great deal of progress.

Without the presence of the laity and without a just, fruitful, balanced, loving collaboration between hierarchy and laity, the life, the activity of a Christian community, whether large or small, would be inconceivable today.

This is maturity!

— Carlo Carretto, from *And God Saw That It Was Good*

It's Never Too Late

"No, it's never too late to heal and start anew." It is not too late because life is this moment, and only this. There is now — this day — and its full potential to open wide a new door. And even though we may tremble at the immediacy and intimacy of the threshold we face, there is within us the power to walk through these new openings. There is within us a power greater than anything we will ever face, greater than anything we have ever done — a power that enables us to learn from our missteps and begin again.

Beginning again is possible because life is possible. We can choose to go on, entering the fullness that is at the heart of all things. Starting over is the step we take because of a small vow we make to ourselves. I choose to live. I choose to heal and grow. I agree to meet the circumstances in my life with the power of spirit that lies within.

— Paula D'Arcy, from *Waking Up to This Day*

"If You Want to Speak to God, Tell It to the Wind"

Gentle breeze from the four corners of the earth,
Bear our prayer on your wings to the court of the most
   high God.
Blazing sun, do not scorch our petition.
Falling rain, do not drown our request.
Flashing lightning, do not strike down our plea.
Roaring thunder, do not scare our supplication . . .

Beaming moon, illumine our prayer before our God.
Twinkling stars, show our prayer the way to the abode
   of God.
Gentle dew, water the path of our prayer to the dwelling of
   God, the most high.
Rustling wind, make our prayer pleasing to the ears of God.

Gentle breeze from the four corners of the earth,
Bear our prayer on your wings to the court of the most
   high God.

— A. E. Orobator, from *Theology Brewed in an African Pot*

MARCH

God Dwells in Us

We say that when we have sanctifying grace, we are in the state of grace and we are using words that mean very little to us. If, instead of saying "in the state of grace," we spoke of God dwelling in us, we might see this wonderful truth in a clearer light. We share in the divine life, we become participators in the divine life, sharers in the Blessed Trinity. There is nothing more startling than this amazing evidence of God's love for us, nothing more worthy of our study.

— Bishop Francis X. Ford, M.M., from *Come, Holy Spirit*

Heaven Is Here

It is a practice in many monasteries to turn and bow to the sister walking in procession with you after bowing to the altar as you enter chapel for prayer. The meaning of such a monastic custom is clear: God is as much in the world around us, as much in one another, as on that altar or in that chapel. God is the stuff of our lives, the breath of our very souls, calling us always to a heightened understanding of Life in all of its forms.

To be enlightened is to know that heaven is not "coming." Heaven is here. We have simply not been able to realize that yet because, like King Arthur and his search for the Holy Grail, we look in all the wrong places, worship all the wrong idols, get fixated on all the wrong notions of God. We are always on our way to somewhere else when this place, the place in which I stand, wherever it is, is the place of my procession into God, the site of my union with the Life that gives Life.

— Joan Chittister, from *Illuminated Life*

We Walk the Path Together

The spiritual pilgrim sets off on the journey of life as a wandering beggar for no other reason than to finally come home.... Interreligious dialogue offers us the opportunity to experience this wonderful truth. I speak from my own experience in this regard. I see my mendicant wanderings into the world of Buddhist and Hindu mysticism as an essential part of my Christian discipleship. It is Jesus himself who has sent me out empty handed, a poor beggar in the spiritual tradition of St. Dominic.... I have shared the scriptures and the music of Jesus with newly found friends, and they have done the same with me. I have heard in the depths of my heart the harmony that springs forth from these blessed encounters. I am beginning to discover that the more my heart becomes a begging bowl, the more wonderfully do I experience the gratuitousness of life.

I would venture to say that I am a better disciple of Jesus because of this journey into the world of interreligious dialogue. Perhaps *better* is not the right word. It is as if I can see Jesus — the living Christ — more clearly now, as he is reflected through the teachings and practices of other spiritual traditions. I am still a wandering pilgrim, and sometimes I feel that the road is as dark and uncertain as the day I began. But I walk with a sense of *presence,* the presence of Jesus, the presence of God, the presence of the Buddha and many other holy men and women throughout the ages. This *presence* becomes more real each time I am able to dwell fully in the present moment.

In no way does this mean that the journey is over. It has only begun. Today is the day of salvation. This moment is the eternal Now. Life is a great gift, a great surprise. Yes, we are home, and yet there is a long road ahead. For this reason we take a step — one step — and we smile and give things. We walk the path together.

— Brian J. Pierce, O.P., from *We Walk the Path Together*

The Coming of a Single Word

One of my Dominican brethren, a rugged Scot called Anthony Ross, was a famous preacher until he was struck down by a stroke that left him wordless. The specialist who came to see him told Fr. Anthony he would never be able to utter a single word again, to which Anthony replied, "Thank you, doctor" — leaving the doctor speechless! Anthony could never say much but every word he struggled to bring out was fruit of awful suffering and victory. People would come hundreds of miles just to hear him speak a single word. You had to wait for it. Before I left for Rome, he gave me a single word: "Courage." And it was food for me for a long time.

— Timothy Radcliffe, from *Just One Year: A Global Treasury of Prayer and Worship*

First Rule of Life

While I was still young I had realized that I would need a point of reference on which to build, references taken from the Gospels which spoke powerfully to me. Without something very central to which I would return throughout my life, how would I ever develop myself within? It was not that I wanted to make some sort of system, but that I hoped to create a little inner unity. If it was going to be a question of taking great risks for God and for Christ — and it was risks and not ease I hoped for — there would be a need to keep a watch on myself, to refer to something which throughout my life would be a point of reference, something constantly to return to.

- Throughout your day, let work and rest be quickened by the Word of God.
- Keep inner silence in all things so as to dwell with Christ.
- Be filled with the spirit of the Beatitudes, joy, simplicity, mercy.

— Brother Roger of Taizé, from *Brother Roger of Taizé: Essential Writings,* edited by Marcello Fidanzio

What Thrills the Heart

We are not human beings trying to become spiritual. That task has already been done for us by our initial creation as "images of God" (Gen. 1:26). We are already spiritual beings. That is God's gift. Our desperate and needed task, the one we have not succeeded at very well after all these centuries, is *how to become human!* Jesus literally turns religion on its head. He is always moving down, descending into the fully human, identifying freely with our tragic and finite situation. We miss him entirely when we are always running up the down staircase. Our task is to follow and imitate him, not offer him incense, titles, and shrines that he never once asked for. All we need to do is take his lead. Most of the world is so tired of "spiritual people." We would be happy just to meet some real human beings. They always thrill the heart, just as he did.

— Richard Rohr, from *Soul Brothers:*
Men in the Bible Speak to Men Today

Listening to the Lives of Others

When we reflect on lives lived well, we see authenticities shaped by spiritual commitments and ethical choices. We see examples or models of what it means to be human; the luminous manner in which this life is lived reveals, at the same time, what it means to be holy. Exquisite humanness *is* holiness. In the examples of the holy ones, we glean hints of being and becoming and these resonate, strike a chord in us, awaken something deep. And so we learn from others — those who ask basic human questions and, following Rainer Maria Rilke, by letting them walk into the answers. The way they live the human questions becomes the cogent word of their lives. For those of us on the path forming our own cogent word, we do well to listen to the lucid expression in the lives of the holy ones. In doing so, we avail ourselves of the opportunity to discover — or recover — something deep, maybe hidden, in our own. Listening to the lives of others allows the question of our lives to surface, and thereby we become rich with possibility.

> —Thomas A. Forsthoefel, from *Soulsong:*
> *Seeking Holiness, Coming Home*

We Thank You, Mary

Your journey
has blessed ours, Mary.
Your Yes dares us
to believe in the impossible,
to embrace the unknown,
and to expect the breaking through of mystery
onto our bleak and level horizons.
The words you heard, Mary,
we will forever remember.
We will not be afraid,
for the life that you birthed
will not be extinguished
in our souls.
And the journey
you took in faithfulness,
we also take.
We the women, the midwives,
and the healers will also,
like you Mary, soul sister,
give birth to God
for our world.

— Edwina Gateley, from *Soul Sisters:
Women in Scripture Speak to Women Today*

The Challenge of Conversion

Change and conversion are not the same thing....

Change is required of us all. No one and nothing can stand still, cemented in the place, the work, the era that we had come to take for granted. However comforting the thought, however desirable the situation, what I am now, where I am now, will not always be.

Change will happen. Our only decision is whether to engage it. If we engage change, we can shape it. If we resist it, we run the risk of being shriveled by it into less than we are meant to be.

The not-so-obvious part of change is that change alone does not define the measure of our growth. Only conversion can do that. Only the willingness to embrace change, to learn from it, and to recognize in it the stuff of my own ultimate development can possibly give change its coinage.

Conversion requires the humility to look again at what we always knew to be true and see new truth in it.

Conversion requires the willing to risk. Stepping out into a new universe of grace and gift is the challenge of conversion. It is the ability to admit that there may be more to life than my own small perspective on it.

— Joan Chittister, from *The Way We Were*

Archbishop Romero
Two Weeks before His Death

I have often been threatened with death. I must tell you, as a Christian, I do not believe in death without resurrection. If I am killed, I shall arise in the Salvadoran people. I say so without boasting, with the greatest humility.

As a shepherd, I am obliged by divine mandate to give my life for those I love — for all Salvadorans, even for those who may be going to kill me. If the threats are carried out, from this moment I offer my blood to God for the redemption and for the resurrection of El Salvador.

Martyrdom is a grace of God that I do not believe I deserve. But if God accepts the sacrifice of my life, let my blood be a seed of freedom and the sign that hope will soon be reality. Let my death, if it is accepted by God, be for my people's liberation and as a witness of hope in the future.

You may say, if they succeed in killing me, that I pardon and bless those who do it. Would, indeed, that they might be convinced that they will waste their time. A bishop will die, but God's church, which is the people, will never perish.

— Oscar Romero, from *The Violence of Love*

Theology — Necessarily Humble

It is of great importance for us to remember that these theological insights are *humble* theological insights. They are *servants*, not masters, to the "inexpressible gift" of God in Christ (2 Cor. 9:15). They cannot exhaust and prove the depth of God's purpose in Christ (Rom. 11:33–35).

Let us remember that...theologies are *humble* theological attempts to express some fragment of the fullness of God's glory in Christ... (Isa. 6:1–8).

Theological contributions made by historical groups of Christians deserve positive evaluation only as long as they are not unduly elevated. That is to say, as long as they all point to the "Christ and him crucified" as *humble* theological insights....

The good news of reconciliation reaches its final realization in Jesus Christ crucified. Theology can only stammer about the person and work of Jesus Christ. It is because the Lord of *agape* crucified is the subject of theology. The one who engages in theology does so to "understand" (Eph. 1:17), "touch" (1 John 1:1–4), and "do the truth" (John 3:21).

— Kosuke Koyama, from *Water Buffalo Theology*

Christ's Redemptive Mystery

The great task of holiness and of following Christ in a consumer society is not a matter of right wing or left, of conservative or liberal. It is a matter of understanding the full message of Christ's redemptive mystery: that having been reaffirmed as persons in the full image and likeness of God, we must actually believe in God's redemption and see that love of one's self, one's neighbor, and God transforms every aspect of our lives and labors. The authentic disciple of Jesus is never pulled between a love of God and thirst for human justice, is never seduced into the delusion that faith somehow has no connection with how we treat our sisters and brothers in this world, and is never presumptuous enough to believe that the great human struggle for justice can ever be resolved without the most profound humility before the God who has created us equal in personhood and destiny.

— John F. Kavanaugh, from *Following Christ in a Consumer Society*

"Do This in Memory of Me"

When I hear the words, "Do this in memory of me," I am riveted. My back stiffens with resolve and my spirit and imagination are stirred. I think of the cloud of witnesses past and present who have modeled how to follow the nonviolent way, resisting oppression, caring for the poor and the sick, the outcast and the imprisoned, reaching out to "the enemy," confident in the love that possesses them. I think also of Gandhi's contention: that it is really *ahimsa* that holds the world together, that violence is the rupture of the normal fabric of life — parents caring selflessly for their children, teachers engaging their students, people helping other people — that daily round of human caring is what is real, not the *maya* of violence....

The "this" in "do this in memory of me" for me now means: "do this way of acting that I have shown you. Do this way of resisting evil and returning good for evil that I lived and taught. Do it even if it is hard and stirs up resistance. Do it filled with love, because you know that you are loved."

— Terrence J. Rynne, from *Gandhi and Jesus:*
The Saving Power of Nonviolence

Embrace Beauty

I found beauty in the rain. Of the thirty-seven days we walked the Camino, the weather often included mist, light rainfall, or steady showers. Except for heavy downpours I found more blessing than burden in rain. The forests and farmlands reached for the wetness. I could almost hear the soil and vegetation sighing with relief after the heat they endured. Those moist days held a stillness and a comforting gentleness. Their wetness wrapped soft arms around my weariness and refreshed me.

Beauty on the Camino revealed itself in more than the layers of misted mountains or the glory of a sunrise. Sometimes we found it in the simplest places, like an old shed. How could it be beautiful? It was. The color of the straw, the shelter from the downpour, the music of the raindrops, the gift of a friend, together these things brought ease and a moment of contentment to body and spirit.

The Camino's beauty strengthened my soul. It restored my attentiveness and reminded me not to miss its blessedness. Wherever I am, I never have to look far for this beauty. Always beauty awaits me. All it needs is my awareness and embrace. Each of us needs to hold on to something beautiful in our heart.

— Joyce Rupp, from *Walk in a Relaxed Manner*

That Mysterious "Must"

A man once said to me, "We need money for all the good that needs to be done at home. I won't give a dime for missionary work." Knowing him well, I asked him whether he gave more for good causes at home, and how much he contributed to these worthy causes. He remained silent. So did I. But since then, the missions have been getting money from him....

What should we answer when they say that missionary work doesn't do any good, that it only squanders money and manpower for nothing? Of course, one could tell a long story about the successes of missionary work in the Great Lakes District of Central Africa, in the South Sea Islands, the hundreds of busy untroubled villages it has created, how it has put a stop to bloodshed.... But no. For missionary work is carried on without thought of success. It goes on because it must, out of a compelling force that is the very nature of things where the Spirit of Jesus is.

Ordinary men in everyday life calculate the changes of success; they will undertake a project only if they are confident of reward. But when something is done in Jesus' name, the only thing to take into account is the "must," that mysterious "must" that Jesus keeps insisting on when he talks of the destiny of the Son of man, of the death that awaited him. The less our prospect of success, the greater the force of that "must."

So, let us not be sparing in our contributions, in money, or manpower. Nothing will ever be wasted.

— Albert Schweitzer, from *Albert Schweitzer: Essential Writings,* edited by James Brabazon

Through the Lens of Jesus

It was 1600 and the Dutch spectacle-maker Hans Lippershey was working in his shop, bent over the table doing the detailed and tedious task of repairing a lens. The door was always open so that as people came into the shop he wouldn't have to get up from his work. Two children who entered were intrigued by the lens and mirrors and strange implements in the window. Curious, they played with everything, delighted with new toys that showed them things so differently.

By accident, chance — grace — they picked up two lenses and looked through both of them at the same time and observed a weathervane on the roof of a church some distance away, but it looked so close! It was magnified in their seeing and they were excited. Laughing, they pointed the lenses at other things. They got so loud that Lippershey went to see what all the commotion was about and he discovered for himself the meaning of depth of magnification. But it was the discovery of the children that set him to making telescopes.

This is what Jesus has done for us. We look through the lens of Jesus, God's telescope, at our world, our church and our lives today and see them magnified and up close. The lens of Jesus draws the distant God of the past near to us. The word of God in the gospels, especially when listened to with others, is a double set of lenses that reveals truth. It's time for us all to start wearing these glasses!

— Megan McKenna, from *On Your Mark*

The Sacred Circle of Life

The Giver of life knows all creation as family. How then can any clan, tribe, or nation be more valuable than another? How can any part of creation be seen as merely a resource for human consumption? How can we claim priorities that undermine relationships of trust? All creation is a gift and all families bear the mark of the Creator's hand. Will we take the time to see it?

We have come so far from a place where grandmothers and grandfathers were needed by the family and where sons and daughters knew aunts, uncles, and cousins. But Joseph took Jesus as his son and showed us that love can make us family where the world sees none. Joseph was not the natural father of Jesus, but he chose to become a father where one was needed. Joseph's strength and manhood were proven by the fire of courage, responsibility, and love.

Will we choose our gadgets and schedules over those who need us to be their family or will we use them to enhance life for all? Will we be able to see relationship as a gift and not just a means to a profitable end? Are we willing to walk the long road of mending the sacred hoop of life? Will we be wise enough to use our creative minds, our compassionate and passionate spirits to meet the needs of our age for the sake of all families? This is not an easy road, but it is a meaningful road. It is the path of becoming a human being. It may be as long as a journey into an unknown land and back again. May we seek the beauty of lifegiving relationships in family and in the creation as we live together on this Earth, our home.

— Judy Wellington, from *Holiness and the Feminine Spirit: The Art of Janet McKenzie,* edited by Susan Perry

Liberation

Christian theology is a theology of liberation. It is a rational study of the being of God in the world in light of the existential situation of an oppressed community, relating the forces of liberation to the essence of the gospel, which is Jesus Christ. This means that its sole reason for existence is to put into ordered speech the meaning of God's activity in the world, so that the community of the oppressed will recognize that its inner thrust for liberation is not only *consistent with* the gospel but *is* the gospel of Jesus Christ. There can be no Christian theology that is not identified unreservedly with those who are humiliated and abused. In fact, theology ceases to be a theology of the gospel when it fails to arise out of the community of the oppressed. For it is impossible to speak of the God of Israelite history, who is the God revealed in Jesus Christ, without recognizing that God is the God *of* and *for* those who labor and are over laden.

—James Cone, from *A Black Theology of Liberation*

Harmony Prayer

O Lord, I cry for peace,
Purify my eyes to see peace,
Purify my mind to understand peace,
Purify my heart to love peace,
Purify my memory to work for peace,
The peace that comes from your
love and compassion.

O Lord, sustain my vision of peace
following your inspiration,
You have many ways of revealing your
presence and love for humanity,
But your style is constant:
You are in dialogue with all,
You care for all.

Make me, O Lord, a sign of your peace,
Living a life-in-dialogue with you
to understand your silence
and seek your presence;
in dialogue with myself
to rediscover the meaning of my life;
in dialogue with others
to move together in harmony with all;
And, in dialogue with creation
to care for the earth.

Give me, O Lord,
the courage to live in dialogue
in the midst of divisions and conflicts
and to build peace with all people
of sincere hearts who believe
in your love and compassion.
Amen.

> —James H. Kroeger, M.M., from *Once upon a Time in Asia,*
> edited by James H. Kroeger and Eugene F. Thalman

The Bread We Break Together

The grace of hope, this consciousness that there is in every person *that which is of God,* comes and goes in a rhythm like that of the sea. The Spirit blows where it listeth, and we travel through deserts and much darkness and doubt. We can only make that act of faith, "Lord, I believe because I want to believe." We must remember that faith, like love, is an act of the will, an act of preference. God speaks, He answers these cries in the darkness as He always did. He is incarnate today in the poor, in the bread we break together. We know Him and each other in the breaking of bread."

> —Dorothy Day, from *Dorothy Day:
> Selected Writings,* edited by Robert Ellsberg

A Prayer to the Living God

Lord, living God, you are the One and the Only, and there is no other beside you. All divinity is yours, and whatever is not properly attributed to you is a theft.

In grace you have revealed your being to us and told us your name. We believe in you. Keep us in the faith, O Lord, and for in it alone are we sustained. Your honor is our honor, and your governance is our salvation.

You have created the world and us in it. Everything — being and existence, life and meaning — comes from your omnipotent and loving world. And so we bow down before you, O Lord, and pray to you.

You are the Holy One. We are however sinful and acknowledge this. We are grateful to you for showing us our sinful condition since this is the truth, and only truth makes it possible for us to begin anew and to overcome our sinfulness.

— Romano Guardini, from *Romano Guardini: Spiritual Writings,* edited by Robert A. Krieg

Witnesses

When Jesus rose from the dead, his first words to his stunned disciples were "Peace be with you." He showed them his wounds and then repeated his greeting: "Peace be with you." Luke tells us that after explaining the scriptures and salvation history, Jesus said to his friends, "You will be my witnesses." With that, he ascended into heaven.

Witnesses are those who testify from personal experience about what they saw or heard. Like a witness who takes the stand in court and pledges to speak the truth, Christian witnesses take the stand in the court of life and speak the truth of God. They tell us that God is alive and at work, that Jesus is risen and calls us to his discipleship journey of compassionate love, and that God's reign of peace and nonviolence is at hand, right now, at this very moment.

— John Dear, from *"You Will Be My Witnesses,"*
Saints, Prophets, and Martyrs

Slow Down, You Move Too Fast!

The creation story reminds us that God took a day off to sit back and enjoy creation, the origin of the Jewish Sabbath, when no work was to be done. It seems as if the heresy called Jansenism has joined hands with a puritanical work ethic to distort the lives of many modern Christians. Jansenism taught that enjoyment was sinful and that we were created to toil and sweat for our living. Doing good works became synonymous with sanctity. "Idle hands are the devil's workshop" is a saying I learned when I was very young. I still feel guilty when I take time off and I find myself needing to make excuses when I go on a holiday.

I marvel at my Zimbabwean friends who can spend the day laughing and talking to one another, even though they barely have enough to eat. No matter how difficult the living conditions, I find people singing, dancing, and praying. There is a tendency for Westerners to call this "laziness" and to condemn African societies to perpetual poverty because they refuse to adopt a Western work ethic. I believe that it is the other way around — that if the West would adopt the African play ethic and give priority to relationships, it would become more human in the process and there might be fewer heart attacks and less high blood pressure.

— Janice McLaughlin, M.M., from *Ostriches, Dung Beetles, and Other Spiritual Masters: A Book of Wisdom from the Wild*

The Beautiful Structure of the Common Good

Everyone can contribute much that is good, and in that way trust is achieved. The common good will not be attained by excluding people. We can't enrich the common good of our country by driving out those we don't care for. We have to try to bring out all that is good in each person and try to develop an atmosphere of trust, not with physical force, but with a moral force that draws out the good that is in everyone, especially in concerned young people.

Thus with all contributing all can build the beautiful structure of the common good, the good that we construct together, and that creates conditions of kindness, of trust, of freedom, of peace.

— Oscar Romero, from *The Violence of Love*

Hail Mary

After I had been told that the girl-mother in the Tuareg encampment [Africa] had been killed because she was caught in adultery, my relations with Mary of Nazareth became much closer.

It was as if she suddenly became my sister. I was not used to seeing her so human, so frail, so near to me.... Yes, I must humbly admit it. It was not until I saw that silent tragedy of the Tuareg encampment in the light of Luke's Gospel that I fully understood Mary's courage in accepting what the angel told her about God's plans for her.

She had to accept the role of a girl-mother. And who was going to believe her?

...Mary had the courage to trust in the God of the impossible and to leave the solution of her problems to him. Hers was pure faith....

To have to believe that the baby in her womb was the son of the Most High. Yes, it was easy enough to conceive him in the flesh, considerably more demanding to conceive him in faith!...

Indeed, God managed to fit into your little womb, Mary, and you kept him warm with your sweet body.

Mary!

My sister!

Blessed are you who believed — I say it to you tonight with rapture, as your cousin Elizabeth said it to you on that hot evening in Ain-Karim.

—Carlo Carretto, from *Blessed Are You Who Believed*

The New Justice

Jesus is the just one (Acts 3:13; 7:52). He embodies, incarnates, and reveals the justice of God (Rom. 1:16–17; 3:21–22; 4:25), and he inaugurates the new historical project of building a just world, what he calls the reign of God and its justice (Matt. 6:33).

Some Christians think that the New Testament says very little about justice and that love replaces justice as the fundamental and all-embracing virtue. But it is only possible to think like that if justice is thought of as one virtue among many. The New Testament is all about justice, and the word occurs very frequently if you remember that "righteousness" means "justice" and that "justification" means making someone or something just, putting right what was wrong.

Jesus made it quite clear from the start that he had not come to abolish the law but to fulfill it. In other words, he had not come to abolish God's demand for justice but to fulfill that demand. This Jesus does by trying to take the people, and especially the scribes and Pharisees, beyond their present, very narrow ideas of what is just and what is not. "Unless your justice goes beyond that of the scribes and Pharisees, you will never enter the kingdom of heaven" (Matt. 5:17–20).

Jesus says this at the beginning of the Sermon on the Mount. He then proceeds to take examples from the law to deepen them, to go beyond them and fulfill them — to preach the new justice. To illustrate this, we might look at what he does about the commandments against killing and adultery. Basically he says our concern should be not only with the external act of murder or adultery but also with the interior act. You could say that he was telling us not to commit "murder of the heart" or "adultery of the heart." Jesus is interiorizing the law, interiorizing justice. He is asking about one's motive for doing justice. What is your motive for not committing adultery or not killing someone you hate? Fear of being caught?

This new justice comes spontaneously from the heart. It is a justice of the heart, motivated by a passion for justice. Now this passion for justice is what we generally call compassion for people.

Compassion, as you know, means "feeling with" people, especially people in need, suffering people. Compassion was very important as the starting point for Jesus. He was moved by compassion for the poor, the sick, and the outcasts.

In short, Jesus' way of deepening and renewing justice was to bring in compassion as the heart of justice, as the motive for a passionate devotion to justice.

— Albert Nolan, from *Hope in an Age of Despair*

Touch Me, O Lord

Lord, help me to see your peace in my turmoil, your compassion in my sorrow, your forgiveness in my weakness, and your love in my needs. Touch me, O Lord, with your healing power and grace.

— Marlene McKinney, Prayer to Christ the Healer,
from *A Maryknoll Book of Prayer*, edited by
Michael Leach and Susan Perry

In the Middle of the Desert

As I was finishing this book I heard that Henri [Nouwen] was planning to leave Yale. Could it be true? How sad and confusing for all of us. I had an image of one Abba, deciding to leave his community, one morning, to get deeper into the desert, seeking to get even closer to the spirit of Jesus.

A few days after an extravagant farewell party for Henri, I received a peculiar call from him. He sounded tense and desperate. "Are you there, Yushi? Do you remember me?" I went straight to the house where he was staying where I found him standing wordlessly. Over a cup of tea he started to talk. "I had a terrible daydream. A lot of good friends gathered and started to dance around me. When the music stopped and the dust settled, there was nobody left. I found myself in the middle of a barren land." "You're not alone, Henri," I said. "You know we've been working together in that desert." "I know, I know. Thank you for reminding me that I'm in the middle of the desert and I'm not alone there."

When one goes into the deepest part of the human soul, one cannot ask someone to accompany him. Step by step, he has to go down all the way to the bottom. When he finds something shining there, he holds it to his bosom, and starts going up the way he came down so that he can share it with others.

— Yushi Nomura, from *Desert Wisdom:*
Sayings from the Desert Fathers

¡Gracias!

Gratitude is one of the most visible characteristics of the poor I have come to know. I am always surrounded by words of thanks: "thanks for your visit, your blessing, your sermon, your prayer, your gifts, your presence with us." Even the smallest and most necessary goods are a reason for gratitude. This all-pervading gratitude is the basis for celebration. Not only are the poor grateful for life, but they also celebrate life constantly. A visit, a reunion, a simple meeting are always like little celebrations. Every gift is shared. "Have a drink, take some fruit, eat our bread" is the response to every visit I make. All life is a gift, a gift to be celebrated, a gift to be shared.

Thus the poor are a Eucharistic people, people who know to say thanks to God, to life, to each other. They may not come to Mass, they may not participate in many church celebrations. But in their hearts they are deeply religious, because for them all of life is a long fiesta with God.

— Henri Nouwen, from *¡Gracias! A Latin American Journal*

Mother of God, She Who Hears the Cries of the World

Mother of Mercy,
the cries of the world keep me awake at night.
I rise from my bed, but I cannot locate the source of the
    wailing.
It is everywhere, Mother, coming from all directions,
and my heart is shattered by the sheer intensity of suffering.
You of boundless compassion,
expand my heart so that I can contain the pain.
Focus my mind so that I can arrive at viable solutions,
and energize my body so that I can engage in effective
    action.
Give me the courage to follow the crumbs of heartbreak
all the way home to the place where I can be of real service.
Let me dip my fingers into the dew of your compassion
and scatter it now over the fevered brow of this world.

—Mirabai Starr, from *Mother of God Similar to Fire*

Discipleship and the Cross

And he began to teach them, that the Son of man must suffer
many things, and be rejected by the elders and the chief priests,
and the scribes, and be killed, and after three days rise again. . . .
— Mark 8:31

Jesus must therefore make it clear beyond all doubt that the
"must" of suffering applies to his disciples no less than to himself. Just as Christ is Christ only in virtue of his suffering and
rejection, so the disciple is a disciple only insofar as he shares his
Lord's suffering and rejection and crucifixion. Discipleship means
adherence to the person of Jesus, and therefore submission to the
law of Christ which is the law of the cross.

Surprisingly enough, when Jesus begins to unfold this inescap-
able truth to his disciples, he once more sets them free to choose
or reject him. "If any man would come after me," he says. For it is
not a matter of course, not even among the disciples. Nobody can
be forced; nobody can even be expected to come. He says rather,
"If any man" is prepared to spurn all other offers which come his
way in order to follow him. Once again, everything is left for the
individual to decide. When the disciples are half-way along the
road of discipleship, they come to another crossroad. Once more
they are left free to choose for themselves, nothing is expected of
them, nothing forced upon them. So crucial is the demand of the
present hour that the disciples must be free to make their own
choice before they are told of the law of discipleship.

— Dietrich Bonhoeffer, from *Dietrich Bonhoeffer:*
Selected Writings, edited by Robert Coles

APRIL

"I Want to Love until I Die"

You can tell a lot about a person by what she chooses to do when she knows her days are numbered. The year 1989 was the last year of Thea Bowman's life and though she couldn't go anywhere without a wheelchair, she lived it as if it were the first.

"There is an urgency about my life," Thea said. "I know that I have not got long. Because of the cancer I am deciding what is important and not important. . . . My role in life is to open people up to life so that they might realize their own talents. So many people have gifts they haven't realized. God has given me a grace to see in people what they have.

"I'm afraid of pain, being helpless and incapacitated. Yet I believe there's a plan and I try to go with the program. All I ask of God is that I be able to live fully until I die. That takes away a lot of the anxiety and what happens doesn't matter. I want to love until I die. And, as I've always said, I want to have a good time!"

— Thea Bowman, from *Thea's Song: The Life of Thea Bowman*
by Charlene Smith and John Feister

Knowing How to Forgive

Some time ago, Eufrasio, an elder of an Aymara clan in the Altiplano of Peru, came to his parish priest and asked if he might use his house for a meeting. The priest assured him that it would be fine. Eufrasio thanked him and said, "We want you to be there as well."

When the day arrived, quite a number of Aymara folks came for the meeting. It seems there had been an incident that had angered people and resulted in many hurt feelings in the group. The elder stood before the group and asked one man to stand and tell his side of the story, which he did. He then asked someone of the opposite opinion to tell his version. After each had spoken, Eufrasio suggested a solution to the problem — and all agreed. He then asked each person present to give a sign of peace to everyone else in the room. When this was done he said, "Now this will never be mentioned again." All left quietly in peace.

Eufrasio then turned to the priest, thanked him for allowing them to use his house, and he too left.

"Now I have truly witnessed the sacrament of reconciliation," said the priest.

> — Helen Phillips, M.M., from *What They Taught Us:*
> *How Maryknoll Missioners Were Evangelized by the Poor,*
> edited by Joseph A. Heim, M.M.

Forgiveness Is a Boomerang

I broke into a sweat every time I thought of the violence, the sin, that happened that night when an eighteen-year-old named Joseph Shadow Clark slid through a basement window into my son and daughter-in-law's home, stealthily went up the stairs to the bedroom where they were sleeping, and shot them to death with his semi-automatic gun.

Every time I saw this in my mind's eye I shrank from the memory, paralyzed and powerless. I knew I had to reclaim my soul, but how? I had to struggle long and hard with whether forgiveness made sense, whether it was even possible. My children helped me as we struggled together with this horror. We had always been opposed to the death penalty, and healing first began when we wrote to the judge, asking that Shadow Clark not be executed.

I learned to see that the minute we say "no" to forgiveness we are gouging Christ out of our life, and from that resulting emptiness of soul we have nothing left to give to anybody else.

To forgive is just what the word itself says — to offer a gift before it's been earned or even deserved. It doesn't mean giving in, it means letting go. If we don't forgive we stay emotionally handcuffed to the person — or the nation — that hurt us. And if we're handcuffed, we are not free, never at peace, never able to do God's work. Forgiveness is a boomerang — the gift we send out is what we're going to get back. This is how God treats us. When we forgive, we act as God does.

— Antoinette Bosco, from *Radical Forgiveness*

Pray for Your Enemy

I find that forgiving one's enemies
is a most curious morbid pleasure.
— Oscar Wilde

Jesus says to pray for your enemy.

But what if the words she spoke still sting within your veins like a cobra's venom, swelling every virgin vessel?

What if the hurtful memories of her action linger inside you like bacteria from spoiled milk, leaving your mouth with a horrible taste?

Or what if the simple mention of her name pierces your heart like cupid's arrow shot the wrong way?

Do you still have to pray?

Yes, Jesus says, especially then?

Especially then.

"Love your enemies
and pray for those who persecute you."
— Matthew 5:44

— Therese Borchard, from *Winging It:*
Meditations of a Young Adult

Honor the Mystery

We belong beautifully to the earth and intimately to the cosmic web of life. Daily we breathe in the odor of sanctity that imbues creation. Our God walks with us in the garden of life, the Originating and Sustaining Mystery who is radically transparent for those who have eyes to see. We need a fresh approach to our theology of God, one that honors the mystery within which everything is held. The divine is written all over creation: the quantum vacuum, the supernova explosions, the recurring cycle of birth-death-rebirth, the process of photosynthesis — these and many more are the chapters of our primary scriptures. Divinity abounds, in and around us.

— Diarmuid O'Murchu, from *Evolutionary Theology*

What Is Scripture Saying to Us?

How are people of faith and good will to respond to the reality of our world? What can be done in the face of such complex and overwhelming challenges and injustices?

As many prophets of our time have testified, the Word of God, as a living book, calls us to respond to these challenges with a radical biblical spirituality, which is both mystical and prophetic.

This spirituality calls for an integral or holistic faith, which seeks to overcome the false dichotomy between faith and life and which recognizes the communal dimension of biblical faith. This is well summarized in the *Kairos Document,* a statement issued by Christian leaders in the midst of the South African apartheid system:

> The Bible does not separate the human person from the world in which he or she lives; it does not separate the individual from the social or one's private life from one's public life. God redeems the whole person as part of his whole creation (Rom. 8:18–24). A truly biblical spirituality would penetrate into every aspect of human existence and would exclude nothing from God's redemptive will. Biblical faith is prophetically relevant to everything that happens in the world.

With such an integral spirituality, we cannot sit idly by in the face of injustices in the world. Our faith in the God of history, as St. James reminds us, must be expressed in concrete action in our world:

> *What good is it, my brothers and sisters, to profess faith without showing works? Such faith has no power to save you. If a brother or sister is in need of clothes or food and one of you says, "May things*

go well for you; be warm and satisfied," without attending to their material needs, what good is that? So it is for faith without deeds: it is totally dead.... So just as the body is dead without its spirit, so faith without deeds is also dead.

— James 2:14–17, 26

As many of the contemporary prophets of justice remind us, such action in the world can be meaningful and effective only if it is grounded in contemplation and prayerful discernment (Rom. 12:2), which will allow us to see and respond to the root causes of the injustices in our world. To understand how to develop and deepen an integral spirituality of action, it may be helpful to start at the beginning — the book of Genesis.

— Kevin Ahern, from *The Radical Bible*

Dailiness

Abba Poemen said about Abba Prior that every single day he made a fresh beginning.

— Joan Chittister, from *Illuminated Life*

Meeting Christ

Every night I try to recover unity with Christ. And with him I relive the meetings of the past day. I think, for instance, about the mother who told me about the problems she has with her husband, with her children, and how hard she finds it to feed them. And, through this very real mother whom I know by name, I think about all the mothers throughout the world, throughout the age; the poor ones, the rich ones, the happy ones, the unhappy ones. Or I think about the man I saw working in the streets, emptying dustbins. I had caught his eye. He didn't dare offer me his hand. I virtually had to force him: "Work isn't what soils our hands, friend. No hand was ever soiled by work. Self-centeredness is what soils them." This man reminds me of working men throughout the world throughout the ages. Then I say to Christ our brother, "Lord, two thousand years after your death injustices are growing worse and worse." Reviewing the day like this, I find time passes very quickly.

— Dom Helder Camara, from *Dom Helder Camara: Essential Writings,* edited by Francis McDonagh

The Infinite Love of Christ

Today, when so many new sources of energy are being discovered, when we stand amazed at all the triumphs of scientific research in atomic physics and in the energy of the atom that may transform the whole universe, we do not sufficiently realize that all human power and natural energy is as nothing when compared with the superatomic energy of this love of Christ, who by giving his life vivifies the world. We, human beings that we are, can only transform already existing energy. But there exists an extraterrestrial source of energy which increases the energy of the world, an energy which has its source in the infinite love of Christ.

If we wish to transform this world of ours under its social and religious aspects, of the individual, the family, and society, here we have the only energy that can achieve this transformation. This is the infinite love of Christ which we acknowledge with St. Paul: "He loved and delivered himself for me" (Gal. 2:20).

— Pedro Arrupe, from *Pedro Arrupe:*
Essential Writings, edited by Kevin Burke

The Book of Job

Only if we know how to be silent and involve ourselves in the suffering of the poor will we be able to speak out of their hope. Only if we take seriously the suffering of the innocent and live the mystery of the cross amid that suffering, but in the light of Easter, can we prevent our theology from being "windy arguments..." (Job 16:3).

In sending his Son, the Father "wagered" on the possibility of a faith and behavior characterized by gratuitousness and by a response to the demand that justice be established. When history's "losers" — persons like Job — follow in the steps of Jesus, they are seeing to it that the Lord wins his wager. The risks accepted in talking about God with the suffering of the innocent in view are great. But, again like Job, we cannot keep quiet; we must humbly allow the cry of Jesus on the cross to echo through history and nourish our theological efforts.

As St. Gregory the Great says in his commentary on Job, the cry of Jesus will not be heard "if our tongues keep silent about what our souls believe...."

This mystery is the one proclaimed by the dead and risen Son of God. It is the mystery that we come to know when his Spirit impels us to say "Abba! Father!" (Gal. 4:6).

— Gustavo Gutiérrez, from *On Job:*
God-Talk and the Suffering of the Innocent

Prayer of Abandonment

This was the last prayer of our Master, our Beloved. May it also be ours. And may it be not only that of our last moment, but also of our every moment:

"Father, I put myself in your hands; Father, I abandon myself to you, I entrust myself to you. Father, do with me as it pleases you. Whatever you do with me, I will thank you for it. Giving thanks for anything, I am ready for anything, I accept anything, give thanks for anything. As long as your will, my God, is done in me, as long as your will is done in all your creatures, in all your children, in all those your heart loves, I ask for nothing else, O God. I put my soul into your hands. I give it to you, O God, with all the love of my heart, because I love you, and because my love requires me to give myself. I put myself unreservedly in your hands. I put myself in your hands with infinite confidence, because you are my Father."

— Charles de Foucauld, from *Charles de Foucauld: Essential Writings,* edited by Robert Ellsberg

The Value of Silence

To sit in silence is often to notice how unsilent the world is and how unstill one's body is. Friends [Quakers] have approached this challenge in many ways. Tayeko Yamanouchi, writing in 1979, recommended her gentle appreciation for the external world.

As I silence myself I become more sensitive to the sounds around me, and I do not block them out. The songs of the birds, the rustle of the wind, children in the playground, the roar of an airplane overhead are all taken into my worship. I regulate my breathing as taught me by my Zen friends, and through this exercise I feel the flow of life within me from my toes right through my whole body. I think of myself like the tree planted by the "rivers of water" in Psalm 1, sucking up God's gift of life and being restored.

— Michael L. Birkel, from *Silence and Witness:*
The Quaker Tradition

Prayer Is a State of Being

Prayer is a state of being before God. Long before it becomes a conscious activity — something we do — it already exists as a necessary condition of inner attentiveness. The Christian tradition teaches us that we are made by God. Our Creator calls us into conversation; or at least to attentive silence, so that we can listen. This relationship does not have to be negotiated; it is a given, and in turning to God in prayer we do no more than give expression to this primary relationship.

Prayer is not our work. It is something the Holy Spirit does in us, opening our hearts and minds and raising them to the Father. We pray in Christ, uniting our prayers with the prayers of Jesus.

— Lavinia Byrne, from *Original Prayer*

Trusting God

Trusting God and being grounded in God does not mean attachment to God. It is not as if we become detached from everything except God, so that in the end we cling desperately to God because there is nothing else left to cling to.

Trusting God, as Jesus did, does not mean clinging to God; it means letting go of everything so as to surrender ourselves and our lives to God. There is a difference between attachment and surrender. In the end we must become detached from God too. We must let go of God in order to jump into the embrace of a loving Father whom we can trust implicitly. We don't need *to hold on* tightly, because we will *be held* — like a child in the arms of its parents.

—Albert Nolan, from *Jesus Today:*
A Spirituality of Radical Freedom

God and Love

God's signature is on the whole of nature. All creatures are love letters from God to us. They are outbursts of love. The whole of nature is bursting with love, set in it by God, who is love, to kindle the fire of love in us. All things have no other reason for existing, no other meaning. They can give us no satisfaction or pleasure beyond this, to stir in us the love of God.

Nature is like God's shadow, reflecting God's beauty and splendor. The quiet blue lake has the splendor of God. God's fingerprints are upon every particle of matter. In every atom is an image of the Trinity, the figure of the triune God. That is why God's creation so fills us with enthusiasm.

And my body was also made for the love of God. Every cell in my body is a hymn to my creator and a declaration of love.

As the kingfisher was made to fish and the humming bird to suck nectar from flowers, so we were made for contemplation and love of God.

— Ernesto Cardenal, from *Abide in Love*

When the Kingdom of God Broke Through

I saw him from a block away. He sat in a motorized chair, his body slight like a child's, hardly fifty pounds in his maturity. His limbs were twisted and contorted like a human pretzel. Even his face was out of his control, gripped by grimaces many times a minute.

I wondered what it would be like, never to be able to smile.

I had never seen suffering so complete. I wanted to cross the street. That way I would not have to see him up close, would not have to share, even for an instant, his reality. But, not liking that feeling, I kept on walking toward him. Could I not give a fellow human being one instant of respect?

I walked forward, my heart trembling. I looked into his eyes and managed a small greeting, a timid smile. It was then that the kingdom of God broke through. This stranger, in his tortured body, attempted to smile out of one corner of his mouth. A crooked little half grin zigzagged across his face like a dancing sun peeping out from behind a cloud. Warmth, joy, and delight spread across his features. Light poured out from him and over me and into the street until it covered the whole scene like a radiant blanket. It happened all in an instant, a quick smile and a greeting, but as he passed by and the sound of his motorized chair buzzed down the street behind me, I broke into tears. I nearly knelt on the sidewalk. O my God, it was Jesus — and I almost missed him.

— Alice Camille, from *Listening to God's Word*

God's Goodness

Abdaraman is accompanying me this evening to the hermitage. . . . I realize that he has something important to say to me and hesitates to do so.

"Speak to me, Abdaraman. You know I am your friend."

Abdaraman bursts into tears, his naked body shaking. Tears stream down his face and then continue down onto his chest and abdomen.

"Brother Carlo, I am crying because you don't become a Muslim!"

"Oh," I exclaim, "and why should I become a Muslim?"

"If you don't become a Muslim you'll go to hell like all Christians!"

"Oh, what a thought, Abdaraman! No, Abdaraman. God is good and will save both of us. He will save your father, too, and we shall all go to heaven. Don't believe that just because I am a Christian I shall go to hell, as I don't believe you'll go there just because you're a Muslim. God is so good!"

— Carlo Carretto, from *Letters from the Desert*

Faith

Abba Doulas, the disciple of Abba Bessarion, said: When we were walking along the sea one day I was thirsty, so I said to Abba Bessarion, "Abba, I am very thirsty." Then the old man prayed and said to me, "Then drink from the sea." And the water was sweet when I drank it. So I poured it into a flask so that I would not be thirsty later. Seeing this the old man asked me, "Why are you doing that?" And I answered, "So that I won't be thirsty later on." Then the old man said, "God is here and God is everywhere."

— Joan Chittister, from *Illuminated Life*

What Is Christian Love?

Christian love is not simply an emotion or feeling. Rather, this love is an active willingness to work on the behalf of others. It is love in the way that parents love their children. In love we see the need in others' lives and seek to meet it from our own strengths.

Love is an attitude of the soul in which we are willing to be a servant to others. But this is not the same as being a doormat! We do not give in to the evil and sin in the human heart. Rather, we seek the good in others and help to nurture that goodness. This is seen in 1 Corinthians, where the apostle Paul sends the church one of the most beautiful meditations on love ever written:

> If I speak with the tongues of mortals and of angels, but do not have love, I am a noisy gong or a clanging cymbal. And if I have prophetic powers, and understand all mysteries and all knowledge, and if I have all faith, so as to remove mountains, but do not have love, I am nothing. Love is patient; love is kind; love is not envious or boastful or arrogant or rude. It does not insist on its own way; it is not irritable or resentful; it does not rejoice in wrong-doing, but rejoices in the truth. It bears all things, believes all things, hopes all things, endures all things. Love never ends. (1 Cor. 13:1–8)

— Sally Bruyneel and Alan G. Padgett,
from *Introducing Christianity*

Transcending Matter

A third experiment, involving the relationship between prayer and healing, seems to indicate that thought and intention may influence biological processes over distance. A cardiologist, Randolph Byrd, divided nearly four hundred cardiac patients into two roughly equal groups. The names of half of these patients were given to prayer groups throughout the United States. Four to seven people prayed for each of these patients — but neither the patients nor their physicians knew this was happening. At the end of the experiment, though, it was found that the group of patients who had received the attention of prayer groups were five times less likely to need antibiotics and three times less likely to suffer from fluid in the lungs. None of the prayed-for patients required endotracheal intubation to assist in breathing, versus twelve persons who needed this in the other group. At the same time, the effect of prayer seemed completely independent of distance (Herbert 1993). Of course, this phenomenon could equally be attributed to divine intervention, but such an explanation also defies purely mechanistic causes. Either the minds of the individuals praying for the patients affected them, or the operation of some kind of larger Mind was at work.

— Mark Hathaway and Leonardo Boff, from *The Tao of Liberation: Exploring the Ecology of Transformation*

The Healing of Community

After the arrest of Jesus in the Garden of Gethsemane, his disciples scattered. Fear probably pushed them into hiding. Frustrated with themselves, and even with Jesus, they must have lost their earlier zeal to work together for the liberation of Israel. Jesus' mission had failed. They had failed him too as friends and followers. They lost their direction. They were separated from each other.

How did the scattered disciples find their way to one another again? What gathered them again as a community? It was their common belief in the Risen Lord who appeared to them. His words were not of condemnation but of peace. He manifested himself to them not to judge but to forgive. The communion shattered by infidelity and selfishness was healed and restored by the one who has triumphed over sin and death. The Risen Lord had gathered them again. Their common experience of having seen the Lord and their common confession of the Risen Jesus as the Christ brought them together as a community of faith.

— Bishop Chito Tagle, from *Easter People: Living Community*

Jesus Carries His Cross

A young Guatemalan carries a heavy load of wood. The wood is for coffins to bury the Indian men who had been kidnapped, murdered, and found dead on the side of the road, or to bury the children who could not survive the diseases that touched them as soon as they were born. It happened many years ago when the international press reported it with great indignation. It happens still today when the subject is no longer newsworthy and remains hidden from the eyes of the world.

...I feel very powerless. I want to do something. I have to do something. I have, at least, to speak out against the violence and malnutrition, the oppression and exploitation. Beyond this, I have to act in any way possible to alleviate the pain I see. But there is an even harder task: to carry my own cross of loneliness and isolation, the cross of rejections I experience, the cross of my depression and inner anguish. As long as I agonize over the pain of others far away but cannot carry the pain that's uniquely mine, I may become an activist, even a defender of humanity, but not yet a follower of Jesus. Somehow my bond with those who suffer oppression is made real through my willingness to suffer my loneliness. It is a burden I try to avoid, sometimes, by worrying about others. But Jesus says: "Come to me all you who labor and are overburdened and I will give you rest" (Matt. 11:28). I might think that there is an unbridgeable gap between myself and the Guatemalan wood carrier. But Jesus carried his cross for both of us. We belong together. We must each take up our own cross and follow him, and discover that we are truly brothers who learn from him who is humble and gentle of heart. In this way only can a new humanity be born.

— Henri Nouwen, from *Walk with Jesus*

Alleluia!

Ah, yes, it is finished in beauty.

Tenacious wild violets erupting year after year no matter how many children are tortured worldwide is a glimmer of hope that God's plan for creation will triumph. Ordinary people participating in a seven-mile peace pilgrimage year after year despite growing lines at soup kitchens and escalating violence in our cities is a hope that death will not have the final word.

It is no mistake, I believe, that Mary Magdalene first looked on the risen Jesus that early morning on the first day of the week, just after sunrise, and saw, of all things, a gardener. Our task is not about death, the empty tomb, and the empty shroud. It is about planting, sowing and caring for hope in whatever garden we find ourselves.

At the Easter Vigil in our chapel, a sister dances the Alleluia banner down the center aisle, accompanied by hand bells and a congregation of hundreds singing "Alleluia."

Two dozen people process down the aisles carrying flowers of every color and fragrance. In less than a minute an empty sanctuary is transformed into an overpowering garden of lilacs, tulips, hyacinths and daffodils. Hold fast to hope, the fragile flowers shout.

Ah, yes, it is finished in beauty.

—Mary Lou Kownacki, from *A Monk in the Inner City*

The Presence of God

When we read the story of Abraham, we see a human being just like us. He too is trying to prosper in life. In and through this effort he came to encounter the true God. But God was no closer to Abraham than God is to us today. Why, then, do we not encounter God today? Perhaps it is because our sight is bad. We are so preoccupied with a particular image of God that we feel that something else cannot possibly be God. Our receiving set is not tuned to the same wavelength that God is using to send out the summons. The God who was revealed to Abraham, our God, is a God of human beings. Moreover, God is not afraid to hide. You may not see a butterfly when you are out hunting eagles; you may overlook the flowers if you are looking for trees.

God is present and is revealed in many things: in a mother's dedication to her family, in the labor of a working man for his children, in the struggle of our people to create a more humane world, in the joy produced by the presence of a friend, and in the mutual interchange of understanding and consolation. It is in such things that we discover the presence of God and gradually trace the lines of God's face.

—Carlos Mesters, from *God, Where Are You?*

The Wager

If Jesus is not in the tomb, where is he?

He is ahead of us, waiting in every situation as a spiritual presence. This presence calls us to join him in making those situations all they can be. We can "see and hear" him because we have studied and meditated on his life; and he is doing now what he did then. Therefore, our prayer-time is preparation for day-time. The day will unfold and we will have "eyes and ears" for the false notes, the lack of integrity, the failure to align the inside and the outside as a son who told his father he would work in the field and had no intention of doing it. In this way, our following of Jesus is not loyalty to a past master; it is staying awake and cooperating with his Spirit who beckons in the next never-before-seen-in-the-world moment. Wagering on the resurrection is betting "he is always with us" (Matt. 28.20).

— John Shea, from *Following Jesus*

Christ Resurrected

Christianity did not present itself to the world as a religion that lives on the nostalgic memory of a happy event in the past. It emerged as an announcement and a joyful celebration of a presence, that of Christ resurrected. Jesus of Nazareth, dead and buried, does not merely live on by means of his remembrance and his message of liberation for the oppressed conscience. He himself is present and lives a way of life that has already surpassed the limitations of our world of death and realized every dimension of all its possibilities. Hence, resurrection is not synonymous with resuscitation, the resuscitation of a body as was the case with Lazarus. Resurrection must be understood as a total, exhaustive realization of human reality in its relationship with God, with others, and with the cosmos.

Christ did not leave this world with the resurrection. He penetrated it in a more profound manner and is now present in all reality in the same way that God is present in all things. Christian faith lives on this presence and has developed a viewpoint that allows it to see all reality as penetrated by the reverberations of the resurrection. Owing to Christ's resurrection, the world became diaphanous and transparent.

In him that which for us will take place only at the end of the world took place in time. He is the anticipated goal.

— Leonardo Boff, from *Jesus Christ Liberator*

The One Who Goes before Us

Easter celebrates the restoration of the narrative of biblical radicalism, which, like Jesus, goes on before us. Whenever the church abandons this story for some other story, it worships an idol. Now idols are deaf and dumb; they cannot hear our brokenhearted cries, and they have nothing to say to us in our historical situation. Churches of the entombed Jesus can only parrot the rationalizing Realpolitik of his executioners. Churches of the enthroned Jesus revere his Way in fresco and stained glass in the sanctuary and then do as they please in the world. And churches that preach Jesus as Lord-of-our-hearts incarcerate the gospel in a subjective house of mirrors. . . .

Only the Nazarene-who-was-executed-but-who-now-goes-on can both hear us and speak to us. Jesus the Interlocutor questions and troubles us; silences our wrong-headed confessions and liberates us from demons that silence us; and calls us to discipleship as many times as it takes. This is the one who reasserted the sovereignty of the exodus God and set about revising the narrative of biblical radicalism: telling the truth and crossing boundaries, retribalizing the community and walking with the poor, healing political bodies and challenging the body politic, and above all, embracing the apocalyptic vocation of the Human One. Only this Jesus can topple our idols, shatter our illusions, show us the way through denial, and transform our dance with death into a tango with the Trinity.

— Ched Myers, from *Who Will Roll Away the Stone?*

Peter and Mary

In John 20:1–2 it is Mary Magdalene who informs both the Beloved Disciple and Peter that they need to pay attention to a new development: Jesus is no longer in the tomb. They not only listen to her — they act on her input. The contemporary implication of this is clear: as long as Peter does not listen to the Marys of the wider church, darkness will continue and the tomb will remain sealed. The fact that women need to be heard does not mean that there has to be competition between Peter and women. The text shows that this woman respected Peter; after all she told him first (20:2). At the same time, however, it also shows that Peter respected Mary and her insight; he acted on it.

— Michael H. Crosby, from *"Do You Love Me?"*

Risen Life

This is what it means to believe in the resurrection.

Every peace treaty is an act of faith in the resurrection.
Every agreed commitment is an act of faith in the
resurrection.
When you forgive your enemy
When you feed the hungry
When you defend the weak
you believe in the resurrection.
When you have the courage to marry
When you welcome the newly born child
When you build your home
you believe in the resurrection.
When you wake at peace in the morning
When you sing to the rising sun
When you go to work with joy
you believe in the resurrection.

—Carlo Carretto, from *Blessed Are You Who Believed*

The Fullness of the Good News of Easter

What then can be the fullness of the good news of Easter and resurrection? Eventually, the resurrection will be *you* with your resurrected body in a transformed universe. More than that, the entire universe will become your resurrected body. The implications are enormous, for the universe will also become Christ's resurrected body. You will now completely enfold, embrace, and compenetrate each other. In the very best sense of the word, you will completely possess and be possessed by each other. And the wonder of the resurrection is that it will not diminish your individual personalities. On the contrary, it will enhance your personal growth to its fullest potential. It will be the ultimate "you" experiencing ultimate intimacy with Christ.

Similarly, the entire universe will also become the resurrected body of every other person gifted with resurrection. Once again, you will completely enfold, embrace, and compenetrate each other. Once again there will be no diminishment of your uniqueness: the result, instead, will be the ultimate personhood and ultimate encounter. The ultimate "you" will experience ultimate intimacy with all others.

Indeed, what is the goal of all religion, mysticism, romance, and love? It is to possess the beloved, whether Christ or others, to such an extent that, paradoxically, you become the beloved. Yet you do not cease to exist so that the beloved can become you. What we have then are the four ultimate heart wishes (to love, to be loved, to share, to blossom out as individual and community) extended to the infinity of their meaning. The result is the fullness of life, the fullness of the Reign of God, and the fullness of the good news of Easter.

—John J. Walsh, M.M., from *Integral Justice*

MAY

. . . .

After Easter

If Schillebeeckx is correct, then the post-resurrection appearance stories are articulations of conversion experiences already undergone by the disciples. This means that one only "sees" the risen Jesus when one has faith in the risen Jesus. In other works, it is not merely a question of visual, sensory input. It is rather a question of identifying the one whom one sees as the risen Christ.

Mary Magdalene on Easter morning sees one whom she mistakes as a gardener. The disciples on the road to Emmaus see one whom they think to be a stranger. Those visual experiences in themselves are not resurrection appearances. It is only when the stranger is recognized in faith as the Christ that we can speak of an Easter narrative. It is only when we understand that the sorrowful, the wayfarer, the hungry, the thirsty, the prisoner, and the sick are really and truly Jesus that we can speak of resurrection.

Easter faith, then, isn't the assurance of things unseen but is rather the unhinged, unjustifiable claim that the panhandler, the homeless on the street corner, and the Jewish boy covered with the slime of the grave are manifestations of Jesus and honored members of the Kingdom of God. Easter faith says that Jesus appears in the poor, the lame, and the dying, and that if we can't see him there, then we shouldn't expect to see him anywhere else.

— Theresa Sanders, from *Tenebrae: Holy Week after the Holocaust*

Hope Does Not End

In the end, three things last — faith, hope, and love. Hope endures and does not end. It is God's gift, God's very life in us eternally. The gift expresses the life of the giver, God's life. God continually gives the gift of hope and yet is never empty of it. God also continues in hope by hoping. Even now, God anticipates and waits. God's coming in flesh waited for the free response of Mary of Nazareth. Her "yes," her hope that God's promise would be fulfilled, changed everything. Likewise, God waits for our "yes." God hopes in us, for us, with us. This is the reason for the hope that lives within us. Yes, even when we cannot see the road ahead of us because the candle has gone out and we are in utter darkness, the lines of our life's story can still be written out in hope.

— Michael Downey, from *Hope Begins Where Hope Begins*

The Material World

Why should we value the material world? All living things? Not because the universe is divine but because it holds a great promise. Because the universe is unfinished, imperfect, a mere installment on an extravagant future. To trash the earth or the creatures of earth is to trash their promise and our own future as well. The things of earth are ultimately not destined to pass away, to vanish without a trace. Christ is Alpha and Omega, the key to the beginning and the end of all creation. If he be raised up, it means all things are raised up. Hence death does not have the last word; it is vanquished. We see but through a glass darkly, we do not apprehend how, but all of creation is somehow taken up in Christ and the promise of the resurrection of the body. This is the vision, however mediated, without which the universe is doomed to futility.

— David Toolan, from *At Home in the Cosmos*

Our Muslim Brothers and Sisters

When I am asked, "What are your thoughts on the Islamic religion?" I respond by talking about the faith of Muslims. I only know a little about Islam, but I am close to many Muslims. First, I need to say that the man who most influenced me to spend my life among my brother and sister Muslims was Blessed Charles de Foucauld. Though he scandalized others in his early life, he had the courage to travel to Morocco in the 1880s, when the fate of many foreigners was death. There he noticed how sincere the Muslims were in their prayer. Muslims praying five times a day certainly impressed de Foucauld. When he returned to France, he decided that he should look into his own faith. He found God again and never turned back.

I also witness the prayers of my neighbors five times a day. This does not mean that everyone prays, but most do. It is impressive. When I first went to Bangladesh some of my Christian companions complained about the noise coming from the amplifiers five times a day. Indeed, some amplifiers were aimed at Christian enclaves. It took me a while to realize that the Muslims were praying to my God, not just irritating the population. I said to myself, "If they are called to prayer five times a day, so am I and so are all Christians."

When you stop to think about it, there are a billion Muslims in the world, spread out in all directions. Many respond to prayer five times daily, if not in the mosques, at least in their own homes. Some even pray in the streets or while riding buses or trains. An Arab astronaut did his prayers in space. Since he passed the sun every ninety minutes, he could not follow the traditional times so he prayed according to the time in Mecca.

Some think such prayers are pharisaical. A billion people? No, we have to accept their sincerity in prayer, as real as our praise of God who made us all. In the end I decided that the call to prayer from the Muslim minarets was meant for me too. When I hear the call, I say, "our Father, thy kingdom come." Just those few words are enough. Yes, our common Father will bring us together if we pray and work for unity with others.

— Douglas F. Venne, M.M., from *What They Taught Us: How Maryknoll Missioners Were Evangelized by the Poor,* edited by Joseph A. Heim, M.M.

Laughter

"Young man," the teacher said, "since you do not think it important to pay attention in this class, please tell us what happened in 1898?"

"The Battleship *Maine* was sunk, Ma'am," the child answered.

"And what happened in 1900?" the teacher persisted.

"The Battleship *Maine* was sunk for two years, Ma'am."

Suddenly life is glorious again, anything is possible, and defeat is not forever.

Most of all, laughter is healthy when we are able to laugh at ourselves, when making a mistake is more a moment of freedom from protocol than it is one of the hidden tragedies of life. When I am laughing at myself, I have crossed the Rubicon of life and given notice that I can risk being mortal and know I shall survive.

Laughter liberates and laughter uplifts. When laughter comes into a life, nothing is impossible; nothing is too difficult, nothing can defeat us. We can survive the noonday sun and the darkness of death and the grinding boredom of dailiness and still find life exhilarating. Other things in life change character like the chameleons on plaid, but laughter is always ornament, always grace.

— Joan Chittister, from *There Is a Season*

Peace of Mind

Every day I experience the benefits of peace of mind. It's very good for the body. As you might imagine, I am a rather busy man. I take many responsibilities upon myself, activities, trips, and speeches. All that no doubt is a very heavy burden, and still I have the blood pressure of a baby.

Last year in Washington, at the Walter Reed Army Hospital, they took my blood pressure. And the doctor said, "Wow, I wish mine were the same!"

What's good for me is good for other people. I have no doubt on that score. Good food, a struggle against every excessive desire, daily meditation, all that can lead to peace of mind; and peace of mind is good for the body. Despite all the difficulties of life, of which I've had my share, we can all feel that effect."

— The Dalai Lama, from *The Dalai Lama: Essential Writings,*
edited by Thomas A. Forsthoefel

A Vision from Below

Aaron Santiago stood on the mountainside. Below him and us stretched the rugged landscape of the villages of Tilantongo in this isolated region of Oaxaca. Looking down at the eroded, rocky hillsides, I could now see that they were girded with row upon row of contour ditches. Aaron and the Mixtec people had revived a millennia-old indigenous technology for holding soils in place and catching rain water to refill thirsty aquifers on steep mountainsides.

He told us to look more closely, and then we began to distinguish them. Stretching across the seeming barren rocks and *arroyos*, we could see a light green blanket of tens of thousands of newly planted native trees.

"In the past five years we have planted over a million tree seedlings in these villages," he explained. "We don't do this just for our children, nor even for our grandchildren. We do it because the world needs it."

— Philip Dahl-Bredine and Stephen Hicken, from *The Other Game: Lessons from How Life Is Played in Mexican Villages*

Waking Up to This Day

How do we come to realize love? By surrendering to life just as it is. Gradually our eyes open. I think of a good friend who buried her young son. Years later someone asked her if she felt that he had been cheated by life because his years were few. Her response was startling. "I don't think in those terms," she replied thoughtfully. "The answer is that I don't know. I don't know what his life should have been. I realize today that this soul had its own journey and its own terms with life. This had nothing to do with me."

I watched her face as she spoke. She was serene and strong. She went on, "But I got to participate for a while in the journey of that soul. For that I am unspeakably grateful."

There was nothing to say in response to her words. The love moving through them was its own flame.

— Paula D'Arcy, from *Waking Up to This Day*

In the Here and Now

To a disciple who was obsessed with the thought of life after death the master said, "Why waste a single moment thinking of the hereafter?"

"But is it possible not to?"

"Yes."

"How?"

"By living in heaven here and now."

"And where is this heaven?"

"In the here and now."

— Anthony de Mello, from *Anthony de Mello: Selected Writings,* edited by William Dych, S.J.

Alive and Thriving
and Living in Harmony

Each spring, not far from where I live, the most spectacular display of beauty presents itself. A very old white dogwood tree stretches out its majestic branches with an Alleluia! That echoes the song of Resurrection; our communities are always singing as this beautiful tree wakens from its winter slumber. It is by far the largest dogwood tree I have ever seen. In its branches for weeks you can hear the songs of birds and the chatter of the squirrels that make it their home. In the fall its generous red berries, inedible to humans, provide a sumptuous feast for other creatures. And its red leaves in the fall are a beautiful auger of the approaching cold.

On the other side of the world in Tanzania there stands another tree, a particular baobab tree whose picture I took a few years ago. Also beautiful, this majestic tree towers over the spectacular landscape of the Tarangire National Park, providing shade, shelter, or food for elephant families and giraffes and baboons and birds and dozens of God's other creatures passing through toward water or staying for a bit of respite from the sun. For humans it provides fruit and bark for baskets and roots for medicine. The baobab is considered a sacred tree.

Like the Mexican and Native American tree of life, it is filled to the brim with creation, alive and thriving and living in harmony.

That is what we are promised if we answer the call.

— Marie Dennis, from *Diversity of Vocations*

One Brief Glimpse

During the eucharist the sign of the kingdom of God is at the same time reality and fulfillment. It still is, when we celebrate it. During its celebration we are one body, one blood, one spirit — his body, his blood, his spirit. Every one of us is able to witness to that reality. For a moment the fights are over, the differences healed, the past overcome.

My most vivid memory of this sharing recalls a Christmas night during the Second World War in the occupied Netherlands. The military commander of the town where I lived lifted the curfew to allow us to go to Midnight Mass. Just before the eucharist a group of German soldiers marched into the church to celebrate with us. No upright Dutch man or woman would ever associate, let alone eat, with them. As kids we stole from them whatever we could, but when they offered us some candy, remembering their own children at home, we would never accept anything, preferring to spit in their faces. At communion time they came to kneel with us at the communion rail — as we did in those days — and nobody objected to those soldiers being there. For a moment all was as it one day will be. We were not enemies. We were interconnected. We were, for a brief moment, at the end of our common journey.

The final gathering, the ultimate reconciliation, the definitive shalom were all realized "already." The future had become real and present just for a moment, just as it always had been in the life of Jesus.

— Joseph G. Donders, from *Charged with the Spirit*

Pray Always

God has given this day into our hands. This is the day in which we pray, but we pray by action and sweat, just as Christ did. He said he "came not to be served but to serve." He also said, "Pray continually." Pray while you work and work while you pray.

The duty of the moment is our strategic place. One day at a time. We have this day in which to open our hearts like doors, and take in everyone that we can. Today we have to love as God loved us.

Some feel as if the routine of our daily duties is not enough, that other things should be added. Stop here. Please stop. Fall on your knees and pray and listen. Walk slowly, in the darkness of faith — because you believe in the Trinity, for no other reason. Then, through hope and love, be faithful to your duty of the present moment. That is the essence of Christianity. That is the heart of the Church. The rest flows from it, but this is to come first, walking in faith while doing our daily routine of duties....

Our daily work, routine or not, exciting or unexciting, monotonous or not, is part of that faith, hope, and love. This workaday world of ours is the outer shell of a deep inner grace that God gives us. It is because we believe, we hope, and we love that we can do what might seem impossible.

Christ wants us to be an icon of himself, to be people of faith beyond reason, to be fools for God in utter simplicity, and to be people who plead for others in prayer.

— Catherine de Hueck Doherty, from *Catherine de Hueck Doherty: Essential Writings,* edited by David Meconi, S.J.

Listening to God

One summer day I sat on the back porch fully immersed in preparing a talk for a conference on "listening to God." As I leaned over my notebook, I heard a bird singing a penetrating, melodious song. The warbling went on and on, but I didn't bother to look or listen because I was concentrating on my work. Finally, an inner stirring drew me to put my pen down. I thought, "Listen! Stop what you are doing! Pay attention to this beautiful song. It is too glorious to miss." I looked up to find the source of the singing and saw a female house-finch seated at the bird feeder and a male finch perched on a branch nearby. The male finch was singing to the female who pretended to peck at the food, seemingly ignoring the enticing song. Finally, the female lifted up and flew away. The moment she left, the other bird's beautiful music stopped.

I thought, "God is always singing a love song, desiring to get my attention, wanting to let me know I am cherished, but I get absorbed in pecking and cleaning. Only by listening to the melody of God will I recognize and respond to what is beneath. Only then will I turn my heart more fully to the One who calls insistently to me."

— Joyce Rupp, from *Prayer*

The Signpost Says Love

The signpost has two words on it. One points to the left and says
"fear." The other directs you to the right and says "love." If you
choose to do nothing the current of life will carry you to the left.
If you take one positive step forward, your foot will land on the
right road.

The magic that occurs when one human being helps another
is that these simple acts of kindness are the footsteps on the road
of happiness. They are what carry us down the dusty roads of
Galilee.

— Bill Mosher, from *Visionaries*

Mary, Follower of Jesus

To use an expression often heard in Latin American Christianity today, Mary appears as one committed to the liberation of all people, particularly the most oppressed. For this reason she experienced poverty, suffering, flight, and exile. The Gospel accounts of her humiliation in Bethlehem, her persecution by Herod, her exile in Egypt, and her sufferings on Calvary, are not pious biblical stories. They are the signs of her faithfulness to the commitment she accepted at the time of the Annunciation. In this, also, Mary is typical of the church, insofar as the church will remain faithful to the integrity of its mission. She is also typical of the Christian communities as "exodus" and as an "Abrahamic minority," and in them she maintains the hope and the strength to await the hour of the liberating God.

It is in this spirit that Mary accompanied the early communities and today continues to accompany all Christian communities that struggle with hope for the coming of the kingdom of God.

— Segundo Galilea, from *Following Jesus*

The Fool in Our Times

The fool in our times honors the Creator in all persons and all things, finds profound joy in the possibility of reconciliation across cultural and racial differences, seeks harmony with the rest of the created order, and is a nonviolent promoter of life.

The fool is in the world but not of the world. The fool finds identity not in that which our society acclaims — appearance, accomplishment, affluence, power, consumption — but rather in the discipleship journey toward God.

The fool knows that we and all created things are sacraments of God. The fool believes in and knows by experience the world of the Spirit.

The fool lives in paradise, ridiculing the powers and principalities, because, with Jesus and Francis, the fool in our times remembers the end of the story, the Reign of God.

— Marie Dennis et al., from *St. Francis and the Foolishness of God*

Are You Sleepwalking through Your Life?

When walking, walk. When sitting, sit.
But don't wobble.

— Zen Proverb

It is said that after the Buddha experienced enlightenment, he passed a man on the road who was immediately struck by the Buddha's appearance. The Buddha had an extraordinary radiance and peacefulness about him. The man knew he was in the company of an unusual person and he wanted to know more about him. Thus, he stopped and asked the Buddha.

"My friend, what are you? Are you a celestial being, or perhaps a god?"

"No," said Buddha.

"Well then, are you some kind of magician or wizard?"

"No," Buddha said again.

"Are you a man?"

"No."

"Well, my friend, what then are you?"

This time the Buddha replied, "I am awake."

One of Buddhism's great insights is that some people — perhaps too many people — are sleepwalking through their lives. Rather than be awake and live mindfully, they simply go through the motions without awareness of their activity. Many individuals operate on automatic pilot. . . . A central message of the Buddha is this: *Wake up!* To be awake and aware is the path to a new life that is happier, more joyous, and more enriching.

— Victor M. Parachin, from *Eastern Wisdom for Western Minds*

An African Creed

We believe in the one High God, who out of love created the beautiful world and everything good in it. He created humanity and wanted humanity to be happy in the world. God loves the world and every nation and tribe on the earth. We have known this High God in the darkness, and now we know him in the light. God promised in the book of his word, the bible, that he would save the world and all the nations and tribes.

We believe that God made good his promise by sending his son, Jesus Christ, a man in the flesh, a Jew by tribe, born poor in a little village, who left his home and was always on safari doing good, curing people by the power of God, teaching about God and humanity, showing that the meaning of religion is love. He was rejected by his people, tortured and nailed hands and feet to a cross, and died. He lay buried in the grave, but the hyenas did not touch him, and on the third day, he rose from the grave. He ascended to the skies. He is the Lord.

We believe that all our sins are forgiven through him. All who have faith in him must be sorry for their sins, be baptized in the Holy Spirit of God, live the rules of love and share the bread together in love, to announce the good news to others until Jesus comes again. We are waiting for him. He is alive. He lives. This we believe. Amen.

— Vincent J. Donovan, from *Christianity Rediscovered*

A Channel of Gentleness and Compassion

The most credible voice for a more compassionate and just community that I have ever heard is the voice of Dr. David Abdulai. David and his wife, a nurse, operate a clinic in Ghana in western Africa. Some have begun to call Dr. David the Mother Teresa of Africa because of the pure altruism he extends to absolutely everyone in need who approaches him.

David told me the story of the recent death of his mother. When she felt the end was near, she went to her son's clinic to say goodbye to her family. She spent the final three hours of her life being held, with utter tenderness, in the arms of her only surviving son. David placed her in his lap just as, when he was an infant, she had held him safely in her lap. He wrapped his arms around her frail body and simply caressed her, gently stroking her body with a loving touch. He gave her a gentle kiss for each of his brothers and sisters. David felt immense gratitude to the Creator for the privilege of being able to serve as a channel of gentleness and compassion for his own mother as she prepared to return to God. After her death in the early evening, he lay down and took the deepest sleep of his life. God filled him with a deep peace. He didn't cry or feel sad. All he knew was peace.

— Donald H. Dunson, from *No Room at the Table:*
Earth's Most Vulnerable Children

Loving Is Success

The only true measure of human success is love, and without it even the ones who appear to be the most successful are nothing more than the cloud that appears great and powerful in the morning but has disappeared by the afternoon. The only true basis of lasting happiness is love, and without it isolated moments of happiness quickly fade into sweet memories of the past. The divine love that I experience in my heart is not just the beautiful love of one person for another; it is the love of God within me that now animates and guides every moment, every feeling, every thought, every desire, and every action of my life. Whether I am dealing with the person whom I love the most in this life, with a stranger, or even with an enemy, it is the love of God within me that will be the driving force of my life. The more this love grows within me, the more I can say with St. Paul: "I live no longer I, but Christ who lives in me" (Gal. 2:20).

— Virgil Elizondo, from *Charity*

God's People All Have Gifts

While a graduate student in Washington, D.C., I saw an exhibit of Michelangelo's sketches. They were his preliminary studies of projects but even so they were already beautiful and filled with graceful movement. Some pieces showed simply circles, or combinations of them, and yet to my amateur eyes they looked like masterpieces. He was brilliant. After going through the whole exhibit, instead of being hopeful, I felt despair because I was envious. I saw an enormous gift and I did not rejoice in it. I actually felt bad about myself for not possessing a gift like his.

At times we are like this. We see a gift and we feel threatened and angry or envious, wondering why that gift was not given to us. My act of despair over the gift of Michelangelo revealed how I have not recognized my own giftedness. In the end, it represented a lack of hope in myself, or of God's hope in me. . . .

We should celebrate the giftedness of each person and remember that someone else's gift is not a diminution of my own gifts. In fact, the gift of another person honors my giftedness to others. Hope lies within these gifts.

— Bishop Chito Tagle, from *Easter People: Living Community*

Spiritual Masters

A spiritual master is ultimately a guide — someone who has traveled the path that lies before us. At the end of the day, such guides do not show us how to be like them, but how to be more truly ourselves, how to find our own hidden gifts, how to respond to the sacred voice that issues from our own hearts and from the challenges of our own time and place. The goal of the spiritual master is not that we should remain forever novices or apprentices, but that we should learn to walk our own path, and perhaps one day become a guide for others.

— Robert Ellsberg, from *Modern Spiritual Masters*

We Have to Choose

I think "freedom" — at least the way we usually think of it — is an illusion. As far as I can tell, absolute freedom doesn't exist. I think we all have some measure of freedom, but in the end we have to choose who or what will be our master. For some people it's their Lexus or their big house or their love of gourmet food or their music. For some people it's their career. For some people it's their family. It's a question of what you want to give your life to, or for.

—Michael P. Enright, from *Diary of a Barrio Priest*

Stories

Our lives unfold in stories. Perhaps the bible has captivated us for such a long time because it is filled with stories — stories that so transcend time and space that they can happen to any of us, any time. They are vivid, colorful stories with which we can identify — being born, being lost, being fed. They are stories of healing and of learning, suffering and dying. They are stories that move us, challenge us, and evoke recognition in our hearts.

Who among us cannot feel the spray of the waves as they crash over the boat during the storm on the lake (Luke 22:23–25), or smell the scent of the ointment or of the woman herself as she dries the feet of Jesus with her hair (John 12:3)? We know the thirst quenching refreshment of a cool drink of water on a hot day, and the deeper thirst that never goes away. We are familiar with dinner parties and wedding feasts, arguments along the way, and the gut-ripping fear of those who wield the sword, whether over our bodies or over our convictions of conscience.

But for anyone who takes this library of stories as a guide for living, the scriptures that we call *sacred* draw us in, inviting us to spend time, entering them deeply enough to be transformed.

— Fran Ferder, from *Enter the Story:*
Biblical Metaphors for Our Lives

Saying the Rosary

Repetition of the rosary prayers deepens reflection on the sacred mysteries of God's relationship with us. When we pray the rosary, we recall that we are joined with God in the unfolding story of redemption. Since its beginnings in the eighth century, praying the rosary has been connected with scripture both as a psalter and as a way of telling the gospel story. Each bead recalls a psalm, each mystery reveals something of Jesus Christ. Praying the rosary makes the gospel story accessible to everyone hungry for a daily connection to faith, regardless of their level of education. That accessibility of the holy has made the rosary a form of prayer offered as often in kitchens, on trains, and at the bedside of a sick child as it is in cathedrals. It is a prayer of life as close as our memories and fingers, an immediacy that reflects God's presence among us as our lives unfold.

— Teresa McGee, from *Mysteries of the Rosary*

The One Prayer of Jesus

In the Lord's Prayer we encounter in a practical way the correct relationship between God and humankind, between heaven and earth, between the religious and the political, while maintaining unity throughout. The first part speaks on God's behalf: the Father, keeping his name holy, his kingdom, his holy will. The second part is concerned with human interests: our daily bread, forgiveness, ever-present temptation, ever-threatening evil.

The two parts constitute the one prayer of Jesus. God is not just interested in what belongs to him: his name, his kingdom, his divine will. He is also concerned about our affairs: bread, forgiveness, temptation, evil. Likewise we are not just concerned with what is vital to us: bread, forgiveness, temptation, evil. We are also open to the Father's concerns: sanctification of God's name, the coming of God's kingdom, the realization of God's will.... It is precisely this mutual involvement that generates the transparency to be found in the Lord's Prayer.

What God unifies — our preoccupation with him and our preoccupation with our own needs — let no one put asunder. God should never be betrayed for the sake of earthly needs; at the same time, it will never be legitimate to anathematize the limitations of our earthly existence because of the grandeur one finds in the reality of God. The two together constitute the material of prayer, supplication and praise. This is why we regard the Lord's Prayer as the prayer of integral liberation.

— Leonardo Boff, from *Praying with Jesus and Mary*

Following Christ

Is it possible to follow Christ while fulfilling the demands of the world, to listen to Christ while paying equal attention to others, to carry Christ's cross while carrying many other burdens as well? Jesus certainly appears to draw a very sharp distinction. "No one can be the slave of two masters" (Matt. 6:24), he insisted, and he did not hesitate to confront us with the uncompromising demands of his call: "It is a narrow gate and hard road that leads to life. . . . Anyone who prefers father or mother to me is not worthy of me" (Matt. 7:14, 10:37).

These challenging words are not meant only for a few of Jesus' followers who have a so-called "special vocation." Rather, they are for all who consider themselves Christians.

— Henri Nouwen, from *The Selfless Way of Christ*

Freedom from Fear

Complete freedom from fear is one of those things we owe wholly to Our Lord. To be afraid is to do him a double injury. First, it is to forget him, to forget that he is with us, that he loves us and is himself almighty, and second it is to fail to bend to his will. If we shape our will to his, as everything that happens is either willed or allowed by him, we shall find joy in whatever happens, and shall never be disturbed or afraid.

So then we should have the faith that banishes all fear. Beside us, face to face with us, within us, we have Our Lord Jesus, our God whose love for us is infinite, who is himself almighty, who has told us to seek for the kingdom of God and that everything else will be given us. In that blessed and omnipotent company, we just go straight along the path of the greatest perfection, certain that nothing will happen to us that we cannot use as a source of the greatest good for his glory and the sanctification of ourselves and others, and that everything that happens is either willed or permitted by him, and therefore, far from lying under the shadow of fear, we have only to say, "Whatever happens — God be praised!" praying that he will arrange everything not in accordance with our ideas but for his greater glory. We should never forget the two axioms: "Jesus is with me" and "Whatever happens, happens by the will of God."

— Charles de Foucauld, from *Charles de Foucauld: Essential Writings,* edited by Robert Ellsberg

Angels Carrying God's Love

Near the entrance of a Catholic seminary in the United States, there is an old weathered statue of a guardian angel. It stands, stone-still, grimy with age and the elements, pious, hovering beside and protective of a young child. I heard a strange story about it from one of the seminarians.

A man, obviously profoundly retarded — or close to the truth — came to visit: he had wandered away from a nearby institution. He saw the angel and climbed up beside it and hung there caressing the angel's hard sculptured, cold face. Sensuously, tenderly, in public but oblivious to all. He stayed there for hours. No one moved toward him, questioned him, cared for him. Some who passed by watched, laughed, made fun of him. Eventually his caretakers found him and took him away. A nobody who touched an angel standing forlornly in a monastery garden.

The angel statue is still there so I went to see it. Where is the man who fingered an angel's face? Does the angel guard and protect him now? Does the angel tenderly, softly caress his face with thanks? Did the gawkers miss the mystery enacted before their eyes and knowingly walk away from two angels caught unawares, communicating in the light of an almost spring day? The story makes me unbearably sad and longing. Am I too seeking an angel?

— Megan McKenna, from *Angels Unawares*

Bullshit and the Buddha

During the Northern Song dynasty in ancient China, a low-ranking official named Su Shi, who was also a renowned and erudite scholar, was persecuted by some court officials and subsequently exiled to a remote southern county. He was very depressed and disappointed, since his dreams of serving his country and the court wouldn't be achieved.

One day, in an attempt to assuage his depression, someone suggested that he pay a visit to his friend, a Buddhist master with sublime virtue at Hua Yan monastery in the forest. Su Shi decided to do this.

When Su Shi arrived at the monastery, he found the master standing in front of the main gate to welcome him. The two old friends were quite happy to see each other, but very soon the master realized that Mr. Su was very unhappy.

"Are you all right, Mr. Su?" asked the master. "Why are you frowning? Is anything wrong?" Mr. Su did not respond. Knowing from other sources that his visitor might be bemoaning his fate, the master changed the subject.

A little while later, a maid served them green tea. While they were drinking the tea and playing chess, the master asked, "Mr. Su, what do I look like?"

Mr. Su, who decided to take this opportunity to make fun of the master, replied, "Oh, revered master, you look like a pile of ugly bullshit, don't you?" Then he laughed. He thought that the master would be very annoyed or irritated. But, to his surprise, the master still smiled amiably at him, seemingly imperturbable and composed.

Mr. Su then asked the master, "Master, what about me? What do I look like?"

The master replied, "Oh, Mr. Su, you look like Buddha."

Mr. Su was surprised at his response. "Why do you say this?" he asked the master. "Why do you speak such nice words to me after I ridiculed you, saying that you look like a pile of ugly bullshit? Aren't you annoyed?"

The master smiled and said, "I see that you look like Buddha because my heart resides in him, or the Buddha is in me. For me, everything looks like Buddha. What you have in your heart is only bullshit. That's why you see others as bullshit. If you set your mind on humanity," the master continued, "you will be free from evil thoughts. If you want to clean or change the nation, you must clean and change your heart first."

Feeling deeply ashamed, Mr. Su immediately bowed and thanked the master for his wise words.

—Traditional story, from *Once upon a Time in Asia*,
edited by James H. Kroeger and Eugene F. Thalman

The Nature of Love

In the epistle to the Philippians, St. Paul tells us to put on the attitude of Christ, who did not consider being of divine condition something to be clung to, but emptied himself, became like other men, even unto death on the cross (Phil. 2:5–11). It is only in the innermost attitude of giving ourselves to others that we will come to the experience of true happiness. It will not always be fun, it will not always be exciting, it might be painful, and could even lead to the ultimate expression of love: that we give our life for the sake of others. Yet it is only in this attitude of total giving that true love will be experienced. We see it in many ordinary ways in people who sacrifice for the sake of their children, for the sake of their elderly parents, for the sake of orphans and abused children, for the sake of the poor and the homeless. In a heroic way we see it in persons like St. Maximilian Kolbe who during the Holocaust gave his life so that another might be free. We see it in the life of Oscar Romero, who sacrificed his life for proclaiming the truth, and in the Maryknoll sisters and Father Stanley Rother of Oklahoma, who were murdered in Central America for helping the poor. Whether it is sacrificing the comfort of a good night's sleep for the sake of caring for the baby to entering into martyrdom for the sake of others, it is through sacrificial love that we obtain what the heart most desires: true and authentic love that is the fundamental basis of lasting happiness. Love is the most beautiful thing there is, but it is never cheap. It is the most precious gift we can ever give, yet money cannot buy it because it is more costly than all the money in the world.

— Virgil Elizondo, from *Charity*

JUNE

· ·

Presence

Lord Jesus,
    teach us to live life fully each day
    to live it from
    the deepest center of our being
    to learn from everything
    and everyone
    most of all, to be grateful.

—Michael D. Bassano, M.M.,
from *A Maryknoll Book of Prayer*,
edited by Michael Leach and Susan Perry

The Violinist

Imagine a violinist. If, without having learned the least bit of music, he were to take his seat in the orchestra and right away begin playing, he would not only be disturbed but would disturb others. No, for a long time he practices by himself alone. As far as possible not a thing disturbs him there; he sits and beats time etc. But his aim is to play with the orchestra. He must be able to tolerate the profusion of the most varied instruments, this interweaving of sounds, and yet be able to attend to his violin and play along just as calmly and confidently as if he were home alone in his room. Oh, this again makes it necessary for him to be by himself to learn to be able to do this — but the aim is always that he play in the orchestra. It is the same with faith and the task of living it out.

— Søren Kierkegaard, from *Provocations: Spiritual Writings of Kierkegaard*

Downwardly Mobile

The way of the cross, the downward mobility of God, becomes our way not because we try to imitate Jesus, but because we are transformed into living Christs by our relationship with his Spirit. The spiritual life is the life of the Spirit of Christ in us, a life that sets us free to be strong while weak, to be free while captive, to be joyful while in pain, to be rich while poor, to be on the downward way of salvation while living in the midst of an upwardly mobile society.

Although this spiritual life may well seem enigmatic, intangible, and elusive to us who live in a scientific age, its fruits leave little doubt about the radical transformation it brings about. Love, joy, peace, patience, kindness, goodness, trustfulness, gentleness, and self-control are indeed the qualities of our Lord himself and reveal his presence in the midst of a world so torn apart by idolatry, envy, greed, sexual irresponsibility, war, and other sin. . . . It is not hard to distinguish the upward pull of our world from the downward pull of Christ. . . .

We will never be without struggle. But when we persevere with hope, courage, and confidence, we will come to fully realize in our innermost being that through the downward road of Christ we will enter with him into his glory. So let us be grateful for our vocation, resist our temptation, and be ever committed to a life of ongoing formation.

— Henri Nouwen, from *The Selfless Way of Christ*

This Once Only Day

There is a moment each day when it is morning before it is morning. Darkness still hovers over the deep. Those who wait for the dawn can hear it even before they see it. At first there are only the slight sounds of attunement as a chorus of birds assembles: twits and trills, chirps and peeps, and even the occasional squawk. Slowly they gather into one great concerted song of supplication. Let it begin! Let us begin! May it begin again!

They are of one accord. They do not take the dawn for granted. When it bursts upon them, once again, as on the first day of creation, they give thanks once again for this once only day, to begin.

The birds know, as we sometimes do, that the light does not dawn because of our singing. We sing because the dawn appears as grace.

—Mary Jo Leddy, from *Radical Gratitude*

A Marvelous Discovery

The essential thing is this marvelous discovery: that all over the world, among all races, languages, religions, ideologies, there are men and women born to serve their neighbor, ready for any sacrifice if it helps to build at last a really juster and more human world.

They belong in their own environment but they feel themselves to be members of the human family. They think of other people everywhere as their brothers and sisters, people from every latitude and longitude, every climate, people of all sizes and colors, rich or poor, whatever their education or their culture.

I beg you, let us try and understand this message with all good will. Let every minority make it its own and translate it into its own language.

— Dom Helder Camara, from *The Desert Is Fertile*

The Importance of the Prayer

There once lived in China a holy woman who knew the location of a sacred tree in a sacred forest. Whenever she prayed at the tree, she received what she wanted.

After the woman died, her daughter also went to pray at the sacred tree in the sacred forest, but, try as she might, she could not recall the words of the prayer. Yet, because she remembered the importance of the prayer, she, too, was given what she sought.

Then the family moved to the city and the woman died. Her daughter could not remember where the tree or forest were, nor did she know the words of the prayer. But because she remembered their importance, she also was rewarded.

— Penny Lernoux, from *Hearts on Fire:*
The Story of the Maryknoll Sisters

On Being a Misfit

Each person has his or her reason for being and feeling like a social misfit... [and] years of feeling like a misfit leave their mark, their scars. It is up to each of us to work at trying to be more interiorly free with the scars. We must learn to perceive and live with these scars as sacraments that reveal the void that brings us to the gateway where the God Who doesn't laugh at us awaits.

... Running away from the gateway to the void is most clearly felt in our trying to fit in to the cultural and social norms set up by others. In doing this we are not only negating our histories, painful as they may be, but we are also negating the waiting God Who doesn't laugh. We are running from the God Whose Son didn't fit this world but didn't run from it. Jesus acknowledged His misfitness and, through all the accompanying feelings and realities of it, walked into the waiting love of the Trinity Whose expression His self-emptying love revealed.

— Larry Lewis, M.M., from *The Misfit*

Choosing Peace

We have got to face the fact that war is not merely the product of blind political forces, but of human choices, and if we are moving closer and closer to war, this is because that is what men are freely choosing to do. The brutal reality is that we seem to *prefer* destructive measures: not that we love war for its own sake, but because we are blindly and hopelessly involved in needs and attitudes that make war inevitable.

— Thomas Merton, from *Peace in the Post-Christian Era*

We Need to Help

Africa is the only continent to produce less food now than it did twenty years ago, which is why so many of Africa's children are hungry. In Asia, the largest and most populated continent, China has managed to cut its proportion of underweight children by more than half. This extraordinary achievement was accomplished in twelve years, from 1990 to 2002, a relatively short period of time. Too many African children are physically stunted: today over a quarter of children under five years are underweight. The extreme poverty felt across the continent is the breeding ground in which diseases such as malaria, tuberculosis, water-borne diseases and parasites, and hunger-related illnesses flourish.

Because severe poverty strikes equally at the body and the spirit, it is also the breeding ground of despair. It is devastating to talk with children who believe that their likely destiny is to die young and to be quickly forgotten.

Hasn't the time come, at long last, to give answer to those who helped bring humanity's treasure to us? Some among those early human beings in Africa had to be the first to foster learning and living in a community, and someone had to be the first to foster love and solidarity in the human family. Hasn't the time arrived for us to turn back toward Africa, to respond to the people whose ancestors propelled all of humanity forward such a long time ago?

— Donald H. Dunson, from *Child, Victim, Soldier:*
The Loss of Innocence in Uganda

In God's Image

We often heard people say, "Oh, I'm just an ordinary this or that...." I have frequently had to say there is in our theology no such thing as an "ordinary this or that." We are all quite special since we are each that marvelous creation, a person created in the image of God. For that reason, we are each a God-carrier, God's viceroy, God's representative. That makes each of us truly special.

— Archbishop Desmond Tutu, from the Foreword,
The Vision of Peace by Mairead Corrigan Maguire

An Invitation to Life

Perhaps the greatest problem affecting our society is that so many people feel that they are not fully alive. They suffer the sense that they are not fully authentic as human beings. A major reason for this is that there are so many living their life secondhand without a real openness to the uniqueness of the gift given to them: their own life.

So many lives are lived by responding to other people's goals for us, society's goals for us, the advertising industry's goals for us. Christian revelation says that each of us is summoned to respond directly to the fullness of our own life in the mystery of God. How then are we to break out of the enclosed circle of inauthenticity and its consequent lifelessness? There is only one way and it is the basic message of the New Testament: to be fully open to the gift of eternal life.

The gift of life to each person is itself an invitation to development — an invitation we deny or refuse at our peril. No matter what fears or desires hinder our acceptance there is no ultimate reason why we should not be open to the "life found in the Son" to be encountered in the deep center of our being.

— John Main, from *John Main: Essential Writings,*
edited by Laurence Freeman

Feed Me, Fill Me

It is forever Pentecost. We seem to prefer that upper room of rationality and cognition, prefer to remain locked into set ways that are essentially of our own making, fearful of relinquishing whatever it is on which we are religiously dependent, women as well as men. The Spirit knows where to find us and precisely how to reach us, and does so, again and again blowing to bits our presuppositions, creating chaos around us and within us, opening a path for preparing a radically new creation in the church and in the world.

We must learn to embrace the chaos of our times as the potential for re-creation, learn to welcome the fire within, no matter how much it burns. We must dare to tell what we have seen and heard when visited by the Spirit, to speak of our experience courageously in public places, no matter what the cost. If this frightens us and others, so be it, for this I really do believe, that "it is God in Christ who has commissioned us, who has put a seal upon us and given us the Spirit in our hearts as guarantee" (2 Cor. 1:21–22). God's "guarantee" will surely guide us and safeguard our fidelity.

—Miriam Therese Winter, from *The Singer and the Song*

Charity

Charity is not about giving what we don't need, like the clothes we no longer wear or the food that has been sitting in our pantries. True charity is about giving even what we need so that others who have less may not go without. Charity can be seen in the women who left their homes to accompany Jesus (Luke 8:1–3). . . . Charity can also be seen in the women and the beloved disciple who stood by Jesus at the cross when everyone else had deserted him (John 19:25–27), very much like those who are willing to stand up for a just yet unpopular cause — like standing up for, sheltering, and defending the undocumented immigrants in our country as the people in the Humane Borders organization are doing by providing water in the desert for those risking death to find work in the United States. . . .

But the best example of true, authentic love is Jesus himself. . . . The entire life of Jesus is a journey of charity, of love in action, of sacrificial love for the sake of others. The more we reflect on the life of Jesus as presented in the Gospel narratives, the more we discover that the only way to truly appreciate authentic love is through the life of Jesus, and the only way we can truly know Jesus is through the optic of unlimited love.

— Virgil Elizondo, from *Charity*

Poverty of Spirit

What does poverty of spirit mean? It is my awareness that I cannot save myself, that I am basically defenseless, that neither money nor power will spare me from suffering and death, and that no matter what I achieve and acquire in this life, it will be far less than I wanted. Poverty of spirit is my awareness that I need God's help and mercy more than I need anything else. Poverty of spirit is getting free of the rule of fear, fear being the great force that restrains us from acts of love. Being poor in spirit means letting go of the myth that the more I possess the happier I'll be. It is an outlook summed up in a French proverb: When you die, you carry in your clutched hand only what you gave away. Poverty of spirit is a letting go of self and of all that keeps you locked in yourself.

— Jim Forest, from *The Ladder of the Beatitudes*

Solitude

Solitude is no longer appreciated in the noisy world of North America. Commuters on planes and trains chat on their cell phones and send text messages. Even walking on the street, many people are intently talking to their phones or have earpieces connecting them to something else.

How often do we take a day off just to be quiet and appreciate the world around us?

I suspect we might feel we were wasting time if we did. Yet it is in solitude and silence that God most often speaks to us. I sometimes envy the herders of sheep and cattle in Africa who spend each day alone with the animals in the fields.

Jesus lived in a pre-industrialized world like these herders. He often took time out from his active ministry to go off alone to pray, and he taught his disciples to do the same.

Bishop Desmond Tutu of South Africa is a very engaged and outgoing person. His schedule is full. When asked how he manages to do it all, he said he takes time for prayer and solitude each day and sets aside a week each month for a silent retreat. With his inimitable humor, he explained how he felt if he failed to meditate each day: "It is worse than having forgotten to brush my teeth."

If such a busy person can take time to be alone with God, why can't we?

— Janice McLaughlin, M.M., from *Ostriches, Dung Beetles, and Other Spiritual Masters: A Book of Wisdom from the Wild*

Love of Brother

The love of the humanity of Our Lord is the love of our brother. I have meditated on this fact during the past month. The only way we have to show our love for God is by the love we have for our brother. And as Father Hugo likes to say, "You love God as much as the one you love the least."

Love of brother means voluntary poverty, stripping one's self, putting off the old man, denying one's self. It also means non-participation in those comforts and luxuries which have been manufactured by the exploitation of others. While our brothers suffer, we must suffer with them.

And we must keep this vision in mind, recognize the truth of it, the necessity for it, even though we do not, cannot, live up to it. Like perfection. We are ordered to be perfect as our heavenly Father is perfect, and we aim at it, in our intention, though in our execution we may fall short of the mark over and over. As St. Paul says, it is by little and by little that we proceed.

— Dorothy Day, from *Dorothy Day: Selected Writings,*
edited by Robert Ellsberg

Finding Our Own Route

Those who suffer unjustly have a right to complain and protest. Their cry expresses both their bewilderment and their faith. It is not possible to do theology in Latin American without taking into account the situation of the most downtrodden of history; this means in turn that at some point the theologian must cry out, as Jesus did, "My God, my God, why hast thou forsaken me?"

This kind of communion in suffering demands watchfulness and solidarity. Commitment to the alleviation of human suffering, and especially the removal of its causes as far as possible, is an obligation for the followers of Jesus. Such a commitment presupposes genuine human compassion, as well as a measure of understanding of human history and the factors that condition it. It also requires a firm and stubborn determination to be present, regardless of the consequences, wherever the unjust abuse the innocent.

How can we talk about God without referring to our own age? . . . Our task here is to find the words with which to talk about God in the midst of the starvation of millions. How are we to preach the love of God amid such profound contempt for human life?

These are our questions, and this is our challenge. Job shows us a way with his vigorous protest, his discovery of concrete commitment to the poor and all who suffer unjustly, his facing up to God. And his acknowledgment of the gratuitousness that characterizes God's plan for human history. It is for us to find our own route.

— Gustavo Gutiérrez, from *On Job:*
God-Talk and the Suffering of the Innocent

The Strength of Weakness

A few things I know now that I didn't [before working with refugees in East Africa]. For one thing I understand that my own struggles — my brief sickness, my worries about my parents, my frustrations in my work — broke open my heart and enabled me to connect with the refugees on a deeper level. I suppose that if I had felt completely in control of things, I might not have experienced the love from the refugees so profoundly, nor have been able to love them as fully. In my weakness, then, I was more able, I think, to meet them as brothers and sisters — as friends. "In my weakness I am strong," said St. Paul. Maybe this is what he meant.

It is also clear that the refugees taught me how to love in a new way. I think it wasn't until I was in Kenya that I understood how satisfying it can be to love chastely, that is, to love many people with your whole heart and to accept the love that comes freely in return.

I also know how connected we remain through the miles and with the passage of time. And I know that if I am connected to my refugee friends thousands of miles away, then I am also connected to the refugee boy huddled under the blanket, that is, to a person I've never met. And, if this is true, then I'm connected to everyone else in the world.

The refugees with whom I worked still accompany me. I close my eyes and remember them when I pray. I hear their voices; I see their faces; I think of their sorrows and their joys; I remember their hope. And I am very grateful.

— James Martin, S.J., from *This Our Exile:*
A Spiritual Journey with the Refugees of East Africa

From a Recent Migrant Who Crossed the Border

If I could say anything to the American people, what I would say is that we are coming because of the poverty that we are forced to live in and that we just want to try to reach that dream, the dream of being able to work and provide for our families. Each one of us that you find in the desert has left behind a family that we loved. Many of us end up lost in the desert, and some of us die. Our families will never hear from us again or know what has happened to us. We who are called wetbacks are just coming to work, so please have some compassion for us when we are risking our lives in the desert. I have twenty brothers and all of us work hard on the farm. They work the land just as I do. Look at my hands. You can see the calluses on them from working the land. My hands are the proof that what I am saying is true.

— Miguel A. De La Torre, from *Trails of Hope and Terror: Testimonies on Immigration*

The Need for Peace

As I journeyed among the refugees and to the nations to which they will return, I became tangibly aware of the centuries it takes to build a culture and a nation and the few years it takes to obliterate the land and the people who gave spirit and life to that particular culture and nation.

Today the beauty is that millions can return home. The pity is that in most cases peace is fragile.

— Judy Mayotte, from *Disposable People? The Plight of Refugees*

All in All

Christ is the power of God among us and within us, the fullness of the earth and of life in the universe. We humans have the potential to make Christ alive; it is what we are created for. To live the mystery of Christ is not to speak about Christ but to live in the surrender of love, the poverty of being, and the cave of the heart. If we can allow the Spirit to really take hold of us and liberate us from our fears, anxieties, demands, and desire for power and control, then we can truly seek the living among the dead; we can live in the risen Christ who empowers us to build this new creation. We can look toward that time when there will be one cosmic person uniting all persons, one cosmic humanity uniting all humanity, one Christ in whom God will be all in all.

— Ilia Delio, from *Christ in Evolution*

Bridging Muslims and Christians

In spite of past hostilities, Catholics are urged by the Church today to promote a spirit of reconciliation with their Muslim neighbors. In the Virgin Mary, they can find one bridge to harmonious existence.

Recently, while I was waiting in an office before formal business hours, I had a fascinating conversation with a charming young lady. Although presently employed in Manila, she originates from Jolo, southern Philippines. In the course of our friendly chat, she proudly told me how her name "Mary Ann" reflects her family which is part Muslim and part Christian.

She narrated her background: "When my parents were choosing my name, it was my Muslim grandfather who insisted on 'Mary' because of his admiration for Mary, the mother of Jesus the prophet. Furthermore, he urged that my second name would be 'Ann' in honor of Mary's mother. Thus, while acceding to my parents' decision that I would be baptized a Christian, he believed that my Muslim heritage would not be lost because of the name he had chosen for me." She concluded her story: "I'm very happy that my own name symbolizes who I am — both Christian and Muslim."

Catholics should be delighted to discover how much Christians and Muslims have in common. Reverence for Mary is a dominant element of Muslim-Christian mutuality, a source of unity and a key for superseding hostilities.

— James H. Kroeger, M.M., from *Living Mission*

Disinterested Love

Aside from Jesus, Bob McCahill draws particular inspiration from the example of Mahatma Gandhi, who renounced all luxury in his selfless service of the poor. Though Gandhi remained committed to the Hinduism of his birth, he wrote a set of challenging reflections on Christianity, *The Message of Jesus Christ*, that had a profound impact on McCahill's own understanding of the Gospel and his view of mission. McCahill says that Gandhi's teachings helped shape his appreciation of other faiths, such as Islam, and the wisdom of totally accepting whatever faith one is called to. For the Maryknoll priest the link between faiths is love or, more specifically, "disinterested love," meaning the love that asks for nothing in return. It is this ideal of pure altruism — the true Christian model that is beyond the need to persuade or proselytize — that fires McCahill's passion. And it seems to strike a chord of wonder in his Muslim neighbors, who are astonished by such acts of genuine kindness by someone of a different faith. He overheard one Muslim man confide to a friend, "This man practices Islam better than we do!"

— Jim Daniels, from *Lives of Service: Stories from Maryknoll*

Do You Love Me?

In December, 1980, Ita Ford, Maura Clarke, Jean Donovan and Dorothy Kazel were brutally murdered on the road between the airport and San Salvador, the capital city of El Salvador. They had been stopped by Salvadoran security forces as they returned to their home after a short stay outside the country. They were raped, tortured, and killed and their bodies thrown into a common grave dug in a cow pasture. What was their crime? They had cared for the poor of El Salvador. They had tried to bring food and medicine to the people who had been driven from their homes and villages and were trying to survive in isolated mountain areas. These four faithful, hardworking churchwomen had no other desire than to alleviate some of the immense suffering of their oppressed neighbors and to show them, in the midst of hatred and violence, that people can truly love one another.

. . . To love is to be willing to embrace sorrow. To love God with all your heart, all your mind, and all your strength is to expose your heart to the greatest sorrow a human being can know. Love for Jesus made the four American churchwomen carry in their hearts the sorrow of the poor of the world, especially those in El Salvador. Their deaths, in turn, caused an immense sorrow in the hearts and minds of their brothers and sisters. The life of a Christian is a life of love for Jesus. "Do you love me?" That is the question he asks us three times. And when we say: "Yes Lord you know I love you," he says: "You will be taken where you would rather not go" (see John 21:15–18). There is never love without sorrow, never commitment without pain, never involvement without loss, never giving without suffering, never a "Yes" to life without many deaths to die. Whenever we seek to avoid sorrow, we become unable to love. Whenever we choose to love, there will be many tears. When silence fell around the cross and all was accomplished, Mary's sorrow reached out to all the ends of the earth. But all those who come to know that sorrow in their own hearts will come to know it as the mantle of God's love and cherish it as the hidden mystery of life.

— Henri Nouwen, from *Walk with Jesus*

It's Not What We Accomplish, but What We Do with It

My grandmother was a major influence both in my life of faith and in nurturing my budding sense of scholarship. I was the first person in my extended family to attend and graduate from college, and my grandmother took special delight in that occasion. She dressed in her "Sunday best" for the commencement ceremony; she would not fail to witness this special event in our family's history. She glowed with pride after the ceremony as I showed her my degree. She took the folder in her hands, stared at it with a little awe, and she said: "Look at that! This sure is something." Then turning to me, with love and pride and affection and wisdom, she asked: "Now, who are you going to help with it? Who are you going to use it for?"

— Bryan N. Massingale, from *Racial Justice and the Catholic Church*

Into the Hands of God

After I had been arrested and interrogated by the secret police for treating a wounded revolutionary [in Chile] I was moved from the torture center to another prison and placed in solitary confinement. Here, left to my own devices, I had sufficient emotional and intellectual space to maneuver, to choose what to do. My immediate inclination was to scream out to God for help, to batter spiritually on the bars of my cage, begging to be released. Then a very curious thing suggested itself to me: while I knew that I was quite right and proper that I should besiege heaven with my prayers to be released, an even better way would be to hold out my empty hands to God, not in supplication but in offering. I would say, not "Please let me out" but, "Here I am Lord, take me. I trust you. Do with me what you will." In my powerlessness and captivity there remained to me one freedom: I could abandon myself into the hands of God.

So for the next three weeks I struggled to let go the strings of my life, to hand myself over to God....

This abandonment experience of mine of course took place in the rather melodramatic context of a Chilean jail, but it could equally well have happened in a British hospital, a convent, or a suburban house. The act was an interior one, a spiritual maneuver taking place within the confines of physical powerlessness. This option for abandonment is available to all who find themselves trapped by circumstances and is the means by which the imprisoned can transcend their bonds. Like a bird in a cage they can choose to exhaust themselves battering their wings against the bars — or they can learn to live within the confines of their prison and find, to their surprise, that they have the strength to sing.

— Sheila Cassidy, from *Sharing the Darkness*

187

"A Patch of Holiness, Please"

Our torn, tattered history needs patching,
Pieces of love to cover the tears,
fabric of affection to heal our hardness of heart.
And patches have come.
Francis mended his time with troubadour songs.
Mother Teresa with her hospice care.
Patches of love holding together
whole nations on the edge of disintegration.

Whether Italy or India,
Wall Street or the monastery,
The halls of parliament or university dorm,
Baghdad or Darfur,
we need a patch of holiness,
a light to shine in our dark universe.

— Robert Morneau, from *The Color of Gratitude*

Your Will Be Done

Lord, you placed me in the world
to be its salt.
I was afraid of committing myself,
afraid of being stained by the world.
I did not want to hear what "they" might say.
And my salt dissolved as if in water.
Forgive me, Jesus.

Lord, you placed me in the world
to be its light.
I was afraid of the shadows,
afraid of the poverty.
I did not want to know other people.
And my light slowly faded away.
Forgive me, Jesus.

Lord, you placed me in the world
to live in community.
Thus you taught me to love,
to share in life,
to struggle for bread and for justice,
your truth incarnate in my life.
So be it, Jesus.

— Peggy M. de Cuehlo, from *Bread of Tomorrow,*
edited by Janet Morley

To Phoebe
Working with Autistic Gabriel

Now how I love you people of the flow
Who bring alive those called dysfunctional
Who only speak within until they know
Another in their rhythm, the sweet fall

Into our loving that the normal miss
Whose inwardness aseptic and quite boring
Prepares them for a sexy goodnight kiss
A loving that knows nothing of adoring.

When Jesus said the last word would be the first
He spoke of the dark world you bring to light
While we the normal stay the God-accursed
Legitimate the world's continued fight.

Phoebe this is of you and Gabriel
Whom without effort you bring out of hell.

— Sebastian Moore, from *The Contagion of Jesus*

Vocational Decisions

Beatitude, the fulfillment of the Promise, the "already and the not yet," is the heart of the Gospel message. Jesus proclaimed the in-breaking of the Reign of God: "Today, this Scripture has been fulfilled in your hearing" (Luke 4:21), and he lived as if that were true, demonstrating for his disciples and all who could "see," the pathway to inclusive community, right relationships and the New Creation, the Reign of God.

Though the stage on which we move through the journey of life may seem stable, though we may have already proclaimed *I have decided to follow Jesus,* the stage settings often change, sometimes dramatically, in response to the multiple opportunities and invitations of a lifetime.

Jesus' Sermon on the Mount lays out a moral framework for vocational decisions in response to these invitations. By his powerful preaching and by his own life, he emphasized over and over again the privileged place of impoverished and excluded peoples; the great need for compassion and social comforting; the centrality to the discipleship journey of the work for social justice or righteousness; and the call to peacemaking and reconciliation.

—Marie Dennis, from *Diversity of Vocations*

JULY

. . . .

Falling in Love

Nothing is more practical than finding God, that is, than falling in love in a quite absolute, final way. What you are in love with, what seizes your imagination, will affect everything. It will decide what will get you out of bed in the morning, what you will do with your evenings, how you will spend your weekends, what you read, who you know, what breaks your heart, and what amazes you with joy and gratitude. Fall in love, stay in love, and it will decide everything.

— Attributed to Pedro Arrupe, from *Pedro Arrupe: Essential Writings,* edited by Kevin Burke

The Language of Contemplation

How are we to talk to God in view of the suffering of the innocent? This is the central question in the Book of Job. The linking of God and the poor has opened up a way of answering the question.

Commitment to those most forgotten is a requirement of the God of the Bible, but this fact need not be completely clear for one to see the urgency of the requirement and put it into practice.... Commitment to the poor gives rise to a way of talking about God that influences the concrete behavior of believers. They thus retain the ethical perspective that is part of the theology of retribution, but they now situate it in a new and different context.

Converging with this prophetic line of thought about God is another that initially appears rather unobtrusively but in the end takes an almost explosive form — the line embodied in the language of mysticism. Its first expression, both simple and profound, is at the level of the faith of the people.

— Gustavo Gutiérrez, from *On Job:
God-Talk and the Suffering of the Innocent*

Ambition Can Be Healthy

Healthy ambition enables us to go beyond the ordinary and the routine to accomplish wonders.... Ambition leads to dreams and to small miracles. I have seen so many during my lifetime that I have lost count! Judy Mayotte, a friend of mine, lived among the displaced and uprooted peoples of the world for two years. She stayed in their makeshift homes, shared their food, ran with them to escape shelling, and listened to their stories, which she wrote about in *Disposable People: The Plight of Refugees.* In 1993 when she returned to Sudan on a mission for Refugees International, she was seriously injured during an air drop of food aid that went amiss.

After her crushed leg was amputated just below the knee and she was no longer able to travel in war zones, she became a special adviser to the Clinton administration on refugee issues.... Judy has never allowed her missing limb to define her or limit her dreams. She has accomplished more than most people with two legs and has been not deterred by the physical challenges she faces each day as moves about in a wheelchair. This kind of ambition enables one to overcome difficulties, to touch many peoples' lives and to have a positive impact on the wider world....

We can all overcome the limitations of age or gender or of limited physical and mental abilities. We too can perform wonders if we only have faith!

— Janice McLaughlin, M.M., from *Ostriches, Dung Beetles, and Other Spiritual Masters: A Book of Wisdom from the Wild*

The Shakertown Pledge of 1973

Recognizing that the earth and the fullness thereof is a gift from our gracious God, and that we are called to cherish, nurture, and provide loving stewardship for the earth's resources, and recognizing that life itself is a gift, and a call to responsibility, joy, and celebration, I make the following declarations:

1. I declare myself to be a world citizen.

2. I commit myself to lead an ecologically sound life.

3. I commit myself to lead a life of creative simplicity and to share my personal wealth with the world's poor.

4. I commit myself to join with others in the reshaping of institutions in order to bring about a more just global society in which all people have full access to the needed resources for their physical, emotional, intellectual, and spiritual growth.

5. I commit myself to occupational accountability, and so doing I will seek to avoid the creation of products which cause harm to others.

6. I affirm the gift of my body and commit myself to its proper nourishment and physical well-being.

7. I commit myself to examine continually my relations with others, and to attempt to relate honestly, morally, and lovingly to those around me.

8. I commit myself to personal renewal through prayer, meditation, and study.

9. I commit myself to responsible participation in a community of faith.

— Adam Daniel Finnerty, from *No More Plastic Jesus*

A Short Sermon

Supposedly St. John the Evangelist constantly gave a six-word sermon.

— Robert Ellsberg, *All Saints*

They say you said,
on every occasion,
regardless of circumstances:
"Brothers and sisters,
love one another."
A short sermon it was
and eventually tiresome.

They asked, your people,
for another topic, a different theme,
to fit differing occasions,
new circumstances.
Supposedly you replied:
"When you've mastered my first lesson,
then we can move on to a second."

— Robert Morneau,
from *The Color of Gratitude*

God

We celebrate the mystery
we call "God,"
the Ground and Sustainer
of everything that exists,
in whom we live and move and have our being.

We acknowledge
this awesome mystery
embodied
in every human person,
aware that
each gives God
unique and personal expression.

Here,
now,
God comes to visible expression
in each of us.

— Michael Morwood, from *Praying a New Story*

Compassion for Others

How do we Christians respond to the manifold human suffering all around us? Do we feel an imperative to become personally involved in the struggle for human dignity? Or do we shrink from conflict and seek in our religion a refuge from turmoil, like the priest who told Henri J. M. Nouwen he had canceled his subscription to the *New York Times* "because he felt the endless stories of war, crime, power games and political manipulations only disturbed his heart and mind and prevented him from meditation and prayer"?

When confronted with controversial issues, such as desegregation, affirmative action, ERA, capital punishment, homosexual rights, abortion, and so on, do we ask ourselves, "What would Jesus do?" Or are our decisions determined by our own self-interests, group loyalties, and the notion of "we" and "they"?

In his deep humanity, Jesus was transparent to God's love and compassion for us. I believe that compassion is a gift of God's grace, our response to God's love. It is the capacity for placing ourselves in another's predicament, feeling "from the inside" what it means to be another person, "feeling with," "suffering with," so that another's pain becomes our pain, another's struggle our struggle. Without compassion, all our good works are meaningless. With it, we become more like Christ.

— Pauli Murray, from *Pauli Murray:
Selected Sermons and Writings,* edited by Anthony B. Pinn

Hospitality

A lovely girl named Aleema, aged seven, came to my door as I was putting up wet clothing to dry. "Bob Brother, I saw you in my dream," she announced. Taken aback, I inquired: "Was I on my bicycle when you saw me?" She replied sweetly: "No. You had come to our home and we were feeding you a good meal."

Now I understand that Muslims are not only hospitable, but that some of them even dream about offering hospitality. It is a dream I cannot remember ever having had. In fact, I do not recall ever having dreamed about eating anything. And so much the less have I ever dreamed about feeding others. If it is true, therefore, that we dream of the things in life that are really significant to us, then the dream of a small Muslim girl, a dream in which wonderful food is offered to a visitor, would seem to say that she, and they, have their priorities in divine order. To offer hospitality to strangers is a requirement of Islam, no less than of Christianity. But to dream about offering hospitality is proof that Allah's holy will has been internalized in one's heart.

— Bob McCahill, M.M., from *Dialogue of Life:
A Christian among Allah's Poor*

Solidarity

I live in Haiti.

The other day in the midst of Port-au-Prince, the great degraded capital city that is my home, I saw a car, an old battered car, a jalopy, falter and sputter and come to a slow halt. It was out of gas; this happens often in my destitute country, where everyone and everything is so poor that the donkeys and horses are starving and even the cars must try to get by on nothing. The man who was driving the car got out and looked at it, stuck there in the middle of traffic, helpless. Then I saw another face, the passenger. A woman. She looked out of the back window with tears in her eyes, and the driver looked around the street at the unemployed loungers who are always there, and said to them, "She is going to have a baby right here." He told them that he had taken the woman from her home because the midwife was unable to help her. The pregnancy was difficult, and the woman needed to go to the hospital to have her baby. Now the tears were coming down the woman's cheeks. "If we do not get to the hospital, she will die," the man told the loungers. "Her baby will die, too."

The loungers — hungry young men who had never had a job and who will never have a job if my country goes on as it has done for the last half century — looked at the car and heard the man's voice and saw the woman's tears. Their backs straightened, their cigarettes fell to the ground, their eyes cleared. They approached the car, eight of them, leaned over, and put their shoulders to the chore. The driver steered. The woman lay back. Down one long dusty road, a left turn, and down another, through the green and white gates of the State Hospital, and she had arrived.

That was the force of solidarity at work, a recognition that we are all striving toward the same goal, and that goal is to go forward, to advance, to bring into this world another way of being. Even if the motor has died, even if the engine is out of gas, that new way of being can be brought into this world through solidarity.

— Jean-Bertrand Aristide, from *In the Parish of the Poor*

Eating Trees and Drinking Stars

When I was in Tucson, we had broccoli stalks for dinner. Helen said it was like eating trees. Indeed. They do look that way. And when I was in Colorado, Dorothy bought a bottle of champagne. As we sat sipping, she exclaimed that she was "drinking stars."

What is it about these two catchy phrases that leap like a little elf inside of me? They bring delight because they connect me with the planet and the universe. Yes, I am eating more than food and drinking more than liquid. Everything is woven together in the loom of life. What feeds me has been fed by Earth. What I drink has been touched by stars. Sun has fed and nurtured grapes, those tiny beginnings of sparkle, as they matured and grew into ripeness. Moon has watched over them in the comforting shade of night, soothing those juicy fruits of vine with her tenderness.

Yes, I eat trees and I drink stars. It is a lovely thought, that one. I want to hold it near to me when I sit down to every meal. Bring on the broccoli and the champagne. It is time to hold hands with the dancing cosmos with every bite I eat and every sip I take.

— Joyce Rupp, from *The Cosmic Dance*

203

Happy Simplicity

She is a lover. There seems no time left for her to collect. The days are given. She opens doors, her open heart a house to strangers. She glides her way through town to visit. She is a Catholic Worker. Her labor is faith. Her work is charity. She travels light through time, and somehow, forsaking all the approvals of high documentation, privileged profession, child or spouse, career or social consequence, she transforms every face she beholds.

They have taken the risks that others only dream of. Home and offspring have not closed them upon the next. They venture boldly: Christmas with their family and like families in Central America, spring breaks in Haiti, summers spent in the hot labors of justice. Their lives are spare, but not Spartan. There are vacancies in them, room for one another, for the poor, for the voiceless. They are not cluttered, neither in their homes nor in their souls. Some of them have launched into downward mobility and they often sail. These couples have time, since they have learned not to hoard it. Their love is both courageous and opportune, since they have realized that love itself is the most renewable of natural and supernatural resources.

She is a doctor and a Sister. A villager who finally accepts a jeep for the sake of the people who might be reached, touched, healed. She lives by the sun and the stars. It is all very un-complex — in the midst of the terrible war around, the helicopters overhead, the future uncertain. She lets go of loves and labors, but they never leave her. She is so distant but so immediate.

They shine for us. They illumine our lives.

And, in our own fleeting moments of lightness, we feel closer to them than we had ever dared to imagine.

— John F. Kavanaugh, from *Faces of Poverty, Faces of Christ*

Simplicity of Life

Many of us have become too dependent on our creature comforts, as those who spend any time in a third-world country quickly discover: the body goes to pieces and peace of mind is shattered when accustomed comforts disappear....

Simplicity of life is never easy for an individual or for a community. Each age group, each type of personality, each human culture has its strong points and weaknesses in this domain. What a powerful witness we would give if we could all share one another's strengths! We must move beyond that kind of accusatory stance which hardens us to one another and immobilizes personal and community good will. If we aim at a more "sparing and sharing" lifestyle, we will surely discover some changes we can make and, in the process, come closer to God, to one another, and to the people of God around us.

—David A. Fleming, S.J., from *Pilgrim's Notebook: An Experience of Religious Life*

Learning from Other Faiths

When I was teaching in Turkey, I had a small apartment in a working-class neighborhood and was known as a Christian monk. One afternoon I returned home to find a man sitting on the steps waiting for me. He said that his wife had stopped by earlier but found the door locked. I said, yes, I usually lock my door when I am not at home. He said that I needn't bother, because the women of the neighborhood were always around and would know if anyone who didn't belong tried to get in.

I realized that locking my door was an indication that I didn't trust my neighbors, so I never locked my door again. Often, I would return from the university to find that someone had left a covered bowl with rice and eggplant, *börek,* or a few kebabs on the counter. After finishing the food, I used to wash the bowl and leave it in the same place and in a few days it would disappear. Some days later, I would receive another gift of food. Other days I would find that my clothes had been washed, floors swept, bed linens changed, shirts ironed and folded, and so on. I never saw who performed this service, although I presume that it was done by women of the neighborhood.

This went on for six months until it was time for me to return to Rome. I told one of the men who had stopped by to wish me a safe journey that I had a final request. I asked if I could meet the neighborhood women to thank them for their generous help during the previous months. He said, "You don't have to meet them. They didn't do this for you; they did it for God, and God who sees all that we do will reward them. The Qur'an teaches that monks are one of the reasons why Christians are the closest community in friendship to Muslims, so it is an act of worship for us to treat you with kindness."

—Thomas F. Michel, S.J., from *A Christian View of Islam,*
edited by Irfan A. Omar

Nothing Is outside the Realm of Your Love

O sweet Lord I want so very much to avoid the bitter cross You ask me to carry, the cross of putting aside everything that is outside the realm of Your love. Actually, nothing is outside the realm of Your love, because You so long for us, so thirst for us, that You follow us into the darkest corners of our lives looking to embrace us with Your mercy and compassion. Yet I so often want to embrace things that You find unhealthy and unfitting for a seeker of God.

O Lord help me see, feel and know that outside of You there is nothing of any worth, and that with You all is priceless. Help me nail to the cross the secret things in my heart that I must sacrifice in order to follow You more closely and love You more dearly.

— Gerard Thomas Straub, from *Hidden in the Rubble:*
A Haitian Pilgrimage to Compassion and Resurrection

Calling

Vocation is not only about "me" and my personal fulfillment, but about "us" and the common good. In Frederick Buechner's words, our callings are found in the places where our "deep gladness" and the "world's deep hunger" meet, on the holy ground where our heart's desire comes together with what the world most needs *from* us. Authentic vocational discernment, therefore, seeks a proper balance between inward listening *to* our hearts and outward, socially engaged listening *with* our hearts to the realities of the world in which we live. These come together in our heart's response to the needs and sufferings of the world. "What matters," writes José Garcia, "is that the world should touch the heart and that the heart should go out towards the world. . . . "

"What does the Lord require of you," asks the prophet Micah, "but to do justice, and to love kindness, and to walk humbly with your God?" Whether we are a doctor or a minister, an artist or a taxi driver, a nanny or a teacher, our fundamental human vocation is to become just, loving, and humble persons during our short lives here on this earth. [This] always begins with how we treat our loved ones and the people in the circles of our everyday lives. As we consider our social responsibilities as citizens of our country and our world, though, our callings extend beyond our personal circle to an ever-expanding network of connection and solidarity with people both far and near.

— John Neafsey, from *A Sacred Voice Is Calling*

Prayer

Prayer is also inseparable from following Jesus because of the motives that inspire it, because of its mystique. What gives quality to any commitment is the mystique that inspires it, or the motives for this commitment If there aren't profound motivations and a stable mystique, the commitment will wither. This is particularly so in Christian spirituality, whose motivations do not come from pure human reason or from analyses and ideologies, but rather from the words of Jesus heard in faith. To have a personal experience of these words in our contemplative prayer is to nourish our mystique and to make of our motives for following these words a "source of living water." The mystique of our discipleship is inseparable from the experience of our prayer.

To address the question of whether prayer still has a place in today's world is not a bad idea. In theory and in practice many Christians doubt the efficacy and meaning of their prayer, in a culture that is becoming secularized, where statistics and technology foresee the near future more and more, where human beings are acquiring a growing responsibility for and dominion over nature and its laws. Moreover, in this context, prayer can be seen as an evasion, an alienation.

— Segundo Galilea, from *Following Jesus*

Death

To save one's life means to hold onto it, to love it and be attached to it and therefore to fear death. To lose one's life is to let go of it, to be detached from it and therefore to be willing to die. The paradox is that the person who fears death is already dead, whereas the person who has ceased to fear death has at that moment begun to live. A life that is genuine and worthwhile is only possible once one is willing to die.

— Albert Nolan, from *Jesus before Christianity*

What Is Saintliness?

Without idealizing or romanticizing the poor, who as a group are as prone to sin as any other group of human beings, liberation theology nevertheless emphasizes the theological significance of their lived faith in the midst of innocent suffering as a place where we encounter the power, the attractiveness, the beauty of Christ's truth. This is what Jon Sobrino calls "primordial saintliness":

> Saintliness does not have to be accompanied by heroic virtues — which are required for canonization; it is also expressed in a life of everyday heroism. We don't know whether these poor who cry out to live are saints-intercessors or not, but they have power to move our hearts. They do not perform "miracles" in the sense of violating the laws of nature, which is also required for canonization. But it is not rhetorical to say that their miracles violate the laws of history; it is a miracle to survive in a hostile world that makes their life exceedingly hard. What we call primordial saintliness is the will to live and to survive amid great suffering, the decision and effort that requires strength, the constancy, defying innumerable problems and obstacles. (Jon Sobrino, *Where Is God?*)

— Roberto S. Goizueta, from *Christ Our Companion*

Kingdom of God

One of the things that marks Jesus as unique among the great spiritual figures in history is the extent, the radical nature of, and fervor with which Jesus applied his vision of the kingdom of God to the society of his time. We find no division in Jesus' teachings or way of life between the social and the spiritual, between his deep inner life and a focused, critical, transformative activity within Israel. When Jesus said "My kingdom is of this world," he did not mean that it belonged to some purely ethereal realm. He was not in any way an escapist or a quietist. What Jesus meant was that the kingdom of God had nothing to do with the banal, violent world created by human greed, power grabs, petty intrigues, ignorance, and frivolousness.

— Gus Gordon, from *Solitude and Compassion*

Only to Love More

The best way — the only way — to truly overcome the fear of death is to live life in such a way that its meaning cannot be taken away by death.

This sounds grandiose, but it is really very simple. It means fighting the impulse to live for ourselves, instead of for others. It means choosing generosity over greed. It also means living humbly, rather than seeking influence and power. Finally, it means being ready to die again and again — to ourselves, and to every self-serving opinion or agenda.

Love is a tangible reality. Sometimes it is born of passion or devotion; sometimes it is a hard-won fruit, requiring work and sacrifice. Its source is unimportant. But unless we live for love, we will not be able to meet death confidently when it comes. I say this because I am certain that when our last breath is drawn and our soul meets God, we will not be asked how much we have accomplished. We will be asked whether we have loved enough. To quote John of the Cross, "In the evening of life you shall be judged on love."

As my great-aunt Else lay dying of tuberculosis, a friend asked her if she had one last wish. She replied, "Only to love more." If we live our lives in love we will know peace at the hour of death. And we will not be afraid.

— Johann Christoph Arnold, from *Be Not Afraid*

Our Search for God

Daniel Barenboim, the classical pianist, John Coltrane, the jazz saxophonist, and Eric Clapton, the rock guitarist, all said the same thing: their best playing occurs when they are no longer playing the instrument, but it is playing them. All three of those figures were meticulously trained, all three had become "masters" of their respective instruments, but they realized that they produced the most beautiful sounds, only at the limit of their striving and accomplishing, when they let the music carry them away. There is something very similar at work in the spiritual dimension, a rhythm between achieving and being achieved, between breathing in and breathing out.... Like these musicians reaching for excellence we can and should seek the Lord in all of our actions and to the limits of our powers, but the richest participation in the divine life occurs only when we stop seeking and we allow God to elevate us.

— Robert Barron, from *The Strangest Way:*
Walking the Christian Path

The Gift of Community

Some people just love to sit in cathedrals. The soaring arches, the light through stained glass, the statues — even those damaged by long-ago bigots — are statements about the people who made all this, their attitudes, their aspirations, and their failures. Just to sit and look at all this is to experience a community. To recognize this unseen community is an important spiritual choice, for it links us not only to the makers but to others who come here searching for something or celebrating something, or just wanting a place to be quiet, or escape, or weep.

Many people are inspired by a forest with its intimation of the community of so many lives — plants, insects, animal and human. Or a movie or a picture gallery can offer amazing revelations of gifts to be chosen. These are personal experiences, yet the gifts they offer us are gifts of community, of shared vision, courage, beauty, hope.

— Rosemary Luling Haughton, from *Gifts in the Ruins:*
Rediscovering What Matters Most

Living for the Promise

"I will be with you." From beginning to end of scripture, the echo never dies. The first promise and the last. With daring we lift the promise from the page and claim it for ourselves.

God with us — we know so little of what the promise might mean in practice, what gift it implies, even what form it takes. God, we are told, stands with the poor, the victims, those buried deep at the base of the human pyramid — and with the friends and champions of these. Still, for all that, history is somber, victims go on being victimized; the best so often go under.

While time lasts, the promise must be taken as ambiguous, dark, all but impenetrable to the logical mind. In this wise: if the power of the Most High is "with us," how comes it that such power so often takes the form of — powerlessness? We look to the martyrs, we hear their outcry.

Perhaps a measure of life dawns when we open the book of Jeremiah. If the promise bears a crucial weight in one thus assured, if the word of Yahweh is accepted as a premise on which a great spirit proceeds to build a life, to risk all — what weight might the same words except on us?

My sense at the outset of the book is that the promise is one matter, the shape of a given life, another. Will the promise shape the life? . . .

No one of us has seen the promise vindicated in the lives that beckon us on, over a long, often bitter, haul. . . . The hearts of such are fixed elsewhere than in the cultural wasteland. Thus they see good work through to the end, quite simply for its own sake: for its goodness, its human substance, its serviceability and good sense — its being "for others." All in virtue of the promise.

Jeremiah, yes. And as to ourselves, we shall see.

— Daniel Berrigan, from *Daniel Berrigan: Essential Writings,* edited by John Dear

Humility and God's Grace

Thank you, Lord,
that your grace
helps us to realize
that rebellion
against weakness, sins, mistakes
is the pride
of those who think themselves perfect
and forget that we are
weakness, weakness, weakness!
Ah! If only our pride understood
that you perform miracles
to sustain
true and genuine humility.

The important thing is to begin again, humbly and courageously, after every fall.

When the not truly humble fall, they are crushed. "How could I possibly have fallen? It's unbelievable! How shameful! I cannot accept it!"

The truly humble laugh at themselves without any bitterness. No surprise. No astonishment. The important thing is not to waste any time in standing up and beginning anew.

At the great judgment the Lord may say to someone: "How horrible! You fell a million times!" But all is salvaged if that person can say: "Yes, Lord, it really is frightful! But your grace helped me to get back on my feet quickly a million and one times!"

— Dom Helder Camara, from *Hoping against All Hope*

Jesus Meets His Mother

This is my son. My son, with thorns piercing his tender flesh, the blood running down his face. He is so young, so handsome. He is my son, my child. I remember so clearly when the angel came to tell me I was to bear a child, a son who would be great among his people. I was overwhelmed. I knew not what to think or say. What would people think? I was betrothed but had never been with a man. How could this be? What would happen to me, to this child? But I knew I would say yes. I was called to this by God, and I trusted in God. So I said yes.

But is this what the angel meant by greatness? What could come of such pain, such indignity? This is my child. I would carry the cross for him as I once I carried him, laughing and crying, on my back. What greatness can come at such at fearful price?

How long, how long, O Lord, must we others watch in silent agony as our children die before their time, weighed down by so many needless crosses not of their own making? Crosses of skin color, of poverty, of language, of sexual orientation, of fear, of lost hopes and discarded dreams. How long, O Lord, how long?

We cannot remain silent. These are our children, whether they came from our wombs or the wombs of others, helpless infants, needing love and care. And now they die, at each other's hands, at the hands of those who were meant to care for them, the hands of indifference, of anger, of corrosive hatred. These are our children, no matter how old or how young. They die. They die senselessly, needlessly, blindly, unknowing, without understanding. Why they must pay such a price. How long, O Lord, how long will this senseless slaughter continue?

— Diana L. Hayes, from *Were You There? Stations of the Cross*

Prayer — The Action of Faith

Faith and prayer are closely intertwined. Faith is the interior disposition of openness to God in face of the impossible. Prayer is the outward activation of this faith through the whole body in words and gestures. The essential quality of prayer is absolute confidence, even in the face of impossible obstacles. Mark has Jesus teach this immediately after the decisive action of the cleansing of the temple — an action that prompted Jesus' enemies to plan his capture and death. How can official Jerusalem, a "mountain" of opposition, be overcome? Jesus said to the disciples:

> Put your trust in God. I solemnly assure you, whoever says to this mountain, "Be lifted up and thrown into the sea," and has no inner doubts but believes that what he says will happen, shall have it done for him. I give you my word, if you are ready to believe that you will receive whatever you ask for in prayer it shall be done for you. (Mark 11:23–24)

— Joseph Grassi, from *Broken Bread and Broken Bodies*

Simon Helps Jesus Carry His Cross

Two men are working together in Bangladesh to build their small huts. These huts are very simple, made of mud, bamboo, rocks and jute sticks, but they are places where people have a sense of home and live together under a protective roof. As I look at these two men carrying together their heavy load of rocks, I am struck by the harmony of their bodies. It seems almost as if they are dancing. Their heavy load seems to become a light burden, a basket of fruit.

. . . I feel within me a strong desire to live my life on my own. In fact, my society praises the self-made people who are in control of their destinies, set their own goals, fulfill their own aspirations, and build their own kingdoms. It is very hard for me to truly believe that spiritual maturity is a willingness to let others guide me and "lead me even where I would rather not go" (John 21:18). And still every time I am willing to break out of my false need for self sufficiency and dare to ask for help, a new community emerges — a fellowship of the weak — strong in the trust that together we can be a people of hope in a broken world. Simon of Cyrene discovered a new communion. Everyone whom I allow to touch me in my weakness and help me to be faithful to my journey to God's home will come to realize he or she has a gift to offer that may have remained hidden for a very long time. To receive help, support, guidance, affection, and care may well be a greater call than that of giving all these things because in receiving I reveal the gift to the givers and new life together can begin. These two men of Bangladesh are not just working together. They are celebrating their shared humanity and so preparing a new home. That is Jesus' call to all people, a call that often comes to us through the poor.

— Henri Nouwen, from *Walk with Jesus*

From an Obscure Corner of Space

My heart has emerged from where it hid slowly, cautiously, fearing that this God of abundance and love is another myth that my intellect will reject and send back through a closing gap in my scientific universe. But I am awash in the abundance of the universe. It shouts at me from the night sky, the Earth, and my own soul. The vast darkness of space is not empty but is filled with the electromagnetic songs of electrons while its very fabric is rippled by gravity waves sent out by the orbital ballets of giant stars. And in this obscure corner of space, the warm, green, tropical sea casts billions of shells upon the shore, each one a life's product. Wading in the sea as the sun sets, I rejoice at the wonders of the sky and sea from which I emerged to sit here, now — in a monastery chapel.

— Aileen O'Donoghue, from *The Sky Is Not a Ceiling:*
An Astronomer's Faith

Who Is My Neighbor?

Neighborliness, for Jesus, consisted of stopping by the scene of disaster, caring for what faces perdition, using one's resources and one's time to restore life where death threatens to take over. It is going out of one's way to seek the well-being of the other. The parable of Luke 10:29–37 is replayed in Matthew 25:31–46, the parable of the Last Judgment, set in an eschatological dimension. The thirsty, the hungry the homeless, and the captives are neighbors, persons calling on our resources of compassion, people whose sufferings are ours by virtue of their humanity and the humanity of Jesus of Nazareth.

The neighbor is not only the person who is geographically "next door," but whoever and whatever is threatened with annihilation and a return to chaos. The planet Earth exists in a "heavenly" neighborhood, the world is a neighborhood of the created, among whom are human beings with their classification into races, classes, and communities of faith. Human existence takes place within concentric circles of relatedness: Family, nurture, culture, nationality, and racial identification make us into particular human beings. The question of who is my neighbor signifies the fact that we often live oblivious of the existence of the other, yet the unacknowledged neighbor is still a neighbor.

— Mercy Amba Oduyoye, from *The Agitated Mind of God: The Theology of Kosuke Koyama,* edited by Dale T. Irvin and Akintunde E. Akinade.

Love One Another

Jesus' message is all about love, love of God and love for neighbor. Like all Christians and people of good will, Catholics are called to love. St. Augustine said it best.

"*Ama Deum et fac quod vis*" (Love God and do what you will). . . . Can you stand before God at the end of your life and, without shame, look Jesus in the eye and say, "This is what I did"? If you can, you are not far from the kingdom of God. If you cannot, reform and conversion are needed. The bottom line is clear: "Love one another as I have loved you. . . . This I command you: to love one another" (John 15:12, 17).

— Richard G. Malloy, from *A Faith That Frees*

Having Lunch with God

A little East African boy in Dar es Salaam wanted to meet God. He knew that it was a long trip to where God lived, so he packed his bag with small, sweet cakes and a large bottle of soda and started on his journey.

He had been on his way for about ten minutes when he met an old woman. She was sitting in a park by the Indian Ocean just staring at some African birds. The boy sat down next to her and opened his bag. He was about to take a drink from his soda when he noticed that the old lady looked hungry, so he offered her a small cake. She gratefully accepted it and smiled at him. Her smile was so pretty that the boy wanted to see it again. So he offered her a drink from his soda. Again she smiled at him. The boy was delighted!

The little East African boy and the old woman sat there all afternoon eating and drinking and smiling, but they never said a word. As it grew dark, the boy realized how tired he was and got up to leave. But before he had gone more than a few steps he turned around, ran back to the old woman and gave her a big hug. She gave him her biggest smile.

When the boy opened the door to his own home a short time later, his mother was surprised by the look of joy on his face.

She asked him, "What did you do today that makes you so happy?"

He replied, "I had lunch with God." But before his mother could respond, he added, "You know what? She's got the most beautiful smile I've ever seen!"

Meanwhile, the old woman, also radiant with joy, returned to her home in the Upanga section of town.

Her son was stunned by the look of peace on her face and he asked, "Mother, what did you do today that makes you so happy?"

She replied, "I ate small cakes and drank soda in the park with God." And then, before her son could respond, she added, "You know, he's much younger than I expected."

—Joseph G. Healey, M.M., from *Once upon a Time in Africa*

AUGUST

· ·

Community

It was early morning on my first day in Irian Jaya. I was trying to get settled in my new home when an old Asmat fellow walked in without knocking and made himself comfortable in one of the chairs.

My previous experience in Indonesia taught me never to go straight to the point with people. We talked a long time, but when the old gentleman gave me no clues as to why he had come, I went back to my work, figuring he would catch on and disappear. He didn't.

I felt uncomfortable having him sitting there, so I came back and blurted out, "Is there something you want?" "No," he answered as he calmly stretched himself out on the short couch. Mildly irritated I said, "Hey, look, if you don't want anything, why are you here?" This ex-headhunter, who was to become one of my dearest friends and mentors, looked puzzled and replied simply, "Because you are alone."

— Vincent P. Cole, M.M., from *What They Taught Us:
How Maryknoll Missioners Were Evangelized
by the Poor,* edited by Joseph A. Heim, M.M.

Forgiveness

Last night I felt that I must ask forgiveness for all the ugly and rebellious thoughts I had about him these last few days. I have gradually come to realize that on those days when you're at odds with your neighbors, you are really at odds with yourself. "Thou shalt love your neighbor as thyself." I know that the fault is always mine, not his. Our two lives happen to have quite different rhythms; one must allow other people the freedom to be what they are. Trying to coerce others, of course, is quite undemocratic, but only too human. It is psychology that will probably pave the way to true freedom. We tend to forget that not only must we gain inner freedom from one another, but we must also leave the other free and abandon any fixed concept we may have of him in our imagination. There is scope enough for the imagination as is, without our having to use it to shackle the people we love.

— Etty Hillesum, from *Etty Hillesum:*
Essential Writings, edited by Annemarie S. Kidder

The Door to Peace

Forgiveness is a door to peace and happiness. It is a small, narrow door, and cannot be entered without stooping. It is also hard to find. But no matter how long the search, it *can* be found.

What does forgiving really mean? Clearly it has little to do with human fairness, which demands an eye for an eye, or with excusing, which means brushing something aside. Life is never fair, and it is full of things that can never be excused.

When we forgive someone for a mistake or a deliberate hurt, we still recognize it as such, but instead of lashing out or biting back, we attempt to see beyond it, so as to restore our relationship with the person responsible for it. Our forgiveness may not take away our pain — it may not even be acknowledge or accepted — yet the act of offering it will keep us from being sucked into the downward spiral of resentment. It will also guard us against the temptation of taking out our own anger or hurt on someone else.

No matter how repeatedly we ourselves stumble or fall, we still want others to forgive us, and to believe that we can change.

Forgiveness is a power. It frees us from every constraint of the past, and helps us overcome every obstacle. It can heal both the forgiver and the forgiven. In fact, it would change the world if we allowed it to.

Each of us holds the keys to forgiveness in our hands. It remains to us whether or not we choose to use them.

— Johann Christoph Arnold, from *Why Forgive?*

Becoming Eucharist

During the meal Jesus took bread, blessed it,
broke it, and gave it to his disciples. (Matt. 26:26)

Mystery of Choosing:

Lord, you have taken and chosen me from among many,
   called me to become your friend.
Such a gracious choice convinces me of your love,
   What a paradox! I belong to you!
From the lowly and insignificant,
   you freely selected me for service.
"Lord, I am not worthy!"
   Your love endures forever.

Miracle of Blessing:

Lord, you have blessed me,
   enriched me beyond measure.
Family, vocation, community, mission:
   all manifesting your generous, loving design.
Your befriending Spirit gently directs my path,
   opening new vistas and broader horizons.
"Goodness and kindness follow me all the days of my life."
   Your love endures forever.

Paradox of Breaking:

Lord, why have you broken me?
   My limitations and failures weigh heavy upon me.
I attempt to speak—my tongue stutters;
   I struggle with community—I'm an outsider;

231

People see me as an enigma — I feel lonely;
Problems and trials bruise and crush me.
"A broken, humbled heart, O Lord, you will not reject."
Your love endures forever.

Wonder of Giving:

Lord, I experience fulfillment as
your servant and herald.
Taken, blessed and broken,
I am now shared and distributed.
May your people find nourishment, strength and consolation
from my humble self-gift.
"Lord, you know all; you know that I love you."
Your love endures forever.

— James H. Kroeger, M.M., from *Living Mission*

Leaps of Faith

I remember being in a seminar on nonviolence in which one of the participants, the daughter of a career Marine officer, talked of her struggle to reconcile violence with the message and life of Jesus. "I always looked upon the military position, the recourse to violence, as logical," she said. Then one day it occurred to her that hell was logical; it made sense to be punished for what we'd done on earth. Heaven, she decided, was illogical. So were forgiveness, mercy, and compassion. The young woman concluded: "I have no trouble accepting heaven. It should be the same with nonviolence. Both are illogical; both are leaps of faith."

— Mary Lou Kownacki, from *A Monk in the Inner City*

Surviving the Atomic Bomb

On the Feast of the Transfiguration, August 6, 1945, the first atomic bomb exploded over Hiroshima. Pedro Arrupe saw the blinding flash of light. Moments later he heard its roar and felt its seismic power.... He was thirty-seven... [and living] in the town of Nagatsuka on the outskirts of Hiroshima. ...

I shall never forget my first sight of what was the result of the atomic bomb: a group of young women, eighteen or twenty years old, clinging to one another as they dragged themselves along the road. One had a blister that almost covered her chest; she had burns across half of her face.... On and on they came, a steady procession numbering some 150,000. This gives some idea of the scene of horror that was Hiroshima.

We continued looking for some way of entering the city, but it was impossible. We did the only thing that could be done in the presence of such mass slaughter: we fell on our knees and prayed for guidance, as we were destitute of all human help....

It is at such times that one feels most a priest.... In light of these facts, a priest cannot remain outside the city just to preserve his life. Of course, when one is told that in the city there is a gas that kills, one must be very determined to ignore that fact and go in. And we did.

— Pedro Arrupe, from *Pedro Arrupe: Essential Writings,* edited by Kevin Burke

At the Heart of God's Reign

Jesus took desire seriously, and wishes all Christians to do the same. We engage desire, not primarily by adopting a moralistic and legal coding, but by working co-operatively for the right relationships that facilitate liberation and growth at every level of life. *Striving to get relationships right is the heart and soul of the New Reign of God.* And it is not merely human relationship, but right relating at every level, from the cosmos to the bacterial realm. Creation is forever held in the embrace of a relational matrix, and from that foundational source all relationships find their true place and purpose.

— Diarmuid O'Murchu, from *The Transformation of Desire*

Where Everything Is Precious

I used to think that happiness was not only random but fairly rare, and certainly not to be counted on. What, after all, is there to feel happy about in a world full of terror, poverty and uncertainty — except at those unusual moments when personal delight overcomes the gloom that so often seems more appropriate.

It took me a long time but I discovered a different way of thinking about happiness. I learned to allow myself to be open to reality as a whole: neither the good nor the bad alone, but the inevitably interwoven nature of both. The joy of a child's laugh and the terrible vulnerability of children; the horror of war and the heights of heroism in it; the pain of illness and the courage and compassion it evokes; the delight of love and the precariousness of it. There is grief hurting in every joy, humiliation behind every achievement and, above all, endings waiting for every beginning. Nevertheless, there is hope surging beyond every failure, compassion and imagination to tackle every disaster. When a tree falls, insects and fungi flourish, and new seedlings grow to take up the space. In the ruins of bombed cities the rubble turns purple with the blazing fireweed.

Nothing lasts, neither evil nor good, but to realize this is not to settle for a resigned detachment. On the contrary, it means that what is good and strong and beautiful must be passionately cherished, loved, praised, wondered at, just because it is fragile and passing. It will pass whether it be a wildflower or a great temple or a mountain or a human life, but that makes it all the more wonderful. A plastic rose, however red, does not give a message of love as does the rose that fades and dies — the ephemeral quality is partly what moves us. The tiny grief implicitly in the beauty makes it more precious.

Conversely, the knowledge that what is evil also has an end gives the courage to fight against it, to try to give goodness and beauty a little longer, to create more space for joy to grow. And if death is the end, at least of the kind of life we know, then we want to cherish and protect that life and give it every chance to discover yet more unexpected loveliness.

Happiness is being able to touch, at least a little, that reality at the heart of the world where nothing is everlasting but everything — everything — is precious.

— Rosemary Luling Haughton, from *Gifts in the Ruins: Rediscovering What Matters Most*

Living in the Present

When you open your eyes,
You open your mind;
When you open your mind,
You open your heart.
You live with dignity;
When you live with dignity,
You share divine life;
When you share divine life,
You can build a community of love;
When you build a community of love,
You enter eternity;
When you enter eternity,
Nothing can harm you;
When nothing can harm you,
You will live forever,
Even now in this present moment.

— Joseph Petulla, from *The Tao Te Ching
and the Christian Way*

The Breath of the Holy Spirit

Jesus' gift of the Sprit to the disciples reminds us of the gratuitousness of God's love, the gratuitousness of life itself. Everything is grace, everything is gift. This is one of the insights the author of the Genesis narrative of God breathing into the nostrils of *adam* attempts to convey, and one that is vital for the Judeo-Christian understanding of God's Spirit. The Spirit always reawakens us to the gift of the first breath, the breath of Genesis. In the resurrection narrative mentioned above, Jesus breathes the Spirit and the Spirit's peace into the disciples as a gift. By the awakening to this gratuitous gift we are freed from the idolatrous notion that we are the source of life and the moving force of the universe.

As St. Paul reminded his friends in ancient Corinth, we are simply vessels formed of clay, containing within us the treasure of the breath of God (2 Cor. 4:7).

— Brian J. Pierce, O.P., from *We Walk the Path Together*

Shine On, Farmer Boy

Shine on, farmer boy, symbol to me of the thousand million like you who drew the Son of God from heaven to smooth and bless your weary anxieties and your puzzled brows. Come to me often in your barefoot squalor and look at me from out of those hopeless and bewildered eyes. Do not let me forget that vision, but stay by me and preside over my dreams. Teach me that souls are people. And remind me everlastingly that they are magnificent people like you.

— Bishop James E. Walsh, M.M., for the people of China,
from *A Maryknoll Book of Prayer*,
edited by Michael Leach and Susan Perry

God Is Love

This is all I have known for certain, that God is love. Even if I have been mistaken on this or that point, God is nevertheless love. If I have made a mistake it will be plain enough; so I repent — and God is love. He *is* love, not he *was* love, nor, he *will be* love, oh no, even that future was too slow for me, he *is* love. Oh, how wonderful! Sometimes, perhaps, my repentance does not come at once, and so there is a future. But God keeps no person waiting, he is love. Like spring-water which keeps the same temperature summer and winter — so is God's love. His love is a spring that never runs dry.

— Søren Kierkegaard, from *Provocations:*
Spiritual Writings of Kierkegaard

Knowing God

Your missionary ancestors told Indian people that they were worshipping a false god when we pray to the sun. The sun is the most powerful physical presence in our lives. Without it we could not live and our world would perish. Yet our reverence for it, our awe, was considered idolatry.

But your missionary ancestors misunderstood even that much, because we never worshipped the sun. We merely saw in it the reflection of the sacred, the Creator, and used its image to focus our prayers of thanksgiving for the Creator's life-giving power. It is, for us, a constant reminder of the creative power of God, as we greet the sun in the morning when we first arise and again in the evening. In between, as we go about our day, we constantly will see our shadow on the ground and will be reminded again of God's creative goodness. We can stop, look up, and say a short prayer whenever this happens.

— Phillip Deere, from *A Native American Theology*
by Clara Sue Kidwell, Homer Noley, and George "Tink" Tinker

The Command to Love One Another

It is our faith that God made all things and makes them all new in the risen Lord who gave us this command: "Love one another. Such as my love has been for you, so must your love be for each other."

When we fear and grieve, time seems to drag cruelly. We delight, and it hurtles by, uncaring. We shall never grasp the meaning of time and its preciousness, or eternity and its promise, if we do not learn to love.

There is a verse, so common it is attributed to many authors, which goes:

> Time is too slow for those who wait.
> Time is too fast for those who fear.
> Time is too long for those who mourn.
> Time is too short for those who rejoice.
> But for those who love,
> Time is eternity.

— John F. Kavanaugh, from *The Word Engaged*

Padre Pio

What I like most about Padre Pio is not his stigmata or his extraordinary experiences that shocked doctors and scientists and psychologists, but the fact that his mysticism was profoundly sacramental. He spent hours in the confessional — Graham Greene did not go to confession to Pio for fear of what he might be told — and the celebration of the Eucharist was his primary mystical experience. This has impressed me because the Eucharist is the center of my prayer and perhaps ultimately I gave up practicing pure Zen because I wanted to pray before the Eucharist.

— William Johnston, from *Mystical Journey*

A Vision in the Subway

I was in an underground train, a crowded train in which all sorts of people jostled together, sitting and strap-hanging workers of every description going home at the end of the day. Quite suddenly I saw with my mind, but as vividly as a wonderful picture, Christ in them all. But I saw more than that; not only was Christ in every one of them, living in them, dying in them, rejoicing in them, sorrowing in them — but because He was in them, and because they were here, the whole world was here too, here in this underground train; not only the world as it was at that moment, not only all the people in all the countries of the world, but all those people who had lived in the past and all those yet to come.

I came out into the street and walked for a long time in crowds. It was the same here, on every side, in every passerby, everywhere — Christ. . . .

The "vision" lasted with that intensity for several days. . . . It altered the course of my life completely.

Christ is everywhere; in Him every kind of life has a meaning and has an influence on every other kind of life. It is not the foolish sinner like myself, running about the world with reprobates and feeling magnanimous, who comes closest to them and brings them healing; it is the contemplative in her cell who has never set eyes on them, but in whom Christ fasts and prays for them — or it may be a charwoman in whom Christ makes Himself a servant again, or a king whose crown of gold hides a crown of thorns. Realization of our oneness in Christ is the only cure for human loneliness. For me, too, it is the only ultimate meaning of life, the only thing that gives meaning and purpose to every life.

— Caryll Houselander, from *Caryll Houselander: Essential Writings,* edited by Wendy M. Wright

Being a Sister and Brother

Every Maundy Thursday before celebrating the Eucharist, we hold a beautiful ceremony; there is always an enormous congregation to see the bishop or priest washing twelve people's feet. Thus we call to mind what the Lord himself did.

However, I always feel a little uneasy when I see our twelve apostles offering themselves with their feet already well washed. The message ought to be: "Dear brothers and sisters, we aren't here today to mime the washing of feet already carefully washed. We're here to tell you we're ready to behave as flesh-and-blood brothers should, ready to help one another and do for our brothers and sisters what is really necessary for them, what they truly need."

Otherwise religion is in danger of being a mere theatrical spectacle. Religion has to be believed, not merely acted. The Lord set us an example that evening, as throughout his life. If we Christians had set an example of always being readier to serve than to be served, the world would already be a better place.

— Dom Helder Camara, from *Through the Gospel
with Dom Helder Camara*

The God-Bless-You Guy

The name Dwight Leeray may not ring a bell in the roll call of the saints. Dwight was just a guy hustling spare change in front of a bank in downtown Berkeley. He was a fellow routinely rebuffed and ignored as he held out a Styrofoam cup while standing the legally required number of paces from the ATM. Those of us in the neighborhood didn't know his name until after he was dead. We just called him the God-Bless-You Guy.

Because that's what Dwight did all day long, just blessed people as they came down the sidewalk. He never asked for money. He blessed us in the name of God and wished us a nice day. He blessed us and cheered us on in every season and our every endeavor as if the victory of one meant victory for all. Until the night, that is, when somebody beat him up for the money in his cup. The thief got two dollars. Dwight died of his injuries.

The newspaper carried no picture of Dwight. But the headlines announcing the death of the "God-Bless-You-Guy" instantly brought his presence to mind. We had never known his name or where he came from, where he slept or why he stood on the same corner every day with his humble cup. We knew him only as a conduit of blessing. No one stands on the corner by the ATM to bless us now.

— Alice Camille, from *Listening to God's Word*

We Are Not Alone

Jesus died a martyr's death, a death not of glory and honor but the shameful death of a criminal. Killed because he brought hope, killed because he, too, was different, hung out with the wrong crowd, didn't say what those in power wanted to hear. But he died a victorious death as well, not in vain, but in sacrifice for the lives of all of us. Jesus died as he lived, a man of faith who refused to lay down his religion, his faith in God, for anyone or anything. Then he rose from the dead to fulfill God' promises of salvation for all of humanity . . . Jesus brought life through his death. That young, robust man, standing there waiting for his cross to be placed on his shoulders, is not a victim but the victor. He is the one who paves the way for us all if we but follow him. We, too, must not lay our religion down. If we are to be like Jesus, in times of difficulty or doubt, we turn not away from the cross but toward it, claiming our faith from its victory and being sustained by that faith. We cannot do it alone, but just as Jesus was not alone, neither are we. . . .

Jesus stands surrounded yet so alone. Who will pray for him? Who will pray for us? Who will stand up for him? Who will stand up for us? Who but us. And our God.

— Diana L. Hayes, from *Were You There? Stations of the Cross*

A Life Poured Out

Pierre Claverie, Dominican friar and the bishop of Oran in Algeria, was assassinated August 1, 1996. It seemed absurd that this man, who had devoted his life to dialogue between Christianity and Islam, should die in such a violent way. The story of Pierre Claverie is of a man who lived with hope. His death did not extinguish that hope but made it shine out more strongly. We have need of that hope more urgently than ever today.

His life and death show that not only can we hope but, as Christians, we must do so. Faced with the prospect of his own death, he did not run away, because he believed that violence never has the last word. That is our faith. He wrote, "Living in the Muslim world, I know the weight of this temptation to withdraw into oneself, the difficulty of mutual understanding and of respecting each other. And I can measure perfectly the abyss that separates us.... We would not be able to bridge this gap by ourselves. But God, in Jesus, gives us the means to measure the length, the breadth, the depth and the extent of his Love. Supported by this revelation, we can regain confidence.... To give one's life for this reconciliation as Jesus gave his life to knock down the wall of hatred which separated Jews, Greeks, pagans, slaves, and free men, isn't that a good way to honor his sacrifice?" Hope is not a naïve optimism, but confidence that for each of us after Good Friday comes Easter Sunday.

— Timothy Radcliffe, from the Foreword, *A Life Poured Out: Pierre Claverie of Algeria* by Jean-Jacques Pérennès

Defending the Poor

Amos and Isaiah are not just voices from distant centuries; their writings are not merely texts that we reverently read in the liturgy. They are everyday realities. Day by day we live out the cruelty and ferocity they excoriate. We live them out when there come to us the mothers and the wives of those who have been arrested or who have disappeared, when mutilated bodies turn up in secret cemeteries, when those who fight for justice and peace are assassinated. . . .

In this situation of conflict and antagonism, in which just a few persons control economic and political power, the church has placed itself at the side of the poor and has undertaken their defense. The church cannot do otherwise, for it remembers that Jesus had pity on the multitude. But by defending the poor it has entered into serious conflict with the powerful. . . .

Early Christians used to say *Gloria Dei, vivens homo* ("the glory of God is the living person"). We could make this more concrete by saying *Gloria Dei, vivens pauper* ("the glory of God is the living poor person"). From the perspective of the transcendence of the gospel, I believe we can determine what the life of the poor truly is. And I also believe that by putting ourselves alongside the poor and trying to bring life to them we shall come to know the eternal truth of the gospel.

— Oscar Romero, from *Voice of the Voiceless*

Holy Humility

From the first moment of his presence in humanity Christ makes *kenosis* (self-emptying) the revelation of the power of the love of the Triune God. He spends the greater part of his human life in the simplicity of everyday labor. . . .

The power of love is totally bound up with *humility*. The opposite of love we usually call hatred. But its real name is egoism. . . . Christ destroys the works of the devil (1 John 3:8), and ransoms us chained in our egoism, by accepting the ultimate humiliation, the cross. By this humility he abolishes on the cross demonic pride and self-centeredness. In that hour the glory of his love shines forth. We are redeemed.

Christian life means continual assimilation of the mystery of the cross in the fight against individual and social selfishness. This holy humility, which is ready to accept the ultimate sacrifice, is the mystical power behind Christian mission. . . .

One of the greatest dangers for Christian mission is that we become forgetful in the practice of the cross and create a comfortable type of a Christian who wants the cross as an ornament, but who often prefers to crucify others than to be crucified oneself. . . .

A mission that does not put at its center the cross and resurrection ends up as a shadow and fantasy.

— Anastasios of Androussa, from *New Directions in Mission and Evangelization: 2,* edited by James A. Scherer and Stephen B. Bevans

Fiestas

Fiestas may be foolishness to those who seek rational discourse; they may be stumbling blocks to those who seek timely, logical, and efficient action. But to those who have participated in the collective mystical experience of Christian faith, they are a celebration of god's power unto new creation. They speak salvation to those who believe — the death unto life of a people . . . the joyful expression and visible sign of God's power unto new life.

— Virgil Elizondo, from *Galilean Journey*

Discerning the Presence

The Gospels are filled with examples of God's presence in the word. Personally, I am always touched by the story of Jesus in the synagogue of Nazareth. There he read from Isaiah:

The Spirit of the Lord is on me,
for he has anointed me
to bring good news to the afflicted.
He has sent me to proclaim liberty to captives,
sight to the blind,
to let the oppressed go free,
to proclaim a year of favor from the Lord.

(Luke 4:18–19)

After having read these words, Jesus said, "This text is being fulfilled today even while you are listening." Suddenly, it becomes clear that the afflicted, the captives, the blind, and the oppressed are not people somewhere outside of the synagogue who, someday, will be liberated; they are the people who are listening. And it is in the listening that God becomes present and heals.

The Word of God is not a word to apply in our daily lives at some later date; it is a word to heal us through, and in, our listening here and now.

The questions therefore are: How does God come to me as I listen to the word? Where do I discern the healing hand of God touching me through the word? How are my sadness, my grief, and my mourning being transformed at this very moment? Do I sense the fire of God's love purifying my heart and giving me new life? These questions lead me to the sacrament of the word, the sacred place of God's real presence.

— Henri Nouwen, from *With Burning Hearts*

Reconciliation

"But God proves his love for us in that while we still were sinners Christ died for us. Much more surely then, know that we have been justified by his blood, will we be saved through him from the wrath of God." (Rom. 5:8–9)

The offer of reconciliation is not given gratuitously but comes to us from a God who has felt the enmity deeply to the point of wrath. This is an important matter to ponder, inasmuch as wrath or anger is a significant but painful moment in overcoming the suffering caused by violence.... Anger can be destructive but we also know that anger is an acknowledgment of the depth of pain and the breadth of the threat that has been made to our well-being. Not to express anger that arises from violence is not to acknowledge the suffering. And unless we do acknowledge it, a new narrative cannot be constructed.

An important corollary flows from this insight that God takes the initiative, that reconciliation is something that we discover rather than achieve. This insight reverses a moment in the process of reconciliation that we usually expect. We expect that evildoers should repent and so seek forgiveness, that those who have wreaked terror and oppression should see the wrongness of their ways and engage in repentance and reparation. However, in the Christian understanding of reconciliation, it works the other way around. We discover and experience God's forgiveness of our trespasses, and this prompts us to repentance. In the reconciliation process, then, because the victim has been brought by God's reconciling grace to forgive the tormentor, the tormentor is prompted to repent of evildoing and to engage in rebuilding his or her own humanity.

— Robert J. Schreiter, from *Reconciliation:*
Mission and Ministry in a Changing Social Order

Mercy

To live truly and humanly in El Salvador inescapably means, as Jesus said in the parable of the good Samaritan, meeting up with a wounded person on the way. But they did not meet up with an individual, but rather an entire people, and not just with a wounded people, but rather with a crucified people. And this meeting is where the human part is decided: Either you make a detour around him, as the priest and the Levite of the parable did, or you heal his wounds.

Our martyrs made no detour. . . . Their hearts were moved and they were moved to mercy. They internalized the suffering of an entire people and responded to it.

Mercy was more for our martyrs than a feeling, or the willingness to alleviate some suffering. It was a principle which guided their entire lives and work. Mercy was there in the beginning, but it stayed there throughout the entire process, shaping *them* as well.

— Jon Sobrino, from *The Principle of Mercy*

Listen to the Poor

When we understand that we are one family, our concern for others becomes both intimate and urgent. Jesus responds in a particular way to the poor and the marginalized. Let us pray for the grace to hear the poor of our world, respond to their cry and value their wisdom and experience.

Oír a los Pobres

Entendemos como una sola familia nos lleva a una preocupación íntima y urgente por los demás. Jesús responde de forma particular a los pobres y los marginados. Oramos por la gracia de escuchar a los pobres de nuestro mundo, responder a su clamor y valorar su sabiduría y experiencia.

—Linda Unger and David Aquije, from *Un solo mundo, una sola familia / One World, One Family*

Play It!

Christianity — like baseball, painting, and philosophy — is a world, a form of life. And like those other worlds, we first approach it because we perceive it as beautiful. A youngster walks onto the baseball diamond because he finds the game splendid, and a young artist begins to draw because she finds the artistic universe enchanting. Once the beauty of Christianity has seized a devotee, she will long to submit herself to it, entering into its rhythms, its institutions, its history, its drama, its visions and activities. And then, having *practiced* it, having worked it into her soul and flesh, she will know it. The movement, in short, is from the beautiful (it's splendid!) to the good (I must play it!) to the true (it is right!). One of the mistakes that both liberals and conservatives make is to get this process precisely backward, arguing first about right and wrong. No kid will be drawn into the universe of baseball by hearing arguments over the infield-fly rule or disputes about the quality of umpiring in the National League. And none of us will be enchanted by the world of Christianity if all we hear are disputes about it. Christianity is a captivating and intellectually satisfying game, but the point is to play it. It is a beautiful and truthful way, but the point is to walk it.

— Robert Barron, from *The Strangest Way: Walking the Christian Path*

It Won't Happen without You

There was a woman who wanted peace in the world and peace in her heart and all sorts of good things, but she was very frustrated. The world seemed to be falling apart. She would read the papers and get depressed. One day she decided to go shopping, and she went into a mall and picked a store at random. She walked in and was surprised to see Jesus behind the counter. She knew it was Jesus, because he looked just like the pictures she'd seen on holy cards and devotional pictures. She looked again and again at him, and finally she got up her nerve and asked, "Excuse me, are you Jesus?" "I am." "Do you work here?" "No," Jesus said, "I own the store." "Oh, what do you sell in here?" "Oh, just about anything!" "Anything?" "Yeah, anything you want. What do you want?" She said, "I don't know." "Well," Jesus said, "feel free, walk up and down the aisles, make a list, see what it is you want, and then come back and we'll see what we can do for you."

She did just that, walked up and down the aisles. There was peace on earth, no more war, no hunger or poverty, peace in families, no more drugs, harmony, clean air, careful use of resources. She wrote furiously. By the time she got back to the counter, she had a long list. Jesus took the list, skimmed through it, looked up at her and smiled. "No problem." And then he bent down behind the counter and picked out all sorts of things, stood up, and laid out the packets. She asked, "What are these?" Jesus replied, "Seed packets. This is a catalog store." She said, "You mean I don't get the finished product?" "No, this is a place of dreams. You come and see what it looks like, and I give you the seeds. You plant the seeds. You go home and nurture them and help them to grow and someone else reaps the benefits." "Oh," she said. And she left the store without buying anything.

— Megan McKenna, from *Parables: The Arrows of God*

Together: No More Us and Them

A number of poor farmers in Brazil were about to lose their land to a government project, and they knew that to lose their land was to lose everything.

The people met to decide what to do. Most were despairing; past protests against big government projects had failed, often with protesters being shot and killed. No one could think how to save their land.

But then some of the women had an idea. They decided to go with their children to the neighborhoods of the rich where the senators lived on the day of the critical Senate vote. When they arrived, they were awestruck by the size of the houses and especially the beautiful green lawns with so many lovely trees. The poor women sat down with their children, making quite a sight in the neighborhood. After a while, the senators' wives sent their servants out to ask if the visitors wanted some food. "No, thank you," replied the women. "We did not come for food."

The wives were perplexed and eventually came out themselves to ask the poor women if they needed some money. "No, thank you, we are not here for your money," they said. The senators' wives became even more confused. Finally, the women in the big houses asked in bewilderment, "What is it that you want?

The poor campesino women looked into the eyes of the wealthy senators' wives and said, "We are going to die. This seems like such a lovely place, so we thought we and our children would just come here to die." The wealthy women were shocked and asked why they thought they were going to die. The campesino women told their story — of what land was so important to them, of how they were about to lose it, and of what that would ultimately mean for them.

Soon, the women and children were invited into the big houses, and their storytelling continued. The senators' wives listened that day, and some also told their own stories. Before long, the phones began to ring at the Senate, and busy legislators were pulled away from their duties to answer urgent calls from home. They were told what had happened and what their wives believed they should do.

The government project was defeated, and the campesinos kept their land. It happened because some people had begun to listen to each other. Compassion always begins with listening, and the listening that leads to compassion is the beginning of understanding.

— Jim Wallis, from *The Soul of Politics*

Transformation

During my long years away from God and the Catholic Church, I had remained friends with a Franciscan friar who always accepted my unbelief, always made time to talk with me. I asked him if he knew where I could stay in Rome and Assisi. He called the guardian of the friary at Collegio Sant'Isidoro, and I was given the rare privilege of being allowed to stay there for a week.

I arrived at the gate of the friary one morning in March of 1995. A woman working in the office escorted me to my tiny, Spartan room. She said I could join the friars for dinner, but the day was mine to wander the vibrant streets of Rome. Before hitting the noisy, hot streets, I decided to sit and rest for a while in the quiet, cool church.

An empty church and an empty man became a meeting place of grace. As I rested in the silence something happened, something highly unexpected: *God broke through the silence* and everything changed. In the womb of the dark church, I picked up a copy of the Liturgy of the Hours and opened it randomly to Psalm 63. In boldface above the psalm it said: "A soul thirsting for God."

Without warning, I felt the overwhelming Presence of God. I didn't see any images or hear any words. I knew — not intellectually, but experientially — that God was real, that God loved me, and that the hunger and thirst I had felt for so long could only be satisfied by God. In that moment of revelation, I was transformed from an atheist to a pilgrim. I went from denying God to wanting to experience more of God.

— Gerard Thomas Straub, from *Thoughts of a Blind Beggar:*
Reflections from a Journey to God

SEPTEMBER

· ·

Preaching the Good News

The world is my cloister,
my body is my cell,
and my soul is the hermit within.
— St. Francis of Assisi

St. Francis said those words more than eight hundred years ago. And they are as powerful today as they were when he found God in the valleys of Umbria. That was the inspiration for Francis to found a religious order known for its love of life, appreciation of silence, and authentic preaching to those who live in towns and cities. A popular story says that when an eager young friar told Francis he couldn't wait to leave the cloister and spread the gospel to the world, Francis smiled at him and said: "We must preach the good news at all times. If necessary, we use words."

— John Michael Talbot, from *The World Is My Cloister*

To Look Like Jesus

I don't know how you can be a human being on this planet today if this growing oppression and poverty is not your central issue. I don't know how we can avoid being ashamed of our being human beings if we don't take this as the central problem of our human family.

To be a Christian today in our world is to look a little bit like Jesus. The task is not simply to imitate him; we can't do that for many reasons. It is to take seriously the reality of creation, to make this so-called option for the poor, to be really compassionate and merciful and to make something ultimate out of that mercy and compassion.

If the churches are not built around this central message of the life and presence of Jesus of Nazareth, then they are simply religious institutions with doctrines and ideologies. Archbishop Romero changed Salvadoran society not because he was an analyst, but because he was convinced that there is a God and that we have to please God. He believed that it is good that there is a God of love, of tenderness, of mercy for the poor, and that this is good news for this world of ours. If you have that conviction, then you act in a different way.

— Jon Sobrino, from *Cloud of Witnesses,*
edited by Jim Wallis and Joyce Hollyday

Our Backyard, the Universe

Where do we live? In a physical sense we live in industrial artifacts designed to keep us inside and the universe outside. It is for this reason that the primary concerns of our hearts and minds are overwhelmingly focused on the requirements imposed on us by life in these industrial artifacts. The resulting American mind of the late twentieth century is a strange brew. It's depressing to realize how easily any of us can talk endlessly about matters of utterly no significance, yet almost all of us become walls of cement when asked the simplest things concerning our actual lives in the universe — such as, "What species of life live in my backyard?" Our eyes and hearts are so crammed full with the many demands of consumerism that we rarely notice even the most basic contours of the life place in which we live.

Our children can reproduce dozens of tinny tunes from advertisements, and yet they cannot distinguish between the song of the meadowlark and the mockingbird. Our pre-schoolers, even before they can speak, can recognize the corporate images of so many of our commercial enterprises, and yet few if any of them can draw the insects or trees or flowers or mammals of our life space. The truly great cosmic event each year of their lives is the rhythmic sequence with which spring explodes into being, but the chance of finding a single child, just one, who knows and celebrates this awesome rebirth of life is much smaller than the likelihood of walking into the executive suites of Nintendo or Sega Genesis and convincing them to stop dumping the relentlessly repulsive violence of their video games into our children's lives.

— Brian Swimme, from *The Hidden Heart of the Cosmos*

Make Me a Window, Not a Wall

The plane banked, the clouds broke, the golden light of late afternoon spilled out of the sky and rushed to embrace the rolling hills of Connecticut. Spirit sang: "God of my childhood and my call." My heart responded: "Make me a window, not a wall." Another song sang itself into life before the day was over.

God of my childhood and my call,
make me a window, not a wall.
So like an icon, may I be
a sign of love's transparency,
and through the love that lives in me,
proclaim Your lasting love for all.

Come, O my Maker, make of me
a mirror, so that all may see
within themselves Your saving grace,
reflection of Your Holy Face,
an image of Your warm embrace
and nurturing reality.

Creator, re-create us all.
Come, lift us up before we fall.
You are the Wisdom and the Way,
the Dawning of Unending Day,
the Word we sometimes fail to say
within our canon of recall.

God of our future, help us see
a vision of the yet-to-be:
in You is freedom from our fears,
a silent strength and no more tears;
in You dissension disappears
into a global harmony.

God of all gods, to You we sing
a song of Your imagining:
a liberating melody,
to set our shackled spirits free,
to tell us that Your canopy
of care is all-encompassing.

— Miriam Therese Winter,
from *The Singer and the Song*

To Martha in the Kitchen

Ah, Martha, you confront us
with the task
of sacralizing our call,
with making holy our work
of home-making
and mothering.
Our voice awakens us
from complacency and submission
to claim the dignity of baking our bread
for the hungry of the world.
Your voice urges us
to claim the right
to bless and break our bread
and offer to all
who come to our table, saying:
Take this,
all of you
and eat it,
This is My Body,
Soul Sister.

> — Edwina Gateley, from *Soul Sisters:*
> *Women in Scripture Speak to Women Today*

Free to Do God's Work

Jesus challenges us to participate in God's Work—as he did. This is not how we commonly see things. What needs to be done has commonly been seen as *our* work. God enters into the picture as someone who can *help us do our work*. We must pray, it is said, for God's grace. In fact what needs to be done is God's Work, and it is we who can be said to help by participating in God's Great Work. God's grace or free gift is best seen as the privilege of participating.

But first we need to become free and humble enough to do so. We need to recognize that we ourselves are products of God's Work. But we are also invited to participate in the process of becoming co-artists and co-creators of the future.

We do this by allowing God to work in and through us. When we are radically free . . . divine energy can flow through us *unhindered*.

God's Work, like God's Wisdom, is revolutionary. It turns the world upside down. We participate by adding our voice to the many prophetic voices that are speaking out boldly in our day and age.

Jesus' Way is a path that will lead us to the radical freedom that enables us to participate in God's Great Work of Art.

God's Work sometimes appears to be very slow. Yet precisely because it is God's Work, the future is secure. There is hope for the universe and for each of us as individuals. When I die, my ego, my false self, will be destroyed once and for all, but my true self will continue forever in God, the Self of the Universe.

— Albert Nolan, from *Jesus Today:*
A Spirituality of Radical Freedom

Work and Prayer

We must join our prayer with work. We try to bring this across to our sisters by inviting them to make their work a prayer. How is it possible to change one's work into a prayer? Work cannot substitute for prayer. Nevertheless, we can learn to make work a prayer. How can we do this? By doing our work with Jesus and for Jesus. That is the way to make our work a prayer. It is possible that I may not be able to keep my attention fully on God while I work, but God doesn't demand that I do so. Yet I can fully desire and intend that my work be done with Jesus and for Jesus. This is beautiful and that is what God wants our will and our desire to be for him, for our family, for our children, for our brethren, and for the poor.

— Mother Teresa, from *Mother Teresa: Essential Writings,* edited by Jean Maalouf

Being Christ-Centered

Throughout this beautiful season, I am praying for you. I pray that the Infant may touch your heart and mind and soul with his tiny hands. I pray that he may open you to his own beauty, and to realize that he needs you in his Mystical Body!

I pray that you might begin to be Christ-centered, not self-centered. Yes, this is my prayer for you — that you become Christ-centered, Love-centered! It is tragic to behold a world that "makes Christ wait" to receive our love. It is even more tragic to behold dedicated Christians — those especially chosen by his love — making him wait.

But when all is said and done, I must come back to this one sentence of John the Beloved: "Little children, let us love one another."

I have nothing else to say, really; Love is the very essence of our religion, our faith.

— Catherine de Hueck Doherty, from *Catherine de Hueck Doherty: Essential Writings,* edited by David Meconi, S.J.

Go and Tell

The Eucharist concludes with a mission. "Go now and tell!" The Latin words "Ite Missa est," with which the priest used to conclude the Mass, literally means: "Go, this is your mission."

Communion is not the end. Mission is. Communion, that sacred intimacy with God, is not the final moment of the Eucharistic life. We recognized him, but that recognition is not just for us to savor or to keep as a secret. As Mary of Magdala, so too the two friends [on the road to Emmaus] had heard deep in themselves the words, "Go and tell." That's the conclusion of the Eucharistic celebration; that too is the final call of the Eucharistic life. "Go and tell. What you have heard and seen is not just for yourself. It is for the brothers and sisters and for all who are ready to receive it. . . ."

The Eucharist is always mission. The Eucharist that has freed us from our paralyzing sense of loss and revealed to us that the Spirit of Jesus lives within us empowers us to go out into the world and to bring good news to the poor, sight to the blind, liberty to the captives, and to proclaim that God has shown again his favor to all people. But we are not sent out alone; we are sent with our brothers and sisters who also know that Jesus lives within them.

It belongs to the essence of the Eucharistic life to make this circle of love grow. Having entered into communion with Jesus and created community with those who know that he is alive, we now can go and join the many lonely travelers and help them discover that they too have the gift of love to share. . . . Every time there is a real encounter leading from despair to hope and from bitterness to gratitude, we will see some of the darkness being dispelled and life, once again, breaking through the boundaries of death.

— Henri Nouwen, from *With Burning Hearts*

273

The Art of Loving

[The] desert monastics did not often speak openly of their piety. Many of their sayings do not mention Christ or God at all, but deal in a very down-to-earth manner with all sorts of practical matters like obedience, discernment, humility, fasting, vigilance, and the like. . . . Living alone or in small groups, they may indeed have had relatively little scope for practicing what the Bible calls love of neighbor, but there are nevertheless numerous sayings that illustrate the centrality of mutual love in their life. One reads as follows:

It was said of a brother that, having made some baskets, he was putting on the handles when he heard his neighbor saying, "What can I do? Marketing day is near and I have no handles to put on my baskets." Then the former took the handles off his own baskets and brought them to the brother, saying, "Here are these handles which I have over; take them and put them on your baskets." So he caused his brother's work to succeed by neglecting his own.

[And another is as follows:]

Two elders had lived together for many years and had never fought with one another. The first said to the other, "Let us also have a fight like other people do." The other replied, "But I do not know how to fight." The first said to him, "Well, look. I'll put a brick between us, and I will say it's mine, and you say, 'No, it's mine,' and so the fight will begin." So they put a brick between them, and the first said, "This brick is mine," and the other said, "No, it's mine," and the first responded, "O.K., if it's yours, take it and go." So they gave it up without being able to find an occasion for argument.

— James A. Wiseman, from *Spirituality and Mysticism*

I Just Want to Tell You How Much I Love You

Until September 11, 2001, we had no sample of any size to tell us what people were like when they faced certain death. Now, however, we know, thanks to dozens of cell phone calls and beyond any doubt, what men and women do in these last seconds of their lives.

They forget themselves as they think of those they love, their spouses and children, their parents and friends. They do not complain or bemoan their fate. Neither do they pray for miraculous deliverance of even for the forgiveness of their sins. They do not think about themselves as they speak their last words.

They just want to tell others how much they love them, that they want them to be safe, that they want them to be happy, that their last will and their true testament is one of utter concern for those they cherish, that they break free of the grasp of death and judgment on their lives by giving themselves away so completely that, before time runs out, they are already immersed in the eternal.

The flaming towers and the skies were not filled with business travelers or tourists that last morning but with lovers, some laying down their lives for their friends, but all of them at their best, drawn fully out of themselves so that we see them as they really were all the time.

— Eugene Kennedy, from *9–11: Meditations at the Center of the World*

Grace Is Everywhere

Father James Martin wrote his book (*In Good Company: The Fast Track from the Corporate World to Poverty, Chastity, and Obedience*), as he told me, "to show how God can work in people's lives wherever they are, how He can lead persons despite themselves." He has spent the last month ministering to the bereaved and the brave at Ground Zero. "Now," he says, "more important than *how* God works is *that* God works in their lives . . . it is an enormous privilege to be with the firefighters and the police where in their unity, concord, and friendship, you feel intensely the presence of the Spirit." Moving through the grotesque reefs of wreckage, Father Martin hears and sees signs of God everywhere. "In the scripture readings of Sunday about searching for the lost sheep and the woman scouring her house for the lost coin, all these symbolize what these rescue workers are doing. The dayliner boat where they feed them is named *Spirit Cruise*, and when you step on board you find the Kingdom of God. There the firemen, nurses, policemen, and emergency workers sit at the table together in a Eucharistic celebration."

"Grace is everywhere," Father Martin quoted French novelist George Bernanos to reassure a young Jesuit co-worker, just as they turned to read in massive letters on the side of a truck, "The Grace Construction Company." Everything, Father Martin says, is a sacrament in this place "where evil has been present and where God is present."

— Eugene Kennedy, from *9–11: Meditations at the Center of the World*

O Gentle God of Vengeance

O Lord,
no matter how much I pray
I cannot forgive them.
No matter how much I try
I cannot bring myself
to forgive you.

You, the All-Powerful,
the All-Knowing,
the All-Merciful God.

Where was your power and mercy
when they did this?

Do you know what it's like
to have people insult you and
want you dead for just being
who you are?

Do you know how it feels
being the object of scorn?

Crucified God,
teach me to pray,
"Forgive us our sins as
we forgive those who
sin against us."

For only in living these words
do I experience freedom and rebirth.

You, Lord have given me the key to unlock the prison
        of my memories in which my salvation lies.
But Pride has rusted shut the door and Spite still stands
        guard.

Help me to see, to understand, to accept that until
    I forgive,
Unless I renounce my urge to retaliate and let go
    of my grudge
I have placed my happiness in the hands of my
    adversary.

Therefore, O God of Justice, font of eternal Wisdom,
    grant that all my enemies may drown in the
    deepest ocean of your Mercy.
Rain down upon their heads the unquenchable fire
    of your Love.
Bind them securely with the unbreakable bonds of
    your Compassion
For only in this way will my wounded soul find
    Healing, my heavy heart find Peace, and my
    crushed spirit the lost Joy of my youth.

—Joseph R. Veneroso, M.M.,
from *God in Unexpected Places*

Holy Ones

The most convincing testament to the truth of the Christian faith are the persons on whose everyday lives have embodied that faith, from the time of Christ to the present — not just those saints officially recognized by the church through its canonization process, but the millions more who toil in the obscurity of their homes, neighborhoods, and communities. Each of us knows who these holy ones are, for they have touched our lives, befriended us, nurtured us, challenged us, inspired us. More than any abstract principle, dogma, or theological proposition, the concrete lives of these exemplary Christians are what have attracted us to Christ. Their lives and testimonies witness to the credibility of the Christian kerygma.

...If we're drawn to Christ, therefore, it will likely not be because we have been convinced by theological arguments, but because we have been inspired by the witness of his martyrs and saints. "From the hope of these people who have been touched by Christ," suggests Pope Benedict XVI, "hope has arisen for others who were living in darkness and without hope." In the final analysis, it is not the rationality of theological arguments that will convince us of the truth of the Christian faith, but the beauty of those lives in which faith is incarnated and made viable and palpable.

— Roberto S. Goizueta, from *Christ Our Companion*

The Mystery of Time

Time is said to betray us by stealing from us our youth, or by taking away old friends. It is the mystery about which Edward Fisher writes:

> We are still . . . realizing more each year how completely everyone is alone, as isolated as a star in space. Many of those who helped us to forget our aloneness have stepped outside of time and let the work of the world go on. As the ritual of requiem grows repetitive, we who are left are reduced. Seeing the many crossed-off names on our Christmas mailing list, and aware that we are living on the outer edge of Nature's permission, we find each day a dividend.

Time is the "familiar stranger" that heals, sooner or later allowing physical pain and unpleasant memories to fade. It offers us repeated new beginnings, not unlike the forgiveness offered to us by the Lord. Ultimately, it is the enabler that allows God's final judgment to overtake us. Please, Lord, with forgiveness!

— Henry A. Garon, from *The Cosmic Mystique*

On the Miracle of Love

Considered solely from the human perspective, the holy and bold undertaking of beginning a joint life of love and fidelity reaches into the mystery of God. When in the freedom of their existence people have free reign over themselves, when they dare to entrust their heart, life, fate, and eternal dignity to another, thus revealing themselves to the ever mysteriously new, unknown and hidden mystery of another, it is possible that such an undertaking, which happens so frequently it may look rather ordinary, still is what it appears to be to the lovers: the unique miracle of love. And such a miracle borders on God, for it encompasses the entire person and his or her entire destiny. To take such an action in freedom always means, regardless of whether one knows it, the drawing near and enduring presence of the perhaps unnamed, silent, all-encompassing and sheltering, rescuing and blessing partner we call God. In true personal love, there is always something unconditional that points beyond the conditional of the lovers; when they truly love, they continually grow beyond themselves, taking part in a movement that no longer has its aim in the nameable finite.

— Karl Rahner, S.J., from *The Mystical Way in Everyday Life,* edited by Annemarie S. Kidder

God with Us

How do we come to Jesus? To experience the heart of God we need Jesus; to experience Jesus, we need to experience that moment in which he sacrificed his heart. And that was the moment when he sealed the surrender of his life with the last drop of his blood, when his eyes dimmed and his heart broke — the hour when he also comforted a criminal. It was Golgotha: that time and place in which we enter into pure, unclouded fellowship with God's eternity, God's heart, God's love. Golgotha is the window through which we can look from this darkened earth into the radiance of God's heart.

"If Christ were born a thousand times in Bethlehem but not in you, you would still be lost eternally." That is what the mystery of religion witnesses to: the uniting of the individual soul with Jesus Christ; the uniting of the individual spirit with the universal Spirit at one moment in time.

— Eberhard Arnold, from *Eberhard Arnold:*
Essential Writings, edited by Johann Christoph Arnold

Heaven

St. Benedict had a keen sense of the inevitability of death and a firm belief in heaven.... Such otherworldly orientation is rare among modern Christians. We neglect Benedict's perspective at our peril. The Christian life always runs along a narrow ridge between angelism on the one side and hedonism on the other. We are made to be immersed in the natural order, though we need training to contemplate its beauty more deeply and truly....

Benedictines have comfortably accepted the optimistic anthropology of the early Church which recognized that we are naturally desirous of the beautiful, but our desires must be challenged and clarified. On the emotional and sexual level the training comes through chastity; the intellect is reformed through *lectio divina* and study; the senses are taught to hear and to see deeply and truly through encounter with the arts. We know the eternal most through its traces in the world, whether in the faces of those we love or in the work of gifted hands. Faith reminds us not to mistake the ephemeral for the enduring. The binocular vision of now and forever, the Zen of the moment and the 'assurance of things hoped for' (Heb. 11:1) lies at the heart of the monastic enterprise. Each monastic day is a lifetime in miniature, just as each lifetime can be seen as dawn and dusk, with strength rising to its zenith and dwindling toward nightfall.

Benedict believed time had been redeemed, and that it went somewhere. Though the path of the commandments leads inevitably to death, there is a door in the wall, a door which opens into the heavenly homeland for which Benedict so longed.

— Columba Stewart, O.S.B., from *Prayer and Community:*
The Benedictine Tradition

Learning from Other Traditions

Here is a Buddhist scripture for meditation:

> May I be a balm to the sick, their healer and servitor,
> Until sickness come never again;
> May I quench with rains of food and drink the anguish
> of hunger and thirst;
> May I be in the famine of the ages' end their drink
> and meat;
> May I become an unfailing store for the poor, and
> serve them
> With manifold things for their need.
> My own being and my pleasures, all my righteousness
> in the past,
> Present, and future I surrender indifferently, that all
> creatures
> May win to their end.

Are these not the words of the heart, even by Christian standards? . . . In these words that come from the Buddhist heart we seem to hear an echo of those marvelous words of Jesus: "Come to me, all whose work is hard, whose load is heavy; and I will give you relief. Bend your necks to my yoke, and learn from me, for I am gentle and humble-hearted; and your souls will find relief. For my yoke is good to bear, my load is light" (Matt. 11:28–30). Here we arrive at the depth of our spiritual quest: a human spirit calling to another human spirit in the bosom of the divine Spirit.

— C. S. Song, from *Tell Us Our Names:*
Story Theology from an Asian Perspective

Come and See

The remarkable journey of the solidarity community [with Central America] began with an invitation — come and see, come and see where I live, how I live, enter into my reality, even for a moment in your lives. Come and see how I and most of the world really live. Hear my language, have a cup of coffee under my leaky thatched roof, sleep on my cot, hold the hand of my impoverished child, the one with the radiant smile. Kneel at my mass graves, visit the blood-stained shrines of my martyrs, share this simple meal — the one we have prepared for you — celebrate in song and dance under the full moon, or pray with me in my little village chapel.

Then go home and carry with you all that you have seen and heard. Go out into the world, denouncing the announcing, holding close to your hears the treasure you have found, preparing the fields for the rich harvest of my New Creation — before it is despoiled forever.

The question that follows, of whether or not it is good to be *here,* depends largely on where we look within our own history and traditions. As Jon Sobrino has told U.S. audiences repeatedly, "Build upon our best traditions, the traditions of solidarity in our country, whether it's the sanctuary movement of nowadays, or Martin Luther King, Jr., or the abolitionists of the last century. This is your tradition, and it's a good tradition."

From the collective reflection of the solidarity community, we can begin to appreciate the importance of this "new tradition" that is being created, and to say in response, "Yes, it is good for us to be here."

— Margaret Swedish and Marie Dennis,
from *Like Grains of Wheat: A Spirituality of Solidarity*

The Gift of Peace

When Cardinal Bernardin announced the news that his cancer had returned, even hard-nosed reporters cried. But Bernardin lifted people's spirits by saying in all sincerity that he was at peace in the face of his impending death, that he considered this as God's special gift to him at that moment in life.

Later as I was working with him on his memoirs, I realized that I had misunderstood what he had said in that press conference. "Cardinal," I apologized, "I made a big mistake in my recent fax. I thought you saw the *cancer* as God's gift, but you were talking about being at *peace* at this time, weren't you?" He smiled an explained that many people had misunderstood. "It's interesting, isn't it? We can understand cancer but peace is less comprehensible." As we worked tirelessly to complete his book, he offered a profound prayer.

> What I would like to leave behind is a simple prayer that each of you may find what I have found — God's special gift to us of peace. When we are at peace we find the freedom to be most fully who we are, even in the worst of times. We let go of what is non-essential and embrace what is essential. We empty ourselves so that God may more fully work within us. And we become instruments in the hands of the Lord.

— Jeremy Langford, from *God Moments*

Peacework

Peacemaking can no longer be regarded as peripheral to being a Christian. It is not something like joining the parish choir. Nobody can be a Christian without being a peacemaker. The issue is not that we have the occasional obligation to give some of our attention to war prevention, or even that we should be willing to give some of our free time to activities in the service of peace. What we are called to is a *life* of peacemaking in which all that we do, say, think, or dream is part of our concern to bring peace to this world. Just as Jesus' command to love one another cannot be seen as a part-time obligation, but requires a total investment and dedication, so too Jesus' call to peacemaking is unconditional, unlimited, and uncompromising. None of us is excused! The tragedy is that, in some demonic way, the word "peace has become tainted. For many people this most precious word has become associated with sentimentalism, utopianism, radicalism, romanticism, and even with irresponsibility....

Christians today, if they want to be Christians, have to find the courage to make the word "peace" as important as the word "freedom." There should be no doubt in the minds of the people who inhabit this world that Christians are peacemakers.

— Henri Nouwen, from *Peacework*

The Heart's Calling

Our sense of vocation is intimately linked to the people and things that move us to passion and compassion. We cannot answer the authenticity question, "Who am I?" without also answering the passion question, "What do I really want?" We discover who we are only by becoming conscious of the most authentic desires, loves, and longings of our hearts. "Who am I?" is also closely related to another question, "*Whose* am I?" We come to know ourselves by recognizing those to whom we *belong*. Whom do we love? With whom do I feel at home? To whom does our heart go out? With whose sufferings and aspirations do we most identify?... The experience of falling in love, for example, is sometimes associated with a profound sense of vocation. There is also the issue of the complex interrelationship between our own desires and God's desires.

In vocational discernment, it is important to pay close attention to our feelings, because authentic callings always begin with a stirring of the heart. Someone or something moves or touches us in some way, and our heart responds with a *feeling*. We may not, at first, be able to articulate or make sense of our heart's response; we know only that something significant has occurred on the affective level of our experience. "The heart has its reasons," wrote Pascal, "that reason does not know."

— John Neafsey, from *A Sacred Voice Is Calling*

Authentic Conversion

Conversion ushers in an intense solitude of communion. We discover that the heart, of itself, is not in the end an ultimate aloneness but a radical solidarity and communion with all God's beloved people. Missioners will know that this communion is a living conversation with the poor, the forgotten, the voiceless, the wounded, the dispossessed.

So we carry in ourselves, wherever we are, a deep suffering, perhaps the social equivalent of that wound of love that St. Teresa and other mystics speak of. We bear wounds of love which never heal, the wounds of the risen Lord.

But we also carry an intense joy because the Christian is not merely a striver for liberation yet to come, but a bearer of a liberation of which the down payment, the pledge, had already been made. It is an enigmatic coexistence of suffering and joy which makes our lives, especially our community lives, living signs....

Conversion always involves a death. Indeed, this side of the grave, it involves a constant dying, but only that new life and freedom may be released in us. We learn what it is to constantly carry the dying of Jesus in the body (our community of faith) so that his risen life may be manifest. And, surprise, surprise, this freedom from fear makes us invincible. You cannot kill me for I have died already.

— Thomas Cullinan, O.S.B., *Trends in Mission: Toward the Third Millennium,* edited by William Jenkinson and Helene O'Sullivan

The Part and the Whole

The whole universe is a sacrament, which mirrors the divine reality. Each created thing, though nothing in itself, is of infinite value and significance, because it is the sign of a mystery which is enshrined in the depths of its being,. Every human being is not merely an isolated individual but a member of a divine society, working out its destiny in space and time and subject to all the tragic consequences of subservience to the material world, but destined to transcend the limitations of time and space and mortality, and to enter into that fullness of life where there shall be "neither mourning nor weeping nor pain anymore." The suffering of this world can have no meaning as long as we attempt to judge it in the light of this present time. We are like people who hear snatches of music, which they have no means of relating to the symphony as a whole. But when we have passed beyond the conditions of this present life we shall then have that integral knowledge in which the whole is known in every part, and every part is seen to mirror the whole.

— Bede Griffiths, from *Bede Griffiths: Essential Writings,* edited by Thomas Matus

Stretchmarks

MARY'S QUESTION

Small, dear heart
nested under mine:
how is it
you are great enough
to encompass all
and everything?

Our son was born by Caesarian section. I had hoped for a natural delivery twice before but again it wasn't to be. Afterward, the young surgically garbed physician took a sharp breath and spoke quietly to me: "You were lucky. The scar tissue was paper thin. Much longer and you two might not have made it."

For a week the baby and I were sequestered in a quiet room away from the worst of the noisy hospital traffic. A steady rain grayed the Boston sunlight and shrouded our thin rectangle of a window. "It would not be a good idea to try this again," the doctors warned. But I wondered at the strange mystery of new life stepping so innocently aside from death's shadow. And I marveled at the angry red wound sliced just a hair's breadth below the twin lines of scar tissue from the two previous births inscribed on the flesh of my belly.

One is never the same. After each birth, the body readjusts. But things are never as they were before. Silver-webbed stretchmarks are only an outward sign. More hidden are the now elastic vessels of the vascular system, the pliancy of the muscle walls, the flat pouch of the once inhabited womb. Each child impresses upon waxen flesh the unique imprints of its life. Inscribes one's own life with an image all its own.

Often I have thought how true that is of the heart as well. Each child occupies its own space and in growing presses and pushes out the bounded contours of one's heart. Each fashions a singular, ample habitation like no other. A habitation crowded with an unrepeatable lifetime sorrow and joy. A habitation inscribed with a name. How could it be otherwise in the heart of God?

— Wendy Wright, from *Sacred Heart: Gateway to God*

A Morning Prayer

God, my Friend,
I offer you each moment of this day:
whatever comes — the unexpected challenges,
    diversions from my plans,
    the need-filled glance,
    the expectations and complaints,
    the being taken for granted,
    the slights and sleights-of-hand.
I'd be grateful if You could keep me aware of my pesky
        habits, like....
And, between us, perhaps we can enliven the spirits of
        those I live and work with, like....
Whatever else befalls,
    I trust we can cope with it,
    together.
Amen.

— William J. O'Malley, from *Lenten Prayers for Busy People*

Change Yourself and You May Change the World

Everyone thinks of changing the world,
but no one thinks of changing himself.

— Leo Tolstoy

Two men who wanted to gain greater spiritual truth learned that at the top of a nearby mountain lived a renowned spiritual teacher. After a very long and difficult climb up the mountain, they found themselves in the presence of the spiritual master. Bowing humbly, they asked the questions which had driven them to the teacher:

"Master, how do we become wise?"

The teacher, who was in meditation, did not answer immediately. Finally, after a lengthy pause, he responded: "By making good choices."

"But teacher, how do we make good choices?" they asked almost in unison.

"From experience," said the teacher.

"And how do we get experience?" they asked.

"Bad choices," said the smiling spiritual master.

The spiritual master was not toying with the two spiritual seekers. He was encouraging them to practice regular, routine self-reflection. Critical reflection on our own thoughts, words, and behaviors is vital for spiritual and emotional growth. That man, who lived and meditated on the mountain, knew how important it was for people to practice self-inquiry. Such self-inquiry, to be most beneficial, must be done in a systematic way. Many spiritual teachers recommend a daily time of recollection and reflection whereby we calmly view our living. The goals of the practice are:

- to learn, not blame;
- to gain insight, not develop guilt;
- to be understanding, not condemning;
- to accept, not judge;
- to maximize strength while minimizing weakness.

This type of regular examination of conscience and spirit helps us to see where we need to make a change or take a corrective step. Doing so will bring about good choices, which in turn lead to good experiences. Another pleasant result is this: when we change ourselves, we often change the world.

— Victor M. Parachin, from *Eastern Wisdom for Western Minds*

The Tree of Life

Trees as a life-form are among the oldest living creatures, long predating humans as a species. Some trees alive today predate all "family trees" as well. Their trunks record every season of a millennium and more.

Just as old and prominent are trees as religious symbols of a sturdy, renewed, and upright way of life. Trees speak and tell stories, stories of life, resistance, death, and new life. Trees breathe of human imagination and history as well as their own....

The tree of life is an old ecumenical symbol discovered anew time and again across innumerable cultures. It is religiously and morally charged.

Perhaps it was also the tree of life that was intimated at a peace gathering in Los Alamos, New Mexico, on August 6, 1989 — Hiroshima Day. A Native American dancer danced against the greatest powers of death ever assembled by humans and prayed for life by giving each of us, in silence, a small green branch. The branch seemed both important and powerful. It was a mere fraction of a tree. But it was juxtaposed, as a strong sign of life, to the mushroom cloud as the towering image of death.

— Larry L. Rasmussen, from *Earth Community Earth Ethics*

Where God Is

The spiritual genius and daring of Jesus are that he finds God in the most universal place of all. He absolutely levels the playing field. *He finds God where the suffering is.* Which is everywhere, on both sides of every war, inside every group and religion, and God is nothing that any group can take to itself as an ego possession, even if they be a Syro-Phoenician woman, a Roman centurion, a Samaritan leper, a woman caught in adultery, drunkards and tax collectors. There is no spiritual loyalty test going on in the ministry of Jesus — just naked humanity responding to naked humanity. This is a religion that can unite and save the world.

— Richard Rohr, from *Soul Brothers:*
Men in the Bible Speak to Men Today

OCTOBER

· ·

Love Is Being Fully Present

A woman I met thirty years ago died recently. We attended the same yearly retreat for twenty years. She turned my heart around long ago when she approached me and told me that I was one of only two people who had ever shown her love. As she spoke I was painfully aware that until that moment I hadn't really looked at her with care, let alone noticed the pain in her eyes. Although I'd apparently been kind, I hadn't seen her apart from the general retreat community — she was on the periphery of my awareness. Her words shot me through the eyes. It was terrible to realize that I was capable of living with such inattention. With that one sentence she taught me to be careful and to take time with people. A real friendship grew between us. Today I consider her to have been one of my significant teachers. Don't turn away from what is in front of you, her life said. Show up. Be fully present. Live into what love means.

— Paula D'Arcy, from *Waking Up to This Day*

Miracles

Miracles are often thought of, both by those who believe in them and by those who do not, as events, or purported events, that contradict the laws of nature and that therefore cannot be explained by science or reason. But this is not at all what the Bible means by a miracle, . . . "The laws of nature" is a modern scientific concept. The Bible knows nothing about nature, let alone the laws of nature. The world is God's creation and whatever happens in the world ordinary or extraordinary, is part of God's providence. The Bible does not divide events into natural or supernatural. God is, in one way or another, behind all events.

Certain acts of God are called miracles or wonders because of their ability to astonish and surprise us. Thus creation is a miracle, grace is a miracle, the growth of an enormous mustard tree from a tiny seed is a miracle, the liberation of the Israelites from Egypt, . . . The world is full of miracles for those who have eyes to see them. If we are no longer able to wonder and marvel except when the so-called laws of nature are broken, then we must be in a sorry state.

— Albert Nolan, from *Jesus before Christianity*

What, Me Worry?

"Why are you crying?" the teacher asked the child. "Are your parents mean to you?"

"No," the child said. "My parents are the kindest people in the world."

"Do they neglect you?" the teacher said.

"No, they don't," the child said. "They play with me and tell me stories every night."

"Do they refuse to get you what you want?"

"No," the little boy went on sobbing. "They get me the best of everything."

"Then why in heaven's name are you crying?" the teacher asked again.

"Because I'm afraid they might try to run away."

Ah, why enjoy what *is* when you can worry about what might be coming?

— Joan Chittister, from *Gospel Days*

The Mystery of Poverty

When I, Francis, heard the call of the Gospel, I did not set about organizing a political pressure-group in Assisi. What I did, I remember very well, I did for love, without expecting anything in return; I did it for the Gospel, without placing myself at odds with the rich, without squabbling with those who preferred to remain rich. And I certainly did it without any class hatred.

I did not challenge the poor people who came with me to fight for their rights, or win salary increases. I only told them that we would be blessed — if also battered, persecuted, or killed. The Gospel taught me to place the emphasis on the mystery of the human being more than on the duty of the human being. . . .

The social struggle in my day was very lively and intense, almost, I should say, as much so as in your own times. Everywhere there arose groups of men and women professing poverty and preaching poverty in the Church and the renewal of society. But nothing changed, because these people did not change hearts. . . .

You can reproach me, go ahead. But I saw, in the Gospel, a road beyond, a path that transcends all cultures, all human constructs, all civilizations and conventions.

I felt the Gospel to be eternal; I felt politics and culture, including Christian culture, to be in time.

I was made always to go beyond time.

— Carlo Carretto, from *I, Francis*

All God's Children

When all God's children get together, what a time, what a time, what a time.... If we come together, bringing our history, our experiences, our survival and coping mechanisms, our rituals of celebration, our unique ways of thinking and planning and relaxing and walking and talking and working, and praying and paying and being, what a gift we can be to one another and to our churches and to our world....

My grandfather was a slave. And he used to talk about slavery, because he said if we understood about slavery we might be able to understand about freedom. My granddaddy said the worst kind of slavery is not the slavery that comes from outside with bonds and chains and forced labor. The worst slavery is slavery that comes in your own heart and your own mind and your own home and in your own church and in your own community.

Let's get in touch with the enslavement that keeps us from reaching out to one another and being to one another the cause of freedom and the cause of strength and the cause of life.

—Thea Bowman, from *Thea's Song: The Life of Thea Bowman*
by Charlene Smith and John Feister

Adventure in Prayer

And now I pick up Thomas Merton's last book, *Contemplative Prayer* which I am starting to read, and the foreword by our good Quaker friend Douglas Steere brought back to my memory a strange incident in my life. He quotes William Blake: "We are put on earth for a little space that we may learn to bear the beams of love." And he goes on to say that to escape these beams, to protect ourselves from these beams, even devout men hasten to devise protective clothing. We do not want to be irradiated by love.

Suddenly I remembered coming home from a meeting in Brooklyn many years ago, sitting in an uncomfortable bus seat facing a few poor people. One of them, a downcast, ragged man, suddenly epitomized for me the desolation, the hopelessness of the destitute, and I began to weep. I had been struck by one of those "beams of love," wounded by it in a most particular way. It was my own condition that I was weeping about — my own hardness of heart, my own sinfulness. I recognized this as a moment of truth, an experience of what the *New Catechism* calls our "tremendous, universal, inevitable and inexcusable incapacity to love." I had not read that line when I had that experience, but that is what I felt. I think that ever since then I have prayed sincerely those scriptural verses, "Take away my heart of stone and give me a heart of flesh." I had been using this prayer as one of the three acts of faith, hope and charity. "I believe, help Thou my unbelief." "In Thee have I hoped, let me never be confounded." "Take away my heart of stone and give me a heart of flesh," so that I may know how to truly love my brother because in him, in his meanest guise, I am encountering Christ.

— Dorothy Day, from *Dorothy Day: Selected Writings,*
edited by Robert Ellsberg

Work for Justice and Peace

The resurrected Jesus greets his disciples saying, "Peace be with you!" Immediately, he sends them out to be messengers of that same peace. Let us pray for the courage that we may also be messengers of peace and justice in our world and in our own day.

— Linda Unger and David Aquije, from *Un solo mundo, una sola familia / One World, One Family*

Obrar por la Justicia y la Paz

Jesús resucitado saluda a sus discípulos diciendo, "La paz esté con ustedes!" Acto seguido, los envía a ser mensajeros de esa misma paz. Oramos por el valor de ser también mensajeros de la paz y justicia en nuestro mundo y nuestro día.

How We See

A guru asked his disciples how they could tell when the night had ended and the day begun.

One said, "When you see an animal in the distance and can tell whether it is a cow or a horse."

"No," said the guru.

"When you look at a tree in the distance and can tell if it is a neem tree or a mango tree."

"Wrong again," said the guru.

"Well, then, what is it?" asked his disciples.

"When you look into the face of any man and recognize your brother in him; when you look into the face of any woman and recognize in her your sister. If you cannot do this, no matter what time it is by the sun it is still night."

— Anthony de Mello, from *Anthony de Mello: Selected Writings,* edited by William Dych, S.J.

Reaching Out

Have you ever felt a call to go out of your familiar world toward the "other," the stranger, the needy one? Think of a particular instance when you have experienced such an invitation. Have you allowed yourself to accept? If not, what held you back?

Upon seeing a leper, Francis of Assisi got down from his horse in order to embrace him. This was a further act of going out. Have you allowed yourself, even forced yourself literally to move to another place in order to embrace a hurting world, to walk in the shoes of a suffering person, to understand the poor?

Let God lead you again and again to the "leper," whoever he or she might be. Let the experience be a reflective one, not a dutiful going among the poor, but a conscious and meditative move out from the familiar to the world of hurt — perhaps in the very same soup kitchen or hospice that you have visited before. Allow the experience to challenge your assumptions about the margins and to push you toward appropriate response.

— Marie Dennis et al., from *St. Francis and the Foolishness of God*

Hope

What is this "thing" without which we cannot live, without which we have no reason to go on? A story told me by my grandmother may capture something of the meaning of hope. As a very poor farm girl growing up in the hinterlands of Ireland's northwesternmost coast, it was quite common for her and the others in the family to go to bed hungry after having worked in the fields from dawn till dusk. Meat was usually in short supply, and potatoes, the staple of the Irish diet, were not always abundant. Milk was often scarce, and butter was sheer luxury.

Year by year, as the days became colder and darker in the drawing near of winter, her father would set a candle in the window in anticipation of Christmas. In the aftermath of one very bad harvest, when nearly everything that had been planted had not yielded fruit, there was hardly anything in the cupboards. But on Christmas Eve, amidst the protests of his family, my great-grandfather took a bit of butter, melted it on a little plate, lit the wick of his makeshift candle, and placed it in the window. The family was shocked. His response to them was quite simple: "We know that we can get by on a little food for several weeks. We've done it before. A little water and milk can keep us going for several days. That we also know. But, listen to me now and listen to me good, we cannot go on for one day without hope."

— Michael Downey, from *Hope Begins Where Hope Begins*

A Humble Leader

On my African sojourns, I have lived among the Ugandan people who bear some of the most crushing burdens in the human family: the preventable deaths of young and old alike from violence, disease, hunger, and abject poverty, and the pain of living without the sense of a peaceful future. Amidst all these intractable foes there is a terrible temptation to place blame solely on others. It must be the fault of the rebels, the government, the international community for its noninvolvement, the greed of those who fail to share food and medicine, and so on.

Some people look to themselves instead of blaming others for a world gone horribly wrong. Archbishop John Baptist Odama, the Roman Catholic bishop of Gulu, is such a person. When he meets with the children he will at times kneel before them and ask for their forgiveness. He says: "Forgive me; I should have done more to build you a safer and more peaceful world." The children are shocked to see their shepherd on his knees before them.

On one occasion, while preaching at a large Confirmation mass at Awach, a sprawling camp for thousands of people displaced by war, Archbishop Odama asked all the children to stand. "Little ones, you stand up!" There were many adults present, even high-ranking military personnel, who were very curious about this unexpected turn of events. In his fatherly tone of voice he spoke directly to the youth and to them alone: "The condition in which you are growing up is wrong. You lack food, you are dressed poorly, and some of you are very sickly. You have missed your future because you are missing education. You walk in fear. I am sure when you grow up you will ask, 'Why did this happen? Where were our elders to help us and protect us?' I say to you: I apologize. I could have done more for you to improve your situation. Forgive me." Then he knelt before them.

I imagine the children received a glimpse of what the disciples felt at the Last Supper when Jesus, their teacher and master, knelt before each of them in order to wash their feet. Peace is built from such humble acts of solidarity and love.

— Donald H. Dunson, from *Child, Victim, Soldier:*
The Loss of Innocence in Uganda

Jeremiah, What Do You See?

Has there ever been a time when the suffering of another person did not affect me? In every day life, if I win an argument, is there any part of me that feels for the person who lost — and wants to reach out? How often do I change the TV channel when the news depicts the tragic plight of others whose lives are remote from mine? Whose story do I block out? Whose pain do I intentionally try to forget? None of us can absorb the sorrow of the whole world, but at some point, and in some situations I need to confront myself with the question God posed to the prophets: *Jeremiah, what do you see?* (Jer. 1:11). In Jeremiah's life, the signs were painful but there was also promise. He would discover the promise not by avoiding the pain but by turning into it. It is the same for you and me.

— Fran Ferder, from *Enter the Feast: Biblical Stories*
as Metaphors for Our Lives

Christ the Fool

Today is a day of processions, circuses, a band of motley followers who are, along with the holy fools of long ago, meant to keep alive the tradition and belief of the Holy Fool who was stripped naked, cursed, beaten publicly and forced outside the city and hung on wood in a garbage dump. St. William of Thierry (1085–1148) calls this "holy madness," madness for the sake of love. This is Jesus. This is God, who is so close to the miserable and wretched of this world; those starving in a world aplenty, those being bombed in Sarajevo, those being hacked to death by neighboring tribes in Africa, those dying slowly of cholera and tainted water and bureaucracy in South America, those on the street in every city, all those outcast from society, culture, and even religion's often narrowly defined boundaries.

Christ, this holy fool, mad with the truth, is part of the ancient tradition of the prophet and the mystic, one who atones for others and refuses to let us keep expecting in systems where there is *truly* madness: insensitivity, hostility toward strangers and the poor, and few of those who are different. The cross cries out loudly that our religion is about uncrucifying the world, about resisting unnecessary pain and humiliation, about standing with those caught in the net of nationalism and ideologies more intent on making their points than lifting up people, about true worship. The cross will not liberate anyone being destroyed while believers spend money and effort on buildings, environments, and ways of spirituality.

— Megan McKenna, from *Lent: The Sunday Readings*

I Will Ask Allah

Word spread very quickly. I had received an emergency phone call in the early morning informing me that my younger sister in the States had been in a serious automobile accident involving a truck. Her injuries were life-threatening and the next forty-eight hours would be critical.

I immediately told the sad news to my fellow faculty members at the seminary in Davao in the southern Philippines. It wasn't long before everyone — including the kitchen staff — had heard the news.

When I finished teaching my two morning classes, I was surprised to see Utol waiting for me outside the classroom. Well known to all, Utol served as our "fish-supplier," personally delivering quality fresh fish three times a week.

Utol lived in a small Muslim costal village near the seminary. In the early morning, he would collect the evening catch from his Muslim neighbors and distribute the fish to several regular customers, including the seminary.

Utol may have finished only one or two grades of school and couldn't read or write well. After years of laboring in the tropical sun, his complexion was very dark. Too poor to afford a dentist, he was missing several teeth. His hands were callused and scarred from years of fishing.

Utol began speaking in Cebuano, the local language. "The cooks in the kitchen told me what happened to your sister. I am so sorry to hear the sad news."

"Thank you very much for your concern and expression of sympathy," I replied. "You are very thoughtful; you waited for me for nearly two hours. You should be at home sleeping, as I'm sure you were up all night fishing."

Utol continued, "I want to tell you that I will pray to Allah for your sister's recovery. Allah will help her, I am sure."

"Thank you. Thank you," I said, holding back my tears.

As Utol turned to go, he assured me, "With Allah, all will be OK."

I was deeply moved. What faith! What trust in divine providence! What beautiful words, coming from the mouth of a man who obviously prays!

And my younger sister is still alive, thirty years later.

— James H. Kroeger, M.M., from *Once upon a Time in Asia,*
edited by James H. Kroeger and Eugene F. Thalman

The Need for Reconciliation

Nelson Mandela, the first president of a democratic multiracial South Africa, spent more than twenty years in prison but emerged without rancor or bitterness. He became a model of reconciliation in a country that had experienced forty-four years of a brutal apartheid system that deprived black people of their rights in their own country. Yet Mandela did not preach hatred and revenge. In his autobiography, *Long Walk to Freedom,* he recounts how he was able to survive prison by finding the spark of humanity in his guards. "I always knew that deep down in every human heart, there was mercy and generosity," he wrote. "No one is born hating another person because of the color of his skin, or his background, or his religion. People must learn to hate, and if they can learn to hate, they can be taught to love, for love comes more naturally to the human heart than its opposite. Even in the grimmest times in prison, when my comrades and I were pushed to our limits, I would see a glimmer of humanity in one of our guards, perhaps just for a second, but it was enough to reassure me and keep me going. Man's goodness is a flame that can be hidden but never extinguished."

This ability to overcome the urge for revenge enabled Mandela to build a new nation from the ruins of apartheid. He was able to unify all races and tribes in the formerly divided country. In his book *God Has a Dream: A Vision of Hope for Our Time,* Bishop Desmond Tutu rightly describes it as a miracle. "Who in their right mind could ever have imagined South Africa to be an example of anything but the most ghastly awfulness, of how not to govern a nation? We were destined for perdition and were plucked out of total annihilation.... We succeeded not because we were smart.... Not because we were particularly virtuous. We succeeded because God wanted us to succeed. . . . This is the principle of transfiguration at work. And so no situation is utterly hopeless, utterly untransfigurable."

The miracle of South Africa's transfiguration is a powerful reminder that healing and reconciliation can take place in even the most hopeless situations. Let us learn to expel the anger and bitterness we carry through life and embrace the possibility of change.

— Janice McLaughlin, M.M., from *Ostriches, Dung Beetles, and Other Spiritual Masters: A Book of Wisdom from the Wild*

A Breakthrough

I will you of my experience when I had a stroke. I was meditating at six o'clock in the morning and something came and hit me on the head. It felt like a sledgehammer. A terrible force was pushing me out of my chair and I did not know what was happening. Apparently I was unconscious for a week. No, I was conscious, but I did not speak, and I have no memory of it at all. But there were some wonderful people in the ashram and they arranged everything for me. At the end of a week I began to come round to normal consciousness, and there as a profound change. . . . I had died to the ego. . . . The ego-mind, and also . . . the discriminative mind that separates and divides, all seem to have gone. Everything was flowing into everything else, and I had a sense of unity behind it all. Then this began to open up. I thought I was going to die, and I . . . let go of the soul and body into the hands of God. . . .

Then somebody came and massaged me, and I came back to normal. A very important experience then happened. I felt rather restless and uncertain, and an urge came to me to "surrender to the mother." I made this surrender, and an overwhelming experience of love came over me. It was like waves of love. I called out to someone who was watching there, "I am being overwhelmed by love!"

I think what happened was a psychological breakthrough to the feminine. . . .

The stroke was a wonderful experience and the greatest grace I have ever had in my life.

— Bede Griffiths, from *Bede Griffiths:*
Essential Writings, edited by Thomas Matus

Christ in the Poor

Christ identifies himself with those in the most urgent conditions of need: the hungry, thirsty, naked, homeless, sick, and imprisoned. The lesson is simple. In responding to the desperate needs of others, we respond to him: "As you did to the last person, you did to me."

Dorothy Day often said, "Those who cannot see Christ in the poor are atheists indeed."

It is not only in words that Christ identified with those who have nothing and are regarded with contempt. He was born in a stable because no better place was offered for his mother to give birth. As a child he was a refugee. He was imprisoned and died a criminal's death. Given all that, is it a surprise that God's hospitality to us is linked to our hospitality to those who have little or nothing. If we avoid Christ in the poor, we are avoiding the gate to heaven.

— Jim Forest, from *Confession: Doorway to Forgiveness*

Family Audience

A few days after his coronation John held a special audience for his family, a privilege granted to each new occupant of St. Peter's Chair. The Roncallis entered the apartments in the apostolic palace timidly. The splendor of the place troubled their simple souls. Finally, bashful and confused, they stood before the white-clad figure of the pope. In their confusion they dropped their little presents. Peasant bread, ham, and wine, packed in brightly colored handkerchiefs, all tumbled to the floor. John looked at their staring eyes and open mouths. Although the comedy of the situation did not escape him, he spoke reassuringly: "Don't be afraid. It's only me."

— Pope John XXIII, from *Pope John XXIII:
Essential Writings,* edited by Jean Maalouf

How to Help End Hunger

Every day somewhere on this earth, 24,000 people — the vast majority of them children — die from hunger. A recent report by the United Nations warns that a hunger crisis currently threatens 8.6 million people in Central America alone. Earthquakes, hurricanes, and plummeting coffee prices have sent this region of the world into deep turmoil; its children are at great risk of malnutrition and hunger-related illnesses. The situation in Africa is even more precarious. It's easy for individuals to feel overwhelmed and helpless in the face of the sheer magnitude of this problem.

Each day I click on the website www.hungersite.com and an image mapping the entire globe appears on my computer screen. Every three seconds a nation in that picture darkens, indicating a death by hunger. . . .

There is a specific, hopeful purpose that lures me and more than 220,000 individuals from around the world to visit this website daily. It is possible to click on a button marked "give free food" and, thanks to generous corporate sponsors whose logos then appear immediately, a cup of food is donated. To date, over two hundred million cups of food have been donated to aid hungry people in over 74 countries.

It is the simplest of actions — a single click, a touch of your finger on the mouse — and in that moment you have joined the worldwide fight against hunger. What is equally important to me is that this action, repeated daily, connects me to the hungriest members of the human family. Millions of voiceless children on our planet sense that their very survival depends on connections such as these.

— Donald H. Dunson, from *No Room at the Table:
Earth's Most Vulnerable Children*

Prayer for the Spirit

Dear Lord, listen to my prayer. You promised your disciples that you would not leave them alone but would send the Holy Spirit to guide them and lead them to the full Truth.

I feel like I am groping in the dark. I have received much from you, and still it is hard for me simply to be quiet and present in your presence. My mind is so chaotic, so full of dispersed ideas, plans, memories, and fantasies. I want to be with you and you alone, concentrate on your Word, listen to your voice, and look at you as you reveal yourself to your friends. But even with the best intentions I wander off to less important things and discover that my heart is drawn to my own little worthless treasures.

I cannot pray without the power from on high, the power of your Spirit. Send your Spirit, Lord, so that your Spirit can pray in me, can say "Lord Jesus," and can call out "Abba, Father."

I am waiting, Lord, I am expecting, I am hoping. Do not leave me without your Spirit. Give me your unifying and consoling Spirit. Amen.

— Henri Nouwen, from *Jesus a Gospel*

God in Broken Things

Like most Catholics, I found the mishandling of the clergy sexual abuse scandal depressing. In a darkened church I vented my frustration. "How can I pray about mission and Maryknoll when everything seems to be falling apart?" I cried. "How can I call young men to serve a church crumbling before my eyes?"

Now I don't normally talk about hearing God, but in the depth of my heart I "heard" these words and leave it to you to discern their origin: "Oh, snap out of it. Stop feeling sorry for yourself. You are exactly where I want you to be. Besides, you're not calling anyone; I am."

Shocked, to put it mildly, I looked up to see the sanctuary lights come on, revealing a mosaic of the Transfiguration and the words from Luke 24:26, "Was it not necessary for the Christ to suffer and so enter his glory?" Not regrettable. Not unavoidable. Necessary. In the midst of the darkest of nights, Jesus took bread and, while breaking it, gave thanks.

"Eucharist" comes from the Greek word for giving thanks. Giving thanks to God, especially in times of trouble, is at the heart of our faith. When we do this in memory of Jesus he is present to us in a unique way. Only broken bread can be shared. Only in the breaking of the bread did the disciples on the road to Emmaus recognize the Risen Lord.

Perhaps the Church, as the Body of Christ, must also be broken for the presence of Christ to be revealed. Perhaps we, as the Body of Christ, must experience suffering and sacrifice in order to share our extraordinary life in God with others.

— Joseph R. Veneroso, M.M., from *God in Unexpected Places*

The Wisdom of St. Augustine

Prayerful hearts: When you pray to God in psalms and hymns, turn over in your heart what you bring forth with your voice.

(Praeceptum II.3)

Simplicity of life: It is better to need less than to have more.

(P. III.5)

The common good: You can measure your progress by your growth in concern for the common good rather than your private good.

(V.2).

Fraternal love as a form of worship: Let everyone live together in oneness of mind and heart, and honor God in yourselves whose temples you have become.

Healing words: Don't exchange harsh words, but if your words do hurt, let your own words become a medicine to heal the wound.

(VI.2)

Authority and love: The one placed over the community should not think himself fortunate because he can dominate by power but rather because he can serve in love. (VII.3)

May the Lord grant that you observe all of these things with love, as lovers of spiritual beauty, with the fragrance of Christ radiating from your good living, not as slaves under the law but as freedmen established under grace. (VIII.1)

— Thomas F. Martin, O.S.A., from *Our Restless Heart: The Augustinian Tradition*

The Gate of Heaven

At the center of our being is a point of nothingness which is untouched by sin and by illusion, a point of pure truth, a point or spark which belongs entirely to God, which is never at our disposal, from which God disposes of our lives which is inaccessible to the fantasies of our own mind or the brutalities of our own will. This little point of nothingness and of *absolute poverty* is the pure glory of God in us. It is so to speak His name written in us, as our poverty, as our indigence, as our dependence, as our sonship. It is like a pure diamond, blazing with the invisible light of heaven. It is in everybody, and if we could see it we would see these billions of points of light coming together in the face and blaze of a sun that would make all the darkness and cruelty of life vanish completely. . . . I have no program for this seeing. It is only given. But the gate of heaven is everywhere.

—Thomas Merton, from *Thomas Merton: Essential Writings,* edited by Christine M. Bochen

The "How" of Presence

How do we remain present,
truly being where we are — here and now?
How do we remain mindful,
truly aware of
 the song of the mourning dove
 the jam on the toast
 the hope of the heart for peace?
Too often we are absent,
inattentive, unaware, insensitive.
We awake one day and discover
that life has passed us by.
So "how,"
how to connect with the moment?
Conversation!
Dialogue with the dove, the jam, the hope.
Speak to them, listen to their message.
Language it is that makes most things present
and, in-between the words, the silence.

— Robert Morneau, from *The Color of Gratitude*

Living in God

Jesus died for what he believed.
He died
in shame and disgrace,
in pain and loneliness,
in failure and defeat,
but also in the conviction
that love is stronger than evil,
that God is present even in darkness and chaos,
that life is stronger than death,
that God is to be trusted absolutely,
that living in love is living in God,
that dying in love is dying into God,
and that resurrection and new life always follow death.

—Michael Morwood, from *Praying a New Story*

Compassion

Toward the end of the morning prayer-time, an ornery six-year-old boy rattled my bamboo door in order to rouse my ire. Stepping outside quickly, I caught the little tease and twisted his ear. Only then did I notice two young mothers standing with their children, waiting to see me. When they observed my mood, one of them, Hamida, faded away. Some hours later she returned to see me.

"What is it, Hamida?" I asked.

"While you were away," she began, "my youngest daughter died." I fastened my attention on Hamida as she unfolded the entire saga of Sorufa's last day, how her breathing became labored, what she said to her mother, and how she did a little dance while delirious. Hamida had been waiting to tell me that story for more than a week.

While Hamida spoke, tears ran down her cheek. I shared her pain. Occasionally, as she whispered her story, I managed to repeat Allah's name. I felt ashamed that I had not attended to her earlier. She had carried with her the wrenching story, waiting for me to bear it with her. All she wanted from me was compassion.

— Bob McCahill, M.M., from *Dialogue of Life:*
A Christian among Allah's Poor

The Merciful Rwandan Wife

In a particular section of Kigali, Rwanda, where people from the Hutu and Tutsi ethnic groups lived together, the genocidal war broke out with a bloody vengeance. Neighbors attacked neighbors. In one area, a Hutu man murdered his Tutsi neighbor.

Some time later, after the Rwandan Pariotic Front had won the war and taken over the government, local investigations of the atrocities started. The wife of the dead Tutsi man was asked to identify her husband's murderer. She refused knowing that the Hutu man would be arrested, imprisoned, and perhaps killed. The woman preferred to remain silent to save another life.

"This is enough," she said. "The killing has to stop somewhere. One murder does not justify another killing. We have to break the cycle of violence and end this genocide."

So she chose to forgive.

— Joseph G. Healey, M.M., from *Once upon a Time in Africa*

326

Learning to Walk

In teaching a child to walk you get in front of the child and turn toward it. You do not walk alongside the child but are the goal toward which the child is to walk. Even though you stand so far away that you cannot reach the child, you stretch out your arms and motion with them as if you already embraced the child, although there is still some distance between you and the child. That much solicitude you have, but more solicitous you cannot be, for then the child does not learn to walk. So it is with Christ. Christ gets in front of us, does not walk beside his disciples, but is himself the goal toward which we are to strive while we are learning to walk alone. There he stands at the goal, turning toward us and stretching out his arms — just as a mother does.

— Søren Kierkegaard, from *Provocations:*
Spiritual Writings of Kierkegaard

Gratitude

Perhaps the most grateful person I've ever heard of was an old woman in an extended care hospital. She had some kind of wasting disease, her different powers fading away over the march of months. A student of mine happened upon her on a coincidental visit. The student kept going back, drawn by the strange force of the woman's joy. Though she could not longer move her arms and legs, she would say, "I'm just so happy I can move my neck." When she could no longer move her neck, she would say, "I'm just so glad I can hear and see."

When the young student finally asked the old woman what would happen if she lost her sense of sound and sight, the gentle lady said, "I'll just be so grateful that you come to visit."

— John F. Kavanaugh, from *The Word Engaged*

Living Water

When we find ourselves adrift in life or storm-tossed on turbulent waters, that is God-given time to turn to serious introspection. When there is nowhere to go to avoid facing our fears and our feelings, no escape from our persistent needs, from our feelings and misgivings, we can plumb the depths to discover the nature and source of disposable cargo. We look back on our lives to discern where and why our things may have gone wrong; decide how to do things differently with the gift of a second chance. We also grab hold of the still point deep within that is our anchor and give thanks for the many blessings that provide us with the stability to ride out any storm. That is what crisis can offer us, opportunity for perspective, so necessary adjustments can be made to save what is worth saving. When the waters had receded in that time before recorded time, God made a covenant with all creation and God still does. The deluge is a rite of passage, the genesis of our coming home to ourselves and to our God. The bridge over troubled waters is the rainbow in our hearts.

Each of us builds our field of dreams, but inevitably a river runs through it. Sometimes that river overflows its banks to completely overwhelm us. We are certain we will not survive. We lose our job. We lose our cool. We lose a friend or a lover. We sink in a whirlpool of emotions. We wallow in our despair. When the floodwaters threaten to destroy us, to wash away all that we cherish, we need to rise above the surface. We need to remember the rainbow, to trust that life will indeed go on, that the life that will be will be worth it.

We need to let go and prepare ourselves to turn and begin again. At times such as these we have to choose the things that are worth saving. As we come face to face with life — or death — we must be able to name those things that we cannot live without.

— Miriam Therese Winter, from *The Singer and the Song*

We're All God's Children

Soon after moving into my two-room, mud-brick house in the village of Pièla in Burkina Faso where I was serving as a Peace Corps volunteer, I realized that I had moved into the section of town where many of the women who worked as prostitutes were also living. They were mostly foreigners like me. Despite this fact, a lot of neighborhood kids would often come and visit me.

One day I started to play Frisbee with a young boy who had stopped by for a visit. While we were playing, one of the young women who worked in a bar as a prostitute started watching us. After a little while, I threw the Frisbee to her, and she joined in with our fun. Then a little while later, an old man came walking by and started watching us play. Pretty soon the young woman threw the Frisbee to him. He dropped the Frisbee and his cane too, but then clumsily picked it back up and threw it to the young boy.

And there we were, the most unlikely mix of people in a little African village: an old man, a prostitute, a little boy, and a foreigner, all standing together in a circle, throwing a Frisbee, and having fun together. When I reflected on this experience later, I realized that I had received a vision of what the reign of God is all about: love, equality, beauty, and enjoyment with no one excluded or left out.

— Dennis Moorman, M.M., from *Why Not Be a Missioner?*
edited by Michael Leach and Susan Perry

NOVEMBER

. . . .

How to Be a Saint

A third grader got it right.
"A saint is someone that
the light shines through."

She was looking at a stained glass window —
the one St. Francis inhabits.
Every morning the light comes
and Francis lets the light pass through.

Saints are bearers of the light
and love
and life.

Just ask any third grader.

— Robert Morneau, from *A New Heart:*
Eleven Qualities of Holiness

Value Is in the Eyes of the Beholder

Kenyans burn all their trash outdoors.... Near every Kenyan house or flat or set of flats — from the president's residence to the simplest shack in the poorest slum — there is a trash pile.... As a result, there is always and everywhere in the city the pungent smell of burning garbage. Often, to start the fire, eucalyptus leaves will be added, which perfumes the city air with an improbably sweet incense. This — combined with the diesel fumes belching out of ancient trucks, the red clay wet by the rain, and the aroma of roasting ears of corn sold on the street corners — is the scent of Nairobi.

Behind the Jesuit Refugee Service office was hidden our own trash dump, fed mostly by garbage, eucalyptus leaves, old folders, letters, and miscellaneous paper products.... You had to be careful what you threw out. Much of what we considered waste was not always considered *takataka,* or trash, by the Kenyans and the refugees. Used envelopes and folders that I had tossed onto our trash pile were cleaned and neatly smoothed down; I would later spy them on someone's desk. After I threw out some old magazines, one of the Kenyan women who worked with us ran outside, walked into the fire, and carefully plucked them out of the conflagration. I made a mental note to ask her if she'd like to read my magazines after I finished them. There was, I found, something inexpressibly sad about my trash being sought after by the friends with whom I worked.

At the Jesuit community one day I tossed out a copy of a Jesuit newsletter, along with old letters and some month-old newspapers that had been brought by a visiting American. I lit the fire with eucalyptus leaves and the wooden matches. As I walked away I noticed our *askari,* our watchman, a Maasai man named Joseph, picking through the smoking garbage.

Not long afterward, as I was chatting with Joseph in his guard shack, I noticed that he had tacked up some pictures from the *Time* magazine I had tossed away, their edges curled black from the fire: a picture of Bill Clinton, and an advertisement for perfume — Ralph Lauren for Men. Next to these was posted a photo clipped from our Jesuit province newsletter: a gathering of a dozen men on the steps of a local Jesuit high school. Joseph caught me staring at the picture. I told him that I knew those people who were pinned on his wall.

"I am so happy," he said, "to be having your friends in my house, Brother."

— James Martin, S.J., from *This Our Exile:*
A Spiritual Journey with the Refugees of East Africa

Where Is God?

The most important question about God is not where God is in the midst of the tragedy, but how he is present. We may answer philosophically or poetically, with resignation or in protest. The answer of Christian faith is that in tragedies, God is on the cross, giving hope. Throughout history this faith has created great, active hope, great commitment, great justice and love; but we cannot ignore the fact that it has also led to cruelty, resignation, and withdrawal on the part of the victims.

As a Christian I believe in the paschal mystery: the cross and resurrection of Jesus as the culmination of a life lived for the poor and for victims. This paschal mystery still gives hope to many people. But I wonder which gives more hope, the moment of resurrection or the moment of the cross. Some will see the answer as obvious, and my reflection as absurd. But there is something about the cross that gives hope.

The main reason is that in the cross there is great love, and love always creates hope.

That hope gives life. And because of that resurgent hope, no matter how hard it is to live through catastrophes, we cannot rule out the possibility of resurgent life in the midst of everything.

The countless victims in this world understand that very well. Against all appearances, they see that life — their life — is possible. As long as this is true, even if the affluent world doesn't know how to take it, the world's poor will still have utopia.

— Jon Sobrino, from *Where Is God?*

Identifying the Sacred in Everyday Life

Everything happening, great and small
is a parable whereby God speaks to us,
and the art of life is to get the message.

— Malcolm Muggeridge

One day God decided to become visible to a king and a peasant, and commissioned an angel to inform them of this blessed event. "O king," said the angel, "God has chosen to be revealed to you in whatever manner you wish. In what form do you want God to appear before you?"

Being pompous and arrogant because he had, for so long, been surrounded by awestruck advisors and subjects, the king said contemptuously, "How else would I wish to see God except in power and majesty? Show God to us in the fullness of power."

God granted the wish and appeared as a powerful, brilliant bolt of lightning, instantly pulverizing the king and his court. Nothing remained, not even a cinder. Everyone and everything was vaporized.

The same angel came to a peasant saying, "God wishes to be revealed to you in whatever manner you desire. How do you wish to see God?"

This puzzled the peasant. Scratching his head and pausing for a few moments, the peasant finally responded, "I am a poor man, not worthy to see God face to face. But if it is God's will and desire to be revealed to me, let it be in those things with which I am familiar. Let me see God in the earth I plow, in the water I drink, in the food I eat. Let me see God in the faces of my family, neighbors, and — if God deems it good for myself and others — even in my own reflection of him as well."

336

God granted the peasant his wish, and he lived a long, happy, healthy, holy life. Each of us would do well to emulate the peasant and seek to indentify the divine presence permeating all of life — to see God in the grass and the flowers, in our pleasures and our pains, in those we love and in those we don't.

— Victor M. Parachin, from *Eastern Wisdom for Western Minds*

The Measure of Kindness

Kindness does not expect to be repaid. That is its real measure.

— Joan Chittister, from *Living Well*

Moments of Prayerfulness

But where shall we start? I can only suggest that we start where we are, that we begin with what comes easiest. Why not start by surveying a typical day? What is it you tend to tackle with spontaneous mindfulness, so that without an effort your whole heart is in it? Maybe it's that first cup of coffee in the morning, the way it warms you and wakes you up, or taking your dog for a walk, or giving a little child a piggyback ride. Your heart is in it, and so you find meaning in it — not a meaning you could spell out in words, but a meaning in which you can rest. These are moments of intense prayerfulness, though we might never have thought of them as prayer. They show us the close connection between praying and playing. These moments when our heart finds ever so briefly rest in God are samples that give us a taste of what prayer is meant to be. If we could maintain this inner attitude, our whole life would become prayer. . . .

— David Steindl-Rast, from *David Steindl-Rast: Essential Writings,* edited by Clare Hallward

Lady Poverty

When I think of the life of Francis, I am reminded of a poor Lutheran pastor and his wife whom I met in a small village in Germany. When he left the room, she spoke of her husband with great love and respect even though his radical commitment to the gospel had brought her great pain and privation. Before he re-entered, she whispered to me solemnly and proudly, "He makes being poor look brilliant! And like brilliance, he lights up everything." So also Francis was not dark ascetic, but a passionate and sensuous Italian, who did not equate poverty with gracelessness or slovenliness. One need only visit his prayer spots throughout central Italy to discover that he chose the most scenic and lovely settings in which to disclose the darkness of his own soul. He knew that he had to surround himself with God's delighting in order to risk such painful truths.

Francis could not just be poor; he had to have a love affair, and even a marriage, with his beloved, "Lady Poverty." His celibacy had to be a passion, not a lack of it. In the twelfth-century tradition of courtly love, the sublimated love of a knight for his idealized lady, Francis insisted that he would marry only "the noblest, the riches, the most beautiful woman ever seen." She turned out to be Lady Poverty.

— Richard Rohr, from *Near Occasions of Grace*

Believing in Jesus

Compassion is the basis of truth. The experience of compassion is the experience of suffering or feeling with someone. To suffer or feel with humanity, nature, and God is to be in tune with the rhythms and impulses of life. This is also the experience of solidarity, solidarity with humanity, nature, and God. It excludes every form of alienation and falsehood. It makes a person at one with reality and therefore true and authentic in himself.

The secret of Jesus' infallible insight and unshakable convictions was his unfailing experience of solidarity with God, which revealed itself as an experience of solidarity with humanity and nature. This made of him a uniquely liberated man, uniquely courageous, fearless, independent, hopeful and truthful....

To believe in Jesus is to believe that goodness can and will triumph over evil. Despite the system, despite the magnitude, complexity, and apparently insolubility of our problems today, humanity can be, and in the end will be, liberated. Every form of evil — sin and all the consequences of sin: sickness, suffering, misery, frustration, fear, oppression and injustice — can be overcome. And the only power that can achieve this is the power of a faith that believes this. For faith is the power of goodness and truth, the power of God.

— Albert Nolan, from *Jesus before Christianity*

Theopoetry

And I saw a man on 126th Street
broom in hand
sweeping eight feet of the street
Meticulously he removed garbage and dirt
from a tiny area
in the midst of a huge expanse
of garbage and dirt

And I saw a man on 126th Street
sorrow sat on his back
sweeping eight feet of the street
Wear and tear showed on his arms
in a city
where only crazy folk
Find something to hope in

And I saw a man on 126th Street
broom in hand
There are many ways to offer prayer
With a broom in the hand
is one I had hitherto
not seen before

— Dorothee Soelle, from *Dorothee Soelle:*
Essential Writings, edited by Dianne L. Oliver

Love for Creation

Living in the middle of a tropical rainforest in Irian-Jaya, as I do, provides ample opportunity to observe first-hand God's creation in its still nearly unadulterated form.

One day some men from one of the villages up near the foothills brought me a baby tree kangaroo, whose mother they had killed while hunting. Thinking that raising it might be fun, I took in the helpless creature.

The news spread quickly through the village, and before long two women were standing at my door to see the newest member of their community. As I opened the door, they brushed past me, scooped up the little fellow from his box, and took him into their arms. They stroked his fine fur and smothered him with kisses. Before long he was resting comfortably on the breast of one of the women, dangling from her neck in a baby sling. The women spent the rest of the day parading him through the village for all to see. Toward evening they returned him to his box and left for the night.

Early the next morning I was startled awake by the sobbing of a death dirge. I assumed that someone had died. When I went outside I saw the two women. They had returned with some food for their little friend, only to find him dead in his box. Their sorrow was genuine and their tears were copious, spontaneous, and totally authentic. They wrapped the small body in the finest piece of cloth they could find and buried the baby kangaroo at the edge of the village, wailing lamentations the whole time.

Since then, this incident has provided me with many rich, wonder-filled moments. How does one fathom the depth of people who can fall so deeply in love with one of God's most humble creatures in less than twenty-four hours? I, on the other hand, might have tossed its body either to my dog or into the river.

— Vincent P. Cole, M.M., from *Once upon a Time in Asia*,
edited by James H. Kroeger and Eugene F. Thalman

Eulogy

She changed the world.

Though orphaned early,
and knowing the Depression's poverty,
she became strong and independent,
wise and compassionate.

She changed the world.
Gave life to five children,
loved her husband for fifty-four years,
cherished her sixteen grandchildren,
put first things first.

She changed the world.
Nursing people back to health,
working and playing with gusto,
embracing God's will with a lively faith.

The world was changed
by one woman who loved
her husband,
her family,
her God.

— Robert Morneau,
from *The Color of Gratitude*

He Fell Down and Can't Get Up

The Zen master teaches that one day Chao-chou fell down in the snow and called out, "Help me up! Help me up!" A monk came by and lay down beside him. Then Chao-chou got up and went away. Point: to be kind does not require us to solve anything for others. It simply requires that, like God, we stay with them long enough in their struggles until they are strong enough to get up and go their own way alone again.

— Joan Chittister, from *Living Well*

Let Your God Love You

Be silent.
Be still.
Alone.
Empty
Before your God
Say nothing.
Ask nothing.
Be silent.
Be still.
Let your God
Look upon you.
That is all.
God knows.
God understands.
God loves you
With an enormous love,
And only wants
To look upon you
With that love.
Quiet.
Still.
Be.

Let your God —
Love you.

> — Edwina Gateley,
> from *In God's Womb*

Two Travelers

An old man named Adaka spent most of his day sitting on the verandah of his mud hut, smoking his pipe. One day, as Adaka watched a stream of strangers coming into the village for the annual harvest festival, a young man who had a spring in his steps and a ready smile approached him and said, "Excuse me, old man, but I have left my village where there is starvation, and I am looking for a place where I can cultivate some fields and settle. I would like to ask your advice. Are the people of this village good, and are they ready to welcome a stranger?"

Adaka asked, "How are the people in the village you left?"

"Well," answered the young man, "they are good. They solve their quarrels with the mediation of the elders, and they work together when there is a need. The evenings of feastdays are wonderful. I get homesick when I think about them."

Adaka smiled and said, "Do not worry, young man. The people in this village are as good as those you have left."

The young man went on with a determined gait and after a few minutes he was lost in the market crowd.

After a while, another young man arrived. He looked around suspiciously, appraised Adaka, and asked, "I would like to settle in this place, but how are the people?"

Adaka asked, "How are the people in the village you left?"

The young man answered with a sneer, "Bad! They are envious and jealous. They never recognized my talent. I am so glad I left them."

Adaka's face took on a worried look, and he slowly said, "Then you had better not even enter this village. Here people are exactly like those you have left behind. You will not find any friends here."

The young man turned away in disgust.

— Joseph G. Healey, M.M., from *Once upon a Time in Africa*

The Value of Contemplation

In the midst of our hectic modern life, many yearn for the serenity of the Dalai Lama or a Thomas Merton. We long to take time out from the daily list of things to be done to replenish ourselves and to silence the inner chatter that makes us anxious and frazzled. Can we learn from the rhythm of nature to stop and be still when we are feeling overwhelmed? Can we eat outside under the trees rather than in a crowded, noisy cafeteria? Can we go for a walk or sit alone, resting our eyes and our brains? Can we listen to the birds and watch the squirrels at play rather than reading a book or a newspaper? Can we take time out, morning and evening, to say thanks to the Creator for the gifts of each day? Can we just take time, instead of rushing and running through our lives? . . .

Jesus also led an active life, healing, preaching, and teaching about God's kingdom. Yet he also took time to rest and to pray. He understood the natural rhythm of life and used images from nature to explain his mission — the world of flowers, birds, wheat, seeds, sheep, pearls, fish, sunshine, and rain. The wind and the sea obeyed him. Children played at his feet. He relaxed with friends over a meal and visited with rich and poor alike. Artists of all nations and all times depict him in various poses, clothing, and cultural settings but almost all capture an inner fire and outer serenity that still attract followers around the world. May we too experience the fruit of contemplation in action.

— Janice McLaughlin, M.M., from *Ostriches, Dung Beetles, and Other Spiritual Masters: A Book of Wisdom from the Wild*

Balance

For American Indians, creation is a matter of give and take. It is never merely a matter of explaining or knowing what happened long ago at the beginning of time but it is rather a matter of knowing our rightful place in the world and of living appropriately. Thus, this give and take is not the stuff of happenstance, but a life and death matter of balancing the world and our place in it, with special attention to maintaining the world for our children who will live seven generations from now. Indian religious thinking, theology, must invariably begin with creation and with understanding our place in the world as human beings. The lessons of creation are multiple. All of creation is filled with our relatives; thus all of creation is alive. Yet we need to eat. Hence, we take whatever we need from the plenty of creation around us; but we always give something back in return to remind us that what we have taken was taken at a cost to our relatives in the world around us.

— George E. "Tink" Tinker, from *A Native American Theology* by Clara Sue Kidwell, Homer Noley, and George E. Tinker

A Letter to Her Niece

A letter to her niece from Maryknoll Sister Ita Ford,
killed in El Salvador on December 2, 1980:

This is a terrible time in El Salvador for youth. A lot of idealism and commitment is getting snuffed out here now.

The reasons why so many people are being killed are quite complicated yet there are some clear simple strands. One is that many people have found a meaning to life, to sacrifice, to struggle and even to death! And whether their life spans sixteen years or sixty or ninety, for them their life has had a purpose. In many ways, they are fortunate people.

Brooklyn is not passing through the drama of El Salvador, but some things hold true wherever one is and at whatever age. What I am saying is I hope you come to find that which gives life a deep meaning for you. Something worth living for, maybe even worth dying for, something that energizes you, enthuses you, enables you to keep moving ahead.

I can't tell you what it might be. That's for you to find, to choose, to love. I just encourage to you to start looking and support you in the search.

—Ita Ford, M.M., from *"Here I Am, Lord":*
The Letters and Writings of Ita Ford, edited by Jeanne Evans

Seeing Jesus

I like to think of Mary Magdalen as the apostle to the apostles — like the Samaritan woman, whose mission was to lead the Samaritans to Christ. But in this instance it's more significant, since it's to proclaim the resurrection. . . .

But knowing how much Mary Magdalen loved the Lord, it's hard to understand why she couldn't recognize him right away. She actually thought he was the gardener. It was the same too with the disciples who met the risen Christ on the way to Emmaus. They had lived with the Lord for three years. When you love somebody, you can recognize them by their voice or even by the way they walk. But no, they walked and talked with him and still they couldn't recognize him. Until he shared the loaf with them.

I was thinking about this one day when someone knocked on my door. It was a poor man. He had interrupted my meditation on the disciples at Emmaus: how was it they hadn't been able to recognize Christ? To get rid of the fellow as quickly as I could, I gave him a little cash, a smile and a good-bye. But the moment the door was shut, I realized: "You've behaved exactly like the disciples at Emmaus. The Lord Jesus knocked on your door, he spoke to you, and you couldn't get rid of the living Christ fast enough to return to your thoughts on the blindness of your brothers, the disciples of Emmaus."

— Dom Helder Camara, from *Through the Gospel
with Dom Helder Camara*

Where the Winds Meet

Foreign missioners are misfits regardless of the culture in which they live and work. Having lived, worked, and loved in both home and host cultures, they feel at home in neither. Missioners arriving in a host culture see that culture from an outsider's viewpoint. They also take into their lives values of the host culture that reveal less than satisfactory truths about their home culture.

Foreign missioners' lives are the locale where the winds meet: the winds of two cultures and the winds of two worlds. Because of this, foreign missioners are profoundly connected to the fundamental mystery of humanity. While serving as beacons for the misfits of this world, they in turn receive direction from the very same misfits.

Called to be beacons for the misfits whose lives carry the void that brings them to the gateway of eternity, foreign missioners need some magnifying of their call. Indeed, it is in the mirror of the misfits that foreign missioners are reminded that they have been called and sent by Jesus, a misfit who stretched *toward* rather than *away from* the waiting void of God's promise. Jesus' life, death, and resurrection offer not protection but the sustenance, the radical support of knowing that God's promise is best remembered in the void.

— Larry Lewis, M.M., from *The Misfit*

Learning from the Children

Three years ago, just after I was ordained bishop, the special novena masses, *Simbang Gabi,* attended at dawn by Filipinos in preparation for Christmas, had already started. After celebrating the Eucharist in the cathedral and still wearing my full vestments, I greeted the people as they went out the door. As I stood there, I saw that little children selling flowers were impeding the progress of the people leaving the church. *"Bulaklak po! Bulaklak!"* (Flowers! Flowers!) I ran after them, scolding them until we reached the road. I was still in my full regalia as I shouted at those children, "Look, we have not forbidden you from selling flowers but let us put some order here! You can sell flowers here at the gate. The people who are attending mass and the people who are leaving the church will certainly pass through the gate."

All the children were trembling before me in fear. I spotted the tallest girl. "You! How old are you?" She softly said, "Fourteen." I replied, "You see! You're fourteen years old. Is it difficult to understand what I'm saying? That you can sell at this point and not beyond it?" And she answered, "No. I understand."

Then I looked at the smallest boy, a very dirty-looking boy. "You! How old are you?" He looked up, smiled and said, "Seven." I said, "You're seven years old. Can you understand what I'm saying?" It was then that he hugged me. He was so small that his hands only reached my waist. He hugged me and again smiled the sweetest smile. He started stroking my back and gently said, "Father, *Obispo ka no."* (Father, you are now a bishop). I stopped and I said, "Yes." God was calling me again and asking me to utter "God" to these children in compassion.

I have never sold flowers, or anything else for that matter. I never wanted for anything; as a child, all I had to do was go to school. These children have to work every day, including Sunday, to have something. There I was, uttering laws, policies, the need for order, and cleanliness. And this young boy uttered a word addressed to my heart, to my identity.

For the next half hour, I just stayed with the children at the gate, still in my full vestments, and had a grand time talking with them. These children taught me how to listen to God and how to say "God."

— Bishop Chito Tagle, from *Easter People: Living Community*

Our Children Need a Peaceful World

A fundamental moral measure of any society is how its youngest and most vulnerable members fare. As we look at our own nation, we must ask: Why is it that the younger you are in the United States, the more likely you are to be poor? Indeed, nearly 20 percent of our preschool children are growing up poor in a land of plenty. We have failed to fully acknowledge that the lives of our children are the truest indicators of the strength and future vitality of our communities. . . .

All of us need to remember that Jesus responded to the question "Who is my neighbor?" with the story of a man whom history calls the "Good Samaritan." Unlike the others before him this man stopped and ministered to a person lying helpless in a ditch. He sensed the silent appeal on the face of the other, the desperate look that said, "I can live if you are on my side."

I wonder why we do not have eyes to see that same look on the faces of the millions of children in our world today, children who need the basic necessities of life — a safe neighborhood in which to grow up, a good education, access to health care, someone to love and protect them.

Jesus of Nazareth lies hidden and helpless in all of humanity's most vulnerable children, those for whom there is no room at the table. May we know the grace of our loving God in them and rebuild our troubled world for them to enjoy as God's beloved daughters and sons.

— Donald H. Dunson, from *No Room at the Table: Earth's Most Vulnerable Children*

eucharist with a small "e"

Not long ago there was a special event in the prison chapel. I had the privilege of awarding a doctor of ministry degree to the chaplain, something that had never happened there before, for something that had not been done before. Laurie had created an interfaith community within the prison complex that would prepare women to return to society with a more informed understanding of other faith traditions as well as their own. Quite a few people had been invited to this significant event, including the women who had been participants in the project. Laurie had decided on a menu that would mean something to the women who ate only prison food. Coffee was eliminated in favor of ice cold cans of soda and a large, rich cake that had lots and lots of icing. The plan had been to serve everyone in the choir room, but there were so many people, including members of the prison choir, that it just wouldn't work. I looked up at the communion table, and said to myself, what would Jesus do? Then I sent two of the women to bring in the cake. When I am old and feeble, I will close my eyes and remember the scene that sent shivers to my heart. The officers had lined up the inmates — we had decided to let them go first because they were the ones who needed the cake — and in a stereotypical communion line, they processed up the aisle and up the steps to the altar-like table, two by two, to receive on a napkin a hunk of cake and to snatch a can of soda from the bucket that stood on the floor. As the line moved forward, one of the women waiting in the pew touched my arm and said to me, "Isn't this eucharist with a small 'e' just like in your book?" Indeed, I had mentioned small "e" eucharist in *The Singer and the Song*. I said to her, "Yes, it is." Then another woman in the front of the chapel who had not heard this exchange, said, "This is like eucharist, like you wrote in your book." Remembering this brings tears to my eyes, for this was precisely what eucharist with a small "e" is all about, and incarcerated women were the first to see it. I was in prison and you visited me. The spirit of Jesus was present there, grabbing a can of soda and carving up the cake.

—Miriam Therese Winter, from *eucharist with a small "e"*

Our Need to Conform

There is a type of obedience that masquerades as freedom: the need for conformity. This is the desire to be myself within the context of the demands of my society. I claim to be myself, to dress as I want, to do what I want, but in reality I have accepted the programming imposed on me by society. It is amazing how much the fashion industry manipulates us into conformity even as they project a certain type of individuality. Even young children are manipulated into wanting only a certain name brand of shoes, clothes and accessories. Take, for example, the need to be beautiful in accordance with the dictates of the fashion magazines, or the need to look eternally young. Society conditions us in many more ways than we can imagine, and we become imprisoned by its norms and dictates. We live in the illusion of freedom when in effect we react like well-programmed robots.

—Virgil Elizondo, from *Charity*

Holiness

Practical experience has now convinced me of this: the concept of holiness which I had formed and applied to myself was mistaken. In every one of my actions, and in the little failings of which I was immediately aware, I used to call to mind the image of some saint whom I had set myself to imitate down to the smallest particular, as a painter makes an exact copy of a picture by Raphael. I used to say to myself: in this case St. Aloysius would have done so and so, or: he would not do this or that. However, it turned out that I was never able to achieve what I had thought I could do, and this worried me. The method was wrong. From the saints I must take the substance, not the accidents, of their virtues. I am not St. Aloysius, nor must I seek holiness in his particular way, but according to the requirements of my own nature, my own character, and the different conditions of my life. I must not be the dry, bloodless reproduction of a model, however perfect. God desires us to follow the examples of the saints by absorbing the vital sap of their virtues and turning it into our own life-blood, adapting it to our own individual capacities and particular circumstances. If St. Aloysius had been as I am, he would have become holy in a different way.

—Pope John XXIII, from *Pope John XXIII: Essential Writings,* edited by Jean Maalouf

Rapture

Alyosha's soul, overflowing with rapture, yearned for freedom, space, openness. The vault of heaven, full of soft, shining stars stretched vast and fathomless above him. The Milky Way ran in two pale streams from the zenith to the horizon. The fresh, motionless, still night enfolded the earth. The white towers and golden domes of the cathedral gleamed out against the sapphire sky. The gorgeous autumn flowers in the beds around the house were slumbering till morning. The silence of earth seemed to melt into the silence of the heavens. The mystery of earth was one with the mystery of the stars.

Alyosha stood, gazed, and suddenly threw himself on the earth. He did not know why he embraced it. He could not have told why he longed so irresistibly to kiss it, to kiss it all. But he kissed it weeping, sobbing, and watering it with his tears and vowed passionately to love it, to love it forever and ever. "Water the earth with the tears of your joy and love those tears," echoed in his soul. In his rapture he was weeping even over those stars, shining at him from the abyss of space, and "he was not ashamed of that ecstasy." There seemed to be threads from all those innumerable worlds of God, linking his soul to them, and it was trembling all over "in contact with other worlds." He longed to forgive everyone for everything, and to beg forgiveness — oh not for himself but for all men, for all echoed again in his soul. But with every instant he felt clearly and tangibly that something firm and unshakable as that vault of heaven had entered his soul. It was as though some idea had seized the sovereignty of his mind — and it was for all his life and forever and ever. He had fallen on the earth a weak boy, but he rose up a resolute champion, and he knew and felt it suddenly at the very moment of his ecstasy. And never, never, all his life long, could Alyosha forget that minute.

"Someone visited my soul in that hour," he used to say afterward, with implicit faith in his words.

Within three days he left the monastery in accordance with the words of his elder, who had bidden him: "Sojourn in the world."

— Fyodor Dostoyevsky (*The Brothers Karamazov*),
from *The Gospel in Dostoyevsky* compiled by The Bruderhoff

The Family of God

Nothing can separate us from the love of God, and nothing can separate us from each other. We are made in the image and likeness of God.

Prayer begins with the awesome recognition of our oneness with God. It continues with the realization of our unity with one another. We are all members of one family — the family of God.

Let us pray...

— Michael Leach, from *A Maryknoll Book of Prayer,*
edited by Michael Leach and Susan Perry

God of My Daily Drudge

I should like to bring my daily drudge before you, O Lord — the long hours and days crammed with everything else but you. Look at this daily drudge, my gentle God, you who are merciful to us men and women for whom daily drudge is virtually all we are. Look at my soul, which is virtually nothing but a street on which the world's baggage-cart rolls along with its innumerable trivialities, with its gossip and fuss, with its noisiness and empty pretension. In face of you and your incorruptible truth isn't my soul like a market, where junk dealers from every direction come together and sell the wretched riches of this world, a market where I, and indeed the world, are spreading sheer nothings in permanent, benumbing restlessness? . . .

Is there a route through the drudge to you? . . .

But — if there is nowhere where you have given me a place to which we can just flee away in order to find you, and if everything can be the loss of you, the One, then I must also be able to find you in everything. Otherwise, humanity couldn't find you at all. Therefore I must seek you in everything. Each day is daily drudge, *and* each day is your day, the hour of your grace.

I must live out the daily drudge and the day that is yours as *one* reality. As I turn outward to the world, I must turn inward toward you, and possess you, the only One, in everything. But how does my daily drudge become the day that is yours? My God, only through you. . . . Your love, my infinite God, the love for you that passes through all hearts and extends out beyond them into your infinite expanses, your love that can still take in everything that is lost as the song of praise to your infinity. For you, all multiplicity is one; all that is dispersed is gathered into you; everything outside becomes in your love something still interior. In your love, all turning outward to the daily drudge becomes a retreat into your unity, which is eternal life. . . .

— Karl Rahner, from *Karl Rahner: Spiritual Writings,*
edited by Philip Endean

Speaking in a Fleshly Way

Within the context of earthly reality we receive the creative, saving, sanctifying acts of Father, Son, and Spirit amidst the humdrum of our often very ordinary lives, lives given to simple acts such as feeding and washing and working. God is with us in our listening, in the sometimes deadening but often consoling silence. The divine presence is to be discerned while we travel, as we teach and learn. God's nearness is to be known in our weeping and in our walking, as we move alongside others through the various stages of life's journey. When we visit the sick, the elderly and the infirm, as he did, God is in our midst. And God is there at our table when we invoke Christ's name and enjoy the fruits of the earth. There, too, in the pain, in the darkness, in the hurt, in the loss, in our very brokenness and vulnerability. God is seen in the healing gaze, touched in the hand that comforts, heard in the word that encourages, and welcomed in offering ourselves as a gift.

— Michael Downey, from *Altogether Gift:*
A Trinitarian Spirituality

Creation

In May 2005 I went off on a solitary journey. . . . I thought I was going to see the wonders of the Petrified Forest/Painted Desert National Park in northern Arizona. But you just never know what will happen when you venture out into creation.

If you have been there you know what I am talking about. The deep reds, roses, pinks, and shades of brown and beige, especially vivid in the late afternoon sun, create a landscape unique in the world reflecting a geological history that goes back millions of years. The land is still taking shape, sculpted by the winds and desert storms. And I wondered how this land had become so dry, why the climate hand changed, what forces were at work over those millions of years to make the rains go away and the animals become extinct and the giant trees disappear. The signs in the park gave me my answer, and altered my perceptions of the Southwest, and this living earth, forever.

The land I was on, whose trails I walked across, was not in that spot back then. It was somewhere around Panama, near the equator, which explains the 200-foot trees now permineralized and buried, land that slowly floated off to Arizona so that on that day, 220 million years later, I could stroll across the footpaths, see what the winds and rain are revealing and gasp in awe.

In that space, in that moment, all that science got out of my abstract thoughts and into every part of my conscious being. I had a powerful sensation of standing on a living planet, one that still seethes, moves, trembles, floats, creates, and re-creates itself, over and over again. I had an almost overwhelming sensation of what it means that there are creatures that can park their cars, take a walk, look out at all of this, know what they are seeing, and pronounce it awesome and beautiful.

That's what we are part of.

—Margaret Swedish, from *Living Beyond the "End of the World"*

Blessed Mourning

Mourning has fallen out of fashion. For people of European ancestry, black was the color for mourning a spouse or parent, and not just during the funeral. Dressing in black for less than six months was disrespectful. People did not attend social functions. They resisted pretending things were normal to let the realization set in that the definition of normal had forever changed.

Such austere practices shielded mourners from the demands of daily social interactions, thus giving their hearts and minds time to heal. Nowadays, in our rush to get back to life as "usual" much has been lost, not the least of which is our mental health.

Nowadays we view death as a rude interruption. In their eagerness to shield a child from the sorrow following the death of a pet, parents may too soon replace it with another one. Denied a chance to grieve, the child is deprived of the emotional opportunity to grow. He or she learns the erroneous lesson that the pain of loss is an inconvenience and, worse, pets and even people are interchangeable.

Such dismissals deaden life. More things than death need grieving. A failed marriage, a lost job, an unsuccessful college application, all demand we admit some doors have closed forever. When we take time to mourn the loss of youth, health and even our dreams, we honor them in order to let them go and let us go on. We do our best when pressing against our limitation.

The cross compels us to become fully alive, not by avoiding pain and loss but by passing through them. The cross, and by extension death, is the ultimate limitation. The Church encourages us to remember those who have died. We bless the emptiness created by their passing. In allowing ourselves time to mourn, we expand our capacity to love and live. We become truly blessed.

— Joseph R. Veneroso, M.M., from *Good News for Today*

DECEMBER

. . . .

Knowing God

It seems there was a bishop whose diocese served many islands in the South Pacific. One day as he was visiting various parishes, he came across an island that he had never seen before, so he had the captain sail over that way and, lowering a dinghy, he went ashore. There he found three fishermen who recognized his religious garb and greeted him. They told him that some twenty years before a missioner had visited them and taught them a prayer, but they had forgotten how it went. They did remember that the missioner told them that God was three. Since they could not remember the prayer he taught them, every day before going fishing they would pray, "You are three, we are three. Have mercy on us."

The bishop thought to himself, "We have a lot of work to do here," so he spent the rest of the morning teaching them the Lord's Prayer.

A few years later the bishop again found himself near that island and decided to stop and visit the fishermen. As his ship drew near, he saw the three men coming toward him, walking on the waters! As they came up to the ship, one of them shouted, "Your Excellency, we have forgotten that prayer you taught us. Would you teach us again how to pray?"

To which the bishop responded, "When you pray, say, 'You are three, we are three. Have mercy on us.'"

— Joseph Heim, M.M., from *What They Taught Us:*
How Maryknoll Missioners Were Evangelized by the Poor

God's Presence

That is why, paradoxically, those who most profoundly experience God's absence, who experience themselves abandoned, are also so often the ones who most profoundly experience God's presence. It is in relationship to God's nearness that we experience God's distance (since "distance" and "absence" are by definition relative terms). Indeed, as Simone Weil observes, the agonizing experience of God's absence is itself a form of presence. "Two prisoners whose cells adjoin communicate with each other by knocking on the wall. The wall is the thing that separates them but it is also their means of communication. It is the same with us and God. Every separation is a link."

It makes perfect sense, then, that the holy person, the person closest to God, is the one who most intimately experiences his or her distance from God. Those who most intimately know God's presence are also those who most profoundly experience God's absence. It is at the moment that Thomas sees Jesus' wounds and is invited to touch them — the moment of conversion — that Thomas simultaneously experiences most intensely the anguish of his, and the other apostles', own sinful distance from God. Thus, our experience of God's distance or silence presupposes a more fundamental experience of God's presence. It is when he witnesses and hears Christ's cry of abandonment on the cross that the Roman centurion realizes that he has seen the form of God's own love: "Truly this was God's Son!"

— Roberto S. Goizueta, from *Christ Our Companion*

Moments of Prayer

Some prayerful moments are as dramatic as bounding across a stage, others as humble as laundry. The common denominator is the spirit of the Creator stirring within us and our response to that Voice. Here are people in beautiful moments of prayer:

- the husband who watches beside the hospital bed of his wife. He says nothing. He holds her hand as he has for the past two weeks.

- the mother who rises to nurse the baby for the third time that night. With half-opened eyes she bumbles toward the crib, scoops up the infant, and feeds him sleepily.

- the student who completes a week of final exams, three term papers, a group project, and the organization of a canned-food drive. He dives into bed but pauses for a moment before falling asleep. Words addressed to the mysterious Holy One come muffled by exhaustion: "Thanks. I got it all done."

- the business executive who knows that a long day looms ahead. She faces the window and lifts both hands in an eloquent gesture. "Thank you for a new day," her hands seem to say. "I am yours, O God. Help me to be kind as well as efficient."

- the two friends who meet over coffee to talk through a dilemma that concerns them both. They listen carefully, lean across the table toward each other, joke, respect each other's truth. They leave knowing clearly what action they must take; the caffeine was in the conversation.

- the protester who takes a deep breath and steps across the line at the nuclear weapons plant, thinking, "If I go to jail, I go to jail. But I can't let conscience lie down and die."

- the artist who launches a new project, excited about its potential while still aware that it will take many long hours to complete. Still, a tantalizing intrigue hovers over the beginning. How will this look when it's finished? What will emerge?

• the older sister who knows it's drudgery, but does it anyway. "Just this once, Sam," she tells her younger brother. "I'll throw your jeans in the wash with my dark load so you'll have clean ones for the party." They grin at each other in the easy camaraderie of people who know they'll fall again, and once again, they'll bail each other out.

These are moments of prayer. Do you recognize yourself in them?

— Kathy Coffey, from *God in the Moment*

Political Love

The development of Christian holiness always presupposes that it is in answer to God's will. This may be different for different persons, but it must, essentially, include what is God's clear will in a particular moment of history. At the moment, God's primary will is that the poor majority should have life, and that they should "build houses and live in them, plant vines and eat their fruits." Or to put it in negative terms: that the poverty and oppression of millions of human beings should stop, that there should be an end to their constant deprivation of human dignity, the horrible violation of their rights, the massacres, mass expulsions, arrests, tortures, and murders. The response to this primary will of God is a specific type of love for persons: love for those most deprived of life and working so that they may have life. This love, which is both a response to God's will and to the present enormous suffering of humanity, is what I call political love. . . .

Political love tries to be *effective*. . . . The political love that seeks to transform the situation of *these* poor must have its specific mechanisms. . . . It must also see the poor not only as the *objects* of beneficial political actions but also the enactors of their own destiny as a people fighting for liberation. . . . For this reason political love must also share in the struggle of the poor, which takes place on the ideological and social level but also on the political level.

— Jon Sobrino, from *Spirituality of Liberation*

Learning to See

Most of his headstrong people were not ready for Moses' inner experience, and they fought him nonstop every step of the journey. . . . Yet, he never stopped leading them. He was a pastor, a prophet, and a true priest all at once, which is most rare. Not only did he hold the people together in life as a pastor does, but he led them beyond their easy comfort zones as a prophet does, and as a priest he made the inner connections and transformations of soul that kept them face to face with God.

Eyes really are, as Jesus says, "the lamp of the body" (Matt. 6:22). How you see is what you see. "If your eye is sound, your whole body will be filled with light. But if your eye is diseased, your whole body will be darkness." I think we could follow Moses' entire development in terms of his learning how to see. This learning began with seeing God's true nature (Exod. 33:13) and daring to look at God "face to face." It had the effect of making others unable to look at Moses, because, as Paul says, "we reflect like mirrors the brightness of the Lord, all growing brighter and brighter as we are turned into the image that we reflect: this is the work of the Lord who is Spirit" (2 Cor. 3:18). Both Moses and Paul became the one they loved, which is of course, true for all of us.

— Richard Rohr, from *Soul Brothers:
Men in the Bible Speak to Men Today*

Thy Kingdom Come

To believe in the kingdom of God is to believe in a final and happy meaning for history. It is to affirm that utopia is more real than the weight of facts. It is to locate the truth concerning the world and human beings not in the past or completely in the present, but in the future, when it will be revealed in its fullness. To pray "thy kingdom come" is to activate the most radical hopes of the heart, so that it will not succumb to the continual brutality of present absurdities that occur at the personal and social level.

How will the kingdom of God come? For the Christian faith there is an infallible criterion that signals the arrival of the kingdom: when the poor are evangelized — that is, when justice begins to reach the poor, the dispossessed, and the oppressed. Whenever bonds of fellowship, of harmony, of participation, and of respect for the inviolable dignity of every person are created, then the kingdom of God has begun to dawn. Whenever social structures have been imposed on society that hinder persons from exploiting others, that do away with the relationships of master and slave, that favor fair dealing, then the kingdom of God is beginning to burst forth like the dawn.

— Leonardo Boff, from *Praying with Jesus and Mary*

Confucius on Wisdom

Confucius lived a life filled with enthusiasm for learning. Although he was just a poor young man in the country of Lu, he earned the respect of many people because of his politeness and love for learning. Aside from studying different things, Confucius spent many years serving in public offices as an advisor and minister. During the last few years of his life, he was again offered a public position, which he declined. Instead, he spent the remaining years of his life teaching and writing. Confucius died at the age of seventy-two.

Confucius said, "To know what you know and know what you don't know is the characteristic of one who knows."

Confucius said, "A man who has made a mistake and doesn't correct it is making another mistake."

Confucius said, "A man who has a beautiful soul always has beautiful things to say, but a man who says beautiful things does not necessarily have a beautiful soul."

Confucius said, "The superior man understands what is right, the inferior man understands what will sell."

Confucius said, "The superior man loves his soul; the inferior man loves his property. The superior man always remembers how he was punished for his mistakes; the inferior man always remembers the gift he received."

Confucius said, "The superior man blames himself; the inferior man blames others."

— From *Once upon a Time in Asia,* edited by James H. Kroeger and Eugene F. Thalman [adapted from *Linking the World through English II* (Philippines: Diwa Scholastic Press, 2006)]

Teachers

Along life's journey, teachers emerge.
Their titles vary: spiritual directors,
coaches, mentors.
Their methods too: direct or indirect,
stern or gentle, demanding or patient.

Another instructor came this week: Pain!
The lesson: "Your passing pain
for many is a chronic condition.
Therefore, have compassion."

I pray that I do not forget
how suffering holds us captive.
I pray that I have compassion
for the suffering ones.

— Robert Morneau,
from *The Color of Gratitude*

Why No One Wins the Race

Some foreigners in East Africa are driven to distraction by the lack of competitive spirit among Africans. Tanzanians seem to have chosen cooperation and togetherness as a way of life.

The first inkling I had of this was during a field day for students at a grammar school. Events did not include the shot-put, javelin throw, or even a tug-a-war. There were only foot races.

After half a dozen heats of fifty-yard dashes, the Catholic sister in charge sensed that something was odd. She had a very hard time determining the winner of each race — the girls were all reaching the finish line at exactly the same time. Before the seventh heat, she asked, "What's going on here? Nobody is winning."

"Oh, Sister," came the reply from the least shy of the youngsters. "It's better when we all come in together."

— Joseph G. Healey, M.M., from *Once upon a Time in Africa*

Take the Time

Take the time to sing a song,
for all those who don't belong:
the women wasted by defeat,
the men condemned to walk the street,
the down and out we'll never meet.

Take the time to say a prayer
for all those people who face despair:
the starving multitudes who pray
to make it through another day,
who watch their children slip away.

Take the time to hear the plea
of every desperate refugee:
the millions who have had to flee
their lands, their loves, their liberty,
who turn in hope to you and me.

Take the time to take a stand
for peace and justice in every land,
Where power causes deep unrest,
come take the part of the oppressed,
and then, says God, you will be blessed.

— Miriam Therese Winter,
from *The Singer and the Song*

Ministering to Others

We must continually remind ourselves that every Christian who is baptized into the church is admitted to the royal priesthood of all believers in Christ, and that each of us has a ministry, whether we are young or old, male or female, lay member or clergy. To be a Christian is to follow Jesus Christ's example of ministry, to be God's representative on earth. Each of us has been called by God to love and serve him and our fellow human beings. However sinful, rebellious, or inadequate we may feel, we cannot escape God's claim on us....

We minister when we pray for others, when we stand before God holding them in our thoughts. We minister by our presence with another in time of trouble, giving reassurance that the other is not alone in adversity. We minister when we simply listen with a sympathetic ear to one who is full of sorrow and grief; or when we telephone a shut-in just to let someone know that he or she is not forgotten; or when we offer a welcoming smile or a welcoming handclasp to a stranger in our midst....

We encounter God in our ministry to others, for only as we love and serve others do we love and serve God.... God is as close to us as our neighbor's hand.

— Pauli Murray, from *Pauli Murray: Selected Sermons and Writings,* edited by Anthony B. Pinn

Hope against Hope

We hope against hope. We continue to hope even when there are no visible signs of hope. We recognize the darkness and apparent hopelessness of the present situation and put all our trust in God. Then, gradually, as our eyes adjust to the darkness of despair, we begin to see the emerging shapes or outlines of God's great and mysterious work — the finger of God, as Jesus called it. These are the paradoxical signs of the time that only become visible once we believe that God is at work in our world, once we learn to look at life with an attitude of hopefulness.

Is that not what the death and resurrection of Jesus is about? Jesus' death plunged his disciples and many others into a state of despair. On the road to Emmaus the two disciples said, "We had hoped that he was the one to redeem Israel. . . . "

But those who continued to trust in God, in spite of all this, gradually came to see the finger of God at work in this terrible tragedy. They began to see that Jesus was alive and active in a surprisingly new way. That he had risen from the dead and that his Spirit was now in them. That the cross was not a total failure. That it was paradoxically the triumph of God's work in the world. That it was our salvation and our hope for the future.

And that is why for Christians the resurrection is the great symbol of our hope.

What matters in the long run, though, is not only that we are hopeful but that we act hopefully. The most valuable contribution that a Christian can make in our age of despair is to continue, because of our faith, to act hopefully, and in that way to be an encouragement to those who have lost all hope.

— Albert Nolan, from *Hope in an Age of Despair*

A Letter from Bangladesh

Postscript for fellow pilgrims: Sometimes I accuse myself: "When are you going to start helping to change structures that oppress people? You're so wrapped up in people's lives that you haven't the time or energy to grapple with the big issues."

Then I beat my scrawny chest, admit my deficiencies, and view myself with calm amusement. Anyway, I say to myself, "Who knows? Maybe God uses even my wee efforts to help transform oppressive structures."

Helping the poor is a work recommended by all the great religions. "Helping the poor" is also an expression so trite that I used to think it described just one among many laudable human activities. No longer do I underestimate that work. The promise of another Great Prophet is fulfilled: "When you give a party, invite the poor, the crippled, the lame and the blind. They have no means of repaying you. In that way lies real happiness for you."

— Bob McCahill, M.M., from *Trends in Mission: Toward the Third Millennium,* edited by William Jenkinson and Helene O'Sullivan

Attentiveness

Learning to sit still, to calm and quiet ourselves enough to be able to hear something other than the surface noise of our lives or the distracting inner chatter of our own egos, is a necessary prerequisite for being able to detect the stirrings of the still, small voice. James Hillman writes: "Prayer has been described as an active silence in which one listens acutely for the still small voice, as if prayer were not asking and getting through to God, but becoming so composed that He might come through to me." There are many things that can get in the way of our composing ourselves and sitting still long enough to hear something other than the usual racket. The still, small voice gets crowded out and drowned out by too much hectic doing and not enough being, too much extroverted activity and too little of the kind of relaxed solitude and leisure that are essential to developing a spiritual life. "To listen for God is a countercultural enterprise," says Margaret Guenther, "for much in our lives works against the patient labor of attentiveness." Such attentiveness requires that we find or make time away from what John Boyle O'Reilly called "the street's rude bustle":

> Oh, no, from the street's rude bustle,
> From the trophies of mart and stage,
> I would fly to the wood's low rustle
> And the meadow's kindly page.

— John Neafsey, from *A Sacred Voice Is Calling*

"Thou Shalt Not Crave Things"

Once upon a time a disciple traveled for miles to sit at the feet of an old nun who had acquired an unusual reputation for holiness. People came from far and wide, simply to watch her work, to listen to her chant, to hear her comment on the scriptures. Here without doubt was a person of substance, an impacting personality, an imposing figure.

What the seeker found when he finally reached the site of her hermitage, however, was only a tiny little woman sitting on the floor of a bare room plaiting straw baskets alone.

Shocked, the seeker said, "Old woman, where are your books? Where are your chair and footstool? Where are your bed and mattress?"

And the old woman answered him back, "And where are yours?"

"But I'm only passing through," the seeker said.

"And so am I," said the old woman knowingly.

— Joan Chittister, from *The Ten Commandments*

Freedom to Love

There is no aspect of human life that is unrelated to the following of Jesus. The road passes through every dimension of our existence. A spirituality is not restricted to the so-called religious aspects of life: prayer and worship. It is not limited to one sector but is all-embracing, because the whole of human life, personal and communal, is involved in the journey. A spirituality is a manner of life that gives a profound unity to our prayer, thought, and action. A spirituality is, in effect, the field in which freedom is exercised — the full freedom that energizes and feeds our option for life and against death.

A particular spirituality always represents a reorganizing of the fundamental foci of Christian life, on the basis of a central intuition or insight. The intuition is that of great men and women of the Spirit as they respond to the needs and demands of their age. Every spirituality is a way that is offered for the greater service of God and others: freedom to love.

— Gustavo Gutiérrez, from *We Drink from Our Own Wells*

The Reign of God

"I have good news for you. The Reign of God is here. Change your lives."   *—Mark 1:14–16*

"Let us move to other towns, that I might proclaim the Reign of God there also, for that is why I came."   *—Luke 4:43*

Jesus saw the Reign of God to be his mission. If it is his, it is also ours.

What Jesus meant by the Reign of God is tied up in his understanding of God as *Abba,* "my own dear Father . . . Dada, Papa." What a closeness and intimacy Jesus had with his Creator and Parent. Living in the Reign of God is to live a God-centered life, in close, intentional relationship with *Abba.*

Life in God's Reign is characterized by unconditional love of all people, service, servant leadership, stewardship of one's resources, mercy, and justice.

Life in God's Reign is about mediating God's healing power to and with each other.

Life in God's Reign is the experience of communion with our fellow human beings.

Life in God's Reign is an endeavor to be happy, to be well, to be whole, to be holy. This was the mission of Jesus. This is the mission of his Church. What could be more beautiful?

— Patrick Brennan, from *The Mission Driven Parish*

The Triumph

Jesus continues to be betrayed, it is true. But it is equally true that Jesus in the person of his disciples, who are willing to go all the way to the Cross with him, continues to proclaim the disturbing but liberating truth about the kingdom of God and every man and woman. The voice and power of God for goodness will continue to challenge the world. The prophets of today's world may well be killed, but they will not be silenced or destroyed. The message of their lives, of their commitment to the real, concrete truth about men and women in society, will continue to be a force for good that no human power can ever destroy. In the betrayal and arrest of Jesus our own betrayals and arrests take on a new meaning. Though horrible and painful, they are necessary risks for the sake of the kingdom of God. And we have the assurance that the kingdom of God, the kingdom of justice and love, the kingdom of community and equality, the kingdom of dignity and appreciation, the kingdom of peace and joy will indeed triumph over this world's kingdom of violence, corruption, avarice, and individualism.

— Virgil Elizondo, from *Way of the Cross*

The Big Picture

The wisdom that imbues the sacred writings of many great religions, the wisdom that Christians perceive to be embodied uniquely in Jesus of Nazareth, is that same wisdom that gave birth to stars, pulsars, planets, and people. The wisdom story is bigger than Christianity and exceeds in grandeur the elegance of all the great religions. It is the prodigiously creative energy of being and becoming. It is the heartbeat of the evolutionary story in its elegant, timeless, and eternal unfolding.

Evolutionary theology requires us to honor the big picture where God in time begins prior to the evolution of the major religions as we know them today The wise and holy God was at work for billions of years before religious consciousness began to develop. And that same creative wisdom will continue to beget radically new possibilities, forever challenging the outstanding theories and inventions of the human mind. To borrow from the Christian story, the light shines still in the darkness, and the darkness cannot overpower it.

— Diarmuid O'Murchu, from *Evolutionary Theology*

Resurrection and Reconciliation

In nearly every country in the world today there are wounds of division that call for healing and reconciliation.

Relief agencies — even secular relief agencies — are turning to the churches to bring the resources of their traditions of reconciliation to bear on societies that have been torn by war and violence.

A spirituality of reconciliation based on the Resurrection is surely a spirituality for these times. In the resurrection of Jesus we see the risen Lord at work in healing divisions and bringing about new life. The call to be ministers of reconciliation, breaking down the wall of hostility that separates us, is a call rooted in truth struggling for justice. It seeks the truth that will not be suppressed, that continues to spring out of the earth among the poor, the dispossessed, the downtrodden. It awaits the justice that goes beyond retribution to create a human society as God intended it.

This understanding of reconciliation illumines what the Resurrection can mean for our time. It is not a forgetting of the past, but a transfiguration of it. It seeks peace; it engages in practices of forgiveness.

The message of the Resurrection is that hope is possible, a hope rooted in the peace of Christ, gained for us in the reconciliation God is effecting. That reconciliation is being brought about in all the smaller acts of reconciliation in the world today, evidence of God being with us.

— Robert J. Schreiter, C.PP.S.,
from *The Ministry of Reconciliation:
Spirituality and Strategies*

Christ in the Margins

On the margins one encounters people who are truly dependent on God and on each other. Late one night I did not have to venture far to encounter such a reality. Walking down a busy street, I was passing a huge old church. Parked at the bottom of its worn concrete steps were three shopping carts piled high with plastic bags full of trophies and bits of junk collected from the streets and the dumpsters. Five elderly homeless women (known as shopping bag ladies) had arranged themselves on the church steps — one at the top and two on each edge of the next two steps going downward. In the center they had placed a large plastic bottle of ginger ale surrounded by some cookies (smuggled, no doubt, from the nearby soup kitchen) and some styrofoam cups from McDonalds. It was almost midnight. I hesitated and looked up at the unlikely gathering.

"We're having a picnic," yelled one of the women above the sound of a passing car. "Come and join us!" I joined them. Sitting on the bottom step I was given a napkin and a cup of ginger ale, then a cookie was decorously passed from hand to hand toward me. It had traveled far — like the ladies themselves.

Night fell. Gradually the ladies ceased to chatter and to laugh. The traffic thinned. We all knew it was time to sleep. Along with the silence, a deep, deep loneliness fell upon our little party. And in me arose a deep shame for the rich country in which I lived, a country that could not share its multiple resources with the very poor even as these very poor shared with me the little they had. How much more clearly the poor can live in solidarity and give us a vision of a new way of being. They had not hesitated to invite me to their party; their fare was meager, but their hearts — broken open — were large enough to invite me in. There was magic on the margins that cold, damp night. Through the homeless women who shared their midnight picnic with me, I myself was drawn into the ranks of the marginalized. For to choose the margins leaves one in a different place than before. One's own social identity shifts and changes as one experiences and becomes part of a new and transforming reality. That reality is compassion. True compassion is not about being at one with one's own social cultural group, but it is being able to see and know oneself as connected to every person without reservation. The words of Jesus, "I am in you and you are in me," became gloriously real and alive on society's edges. That experience itself is the magic of the margins.

— Edwina Gateley, from *Christ in the Margins*
by Robert Lentz and Edwina Gateley

Love in Action

Charity is love in action. It is action on behalf of others arising spontaneously out of a loving heart, a heart that has experienced love and in a very special way has experienced the love of God who is unconditional and unlimited love. These acts of benevolence are not looking for recognition or reward; they simply and very naturally flow out of the generosity of a loving heart.

— Virgil Elizondo, from *Charity*

Follow a Star

The Gospel of Matthew tells the story of three wise kings who leave their own land to follow a star. They set out to find and honor the newborn King of the Jews. Their wisdom is tested when the star brings them to a poor child lying beside his mother in a stable. Logic would have told these men that their calculations were off, that they followed the wrong star and that their entire journey was folly. But their openness told them to accept this truth turned upside down. Although their image of king and messiah was challenged by what they saw, they trusted their hope and knew that they were exactly in the right place and they paid homage to the child they found.

These wise men tug at my heart because they were not afraid to leave their comfortable homes to follow their dreams. They were receptive to truths that went beyond logic. Their star-gazing took them to a different culture where their perception of the Holy was stretched to unbelievable limits as they bowed down to adore the king and messiah found in the face of a poor child.

— Kathleen McNeely, from *Why Not Be a Missioner?*
edited by Michael Leach and Susan Perry

A Christmas Story

It was Christmas Eve at the famed Riverside Church in New York City, and with William Sloane Coffin Jr. scheduled to preach, the pews were packed. The Christmas Pageant was on and had come to the point where the innkeeper was to say that there was no room at the inn for Joseph and Mary pregnant with Jesus.

The part seemed perfect for Tim, an earnest youth of the congregation who has Downs Syndrome. Only one line to memorize and he had practiced it again and again with his parents and with the pageant director. He seemed to have mastered it. So there Tim stood at the altar, a bathrobe over his clothes, as Mary and Joseph made their way down the center aisle. They approached him, said their lines, and waited for his reply. "There's no room at the inn," he boomed out, just as rehearsed. But then, as Mary and Joseph turned to travel further, Tim suddenly yelled, "Wait!" They turned back startled. "You can stay at my house," he called.

Bill Coffin strode to the pulpit, said, "Amen," and sat down. It was, as Miriam Wright Edelman says, the best sermon he never preached.

— Walter J. Burghardt, S.J., from *Short Sermons for Preachers on the Run*

What's a Nice God Like You Doing in a Place Like This?

Jesus' birth has inspired countless Nativity sets — from gaudy plastic lawn ornaments to exquisite porcelain figurines. I set up a wooden crèche from Korea with a Confucian scholar, a Buddhist monk and a Taoist priest representing the wise men from the East. Viewing the Nativity scene through the eyes of another culture helps us take a fresh look as the meaning of Jesus' birth.

Unfortunately, the Nativity scene no longer shocks us. A crèche from Mexico, Kenya or China might charm us, but we may miss the essential message: God became human; not plastic, not wooden, not marble. In our efforts to retell the Christmas story, we run the risk of sanitizing it.

Stables stink. Moldy hay, cow dung, smelly sheep and all. What kind of place is that for the Son of God to be born? Who would look for God in a place like that?

I've often wondered about the characters not portrayed. Where is the High Priest? Where are the Pharisees? Maybe these "respectable" people were invited, just like the shepherds, but they got to the entrance to the barn and couldn't get past the smell.

Jesus' birth in a lowly stable shows God's desire not just to become human but also to be poor. Angels announce the Good News to social misfits. Shepherds were regarded as religious outcasts because their job prevented them from keeping all the commandments. The wise men? So-called pagan foreigners who found God using superstitious astrology while the religious leaders of Jerusalem did not.

The Christmas crib should shake us from our complacency. The scene is an indictment of our judging people by their wealth, looks, youth or positions of power. The Nativity invites us to search for God in the least likely places: among the poor, the mis-fits, foreigners and nonbelievers. Above all, in our humanity. That is the portal through which God entered the world and through which we enter into life with God.

— Joseph R. Veneroso, M.M., from *Good News for Today*

God Will Multiply Them

One of the great evils of the day is the sense of futility. Young people say, What good can one person do? What is the sense of our small effort? They cannot see that we must lay one brick at a time, take one step at a time, we can be responsible only for the one action of the present moment. But we can beg for an increase of love in our hearts that will vitalize and transform all our individual actions, and know that God will take them and multiply them, as Jesus multiplied the loaves and fishes.

— Dorothy Day, from *Loaves and Fishes*

Children of the Same Parents

In every movement of peoples, whether it be migration, exile, or conquest, there is a mutual and yet unbalanced cultural influence — the dominant group has the greater impact because they control the image of the good, the true, and the beautiful human beings and have the means to enforce and impose their cosmovision on everyone else. The early Christian movement went against this current and, working from the perspective of the new cosmovision of the converted poor and disenfranchised who now saw themselves and everyone else in a radically new way, started to change all the people it encountered, regardless of the perceived superiority of these peoples.

Through the force of their conversion to the way of Jesus, the poor, the slaves, and the servants were no longer ashamed of who they were. They gained a new pride and a new confidence in their new identity and status as children of God. . . .

In the new universal fellowship from below, based on the "little stories" of Jesus of Nazareth, a new identity and status emerged that would transcend the previous identity struggles and dehumanizing divisions between men and women; Greeks, Jews, and Romans; masters and slaves; intellectual elites and the ignorant rabble; saints and sinners; citizens and foreigners; legals and illegals — for beyond all those worldly classifications, they were all first and foremost creatures of the one Creature and children of the same Parents.

— Virgil Elizondo, from *Guadalupe*

The Oldest Profession

Motherhood is the *real* "oldest profession"; the daily, countless acts which every mother performs for her child comprise the first human experiences of solidarity. The nine months of feeding, sheltering and cradling a baby in one's belly under a protective mantle of flesh extend into other nurturing tasks whose lasting value will be played out over the child's lifetime.

Prayer, too, can be an act of solidarity: I know with utmost certainty that every night of my life until she died, my grand-mother prayed for me. Sometimes I feel as if her rogation cloaks me posthumously — whether because prayer transcends limits of time and space or due to her elevated position as one of the Com-munion of Saints, I don't know. What I *do* know is that her prayer still covers me, a blessing over the years of my life to come.

— Deirdre Cornell, from *American Madonna: Crossing Borders with the Virgin Mary*

God's Activity in Our Lives

God exists in movement. God lives, and God's living is love. I begin to understand God's love when I see it directed not to the world in general but to me. God is acting in love toward me. When Holy Scripture says, "Come, Lord," it is referring not to an image or idea of God but to the living God. This thought should not confuse us: God is present everywhere. Surely God is everywhere; everything exists through God, and God sustains everything. Nevertheless, God comes to each of us. God always comes to us. God is the One coming to us — coming to human beings, and through human beings coming to the world which God will eventually raise into eternal newness.

— Roman Guardini, from *Romano Guardini: Spiritual Writings,* edited by Robert A. Krieg

The Color of Gratitude

My choice is purple,
   recalling the clover in a boyhood meadow.

   Deo Gratias!

Others might choose red,
   watching the fireball sun sink into the ocean.

   Deo Gratias!

Still others opt for blue,
   robin-egg blue telling of hidden life.

   Deo Gratias!

Gratitude is a rainbow
   sun and rain shining in the same room.
Gratitude is a peanut-butter sandwich (toasted),
   knowing that it is enough.
Gratitude is to dwell in mystery,
   the enigma of being loved,
   of just being.

— Robert Morneau, from *The Color of Gratitude*

Praise God!

God has made us and takes responsibility for what he has created. He takes responsibility for the history of this world and even for every single person's life. He has enveloped us in his grace, his love, and his faithfulness. When we bring with us into the new year our past and our worries, with all our foibles and weariness, our faithful and merciful God goes with us. . . . So, let us say good-bye to the past year! It was a year of the Lord, a year of grace, a year of inner growth, even if we did not feel it. After all, God's strength achieves victory in our weakness. Thus we really can praise God at the end of the year, and thank him, and give him honor, for he is good, and his mercy everlasting.

— Karl Rahner, S.J., from *The Mystical Way in Everyday Life,*
edited by Annemarie S. Kidder

Author Index

Thank You!

Thank you for reading *A Maryknoll Book of Inspiration.*

If any of the selections interest you in the original book from whence they came, please check for the book title on our web page, *orbisbooks.com,* or call us at 1-800-258-5838. Some of the books may be out of print, but most are still available. Please support your local bookstore, and let them know about Orbis Books. For a free catalog you may also write us at

Orbis Books
Box 302
Maryknoll, NY 10545-0302

If you liked this book, you may also enjoy *A Maryknoll Book of Prayer,* an anthology of hundreds of favorite prayers, both traditional and contemporary, from all around the world selected by hundreds of people in the Maryknoll family.

Do visit us at *www.maryknollsociety.org* to learn more about Maryknoll's work around the world, and how you can help. Thanks again!